MW00611855

CUCINA
POVERA

CUCINA POVERA

The Italian Way of Transforming
Humble Ingredients into Unforgettable Meals

GIULIA SCARPALEGGIA

PHOTOGRAPHS BY TOMMASO GALLI

Artisan | New York

Copyright © 2023 by Giulia Scarpaleggia
Photographs copyright © 2023 by Tommaso Galli

All rights reserved. No portion of this book may be reproduced—
mechanically, electronically, or by any other means, including
photocopying—without written permission of the publisher.

Library of Congress Cataloging-in-Publication Data

Names: Scarpaleggia, Giulia, author.
Title: Cucina povera : the Italian way of transforming humble
ingredients into unforgettable meals / Giulia Scarpaleggia ;
photographs by Tommaso Galli.
Description: New York : Artisan, [2023] | Includes index.
Identifiers: LCCN 2022027919 | ISBN 9781648290565 (hardback)
Subjects: LCSH: Cooking, Italian. | LCGFT: Cookbooks.
Classification: LCC TX723 .S3557 2023 | DDC 641.5945—
dc23/eng/20220729
LC record available at https://lccn.loc.gov/2022027919

Cover and book design by Shubhani Sarkar

Artisan books are available at special discounts when purchased
in bulk for premiums and sales promotions as well as for
fundraising or educational use. Special editions or book excerpts
also can be created to specification. For details, please contact
specialmarkets@hbgusa.com.

Published by Artisan,
an imprint of Workman Publishing Co., Inc.,
a subsidiary of Hachette Book Group, Inc.
1290 Avenue of the Americas
New York, NY 10104
artisanbooks.com

Artisan is a registered trademark of Workman Publishing Co.,
Inc., a subsidiary of Hachette Book Group, Inc.

Printed in China on responsibly sourced paper

First printing, March 2023

10 9 8 7 6 5 4 3 2 1

To my family

CONTENTS

Introduction 9

The Italian Pantry 15

VEGETABLES
Cooking from the Garden 18

BEEF, PORK, AND LAMB
Offal and Affordable Cuts of Meat 56

POULTRY AND RABBIT
Recipes from the Farmyard 86

FISH AND SEAFOOD
Italian Pesce Povero 112

MILK AND CHEESE
Dairy-Based Meals 140

BEANS AND LENTILS
Plant Proteins 168

POTATOES, CORN, AND CHESTNUTS
Staples from the Mountain Regions 200

LEFTOVERS
Making the Most of What You've Got 232

DESSERTS
*Making Do for Cakes,
Tarts, Puddings, and Cookies Too* 264

BASICS
Breads, Stocks, and Sauce 300

Acknowledgments 313

Index 314

INTRODUCTION

Cucina povera, Italian peasant cooking, is the way people have been cooking in Italy for centuries, in both the cities and the countryside. Cucina povera is not just a unique approach to cooking and ingredients; it's the highest expression of the Italian *arte dell'arrangiarsi*, the art of making do with what you've got.

Traditional cucina povera dishes are immediately recognizable from some common traits: the use of humble ingredients, seasonal vegetables, and simple cooking techniques, along with a healthy dose of imagination. This culinary approach may be ancient, but it is still relevant today; it is a way of cooking that transforms simple ingredients into hearty meals that are more than the sum of their parts.

Italian cucina povera relies on basic, affordable ingredients that are available no matter where you live, from a loaf of sturdy bread to different types of dairy and cheese, as well as seasonal vegetables, grown in your garden or obtained from a local market. Leftovers of all sorts, from the remains of a Sunday roast to scraps from homemade fresh pasta, are reinvented to make a second (or even third) meal that is just as tasty and nutritious as the original one. Day-old bread and leftover pasta, rice, and boiled meats are transformed with inventiveness and an innate sense of taste into treats like fried arancine, spaghetti frittata, beef stew with onions, and meatballs. Cucina povera brings excellent value to your cooking, and who doesn't need that?

Meat is eaten only on rare occasions. Rather, the cuisine is centered around dishes with fish or vegetable and plant proteins such as chickpeas and fava beans, along with basic ingredients like chestnuts, potatoes, and pasta. These ingredients may be simple, but when you use them the Italian way, you will never feel like you are missing out. And some of the most popular Italian dishes, those that are some of the best examples of cucina povera, require only a few ingredients. Think of cacio e pepe or polenta.

Cucina povera employs some clever strategies to make the most of what you have in your pantry. Stale bread soaked in water or in a tasty vegetable stock makes soups more filling and nutritious; Tuscany's hearty ribollita and Apulia's pancotto both incorporate this trick. Breadcrumbs become a filling for stuffed vegetables, another layer in a cod and potato bake, or, when fried until golden, a crisp, tasty seasoning for orecchiette. A boiled chicken will give you more than one meal: the next day, toss the shredded meat into a colorful salad with radicchio and pickled vegetables, and then use the golden stock to cook risotto or passatelli, or to make stracciatella. The most important principle of Italian cucina povera is an economical, waste-not approach, which is still practiced today in most Italian households.

There are recipes for weeknight suppers and Sunday gatherings, recipes to celebrate the season with a group of friends, and recipes you'll find yourself making time and time again as they become new favorites. With their short lists of affordable ingredients and simple cooking techniques, cucina povera dishes easily fit into our modern lives, with a traditional yet contemporary attention paid to sustainability, budget, and inclusiveness, with dishes that are naturally gluten-free, vegetarian, or vegan.

CUCINA POVERA IN ITALIAN HISTORY

Nowadays Italian cooking is often viewed as fragmented into different regional cooking styles, based in part on the local preference for particular ingredients, such as butter rather than olive oil (or vice versa), meat over fish, and pasta rather than polenta. These differences are influenced both by availability and historical political domination: Arab and then Spanish in the South, Austrian and French in the North. There is a common ground, though, that characterizes all Italian cuisine, that makes it unique and recognizable, and that is an allegiance to the principles of cucina povera.

Historically, Italian cucina povera was considered the cuisine of poor people, as opposed to the cuisine of the elite. Throughout time, different cuisines were classified as cucina povera: the cuisine of the countryside, that of poor mountain people, that of nomad shepherds, and that of city dwellers struggling to make ends meet in an impoverished environment. In cucina povera, you can find recipes, ingredients, and techniques that go back to medieval times or even before, as well as more recent recipes that sustained people through the hardship of postwar Italy.

Every Italian region has its own traditional ingredients and foods: polenta and rice are the staples of the cucina povera in the North of Italy, where dishes such as risi e bisi and polenta concia are a source of pride and identity. Tuscany has its pane sciocco, a bread made without salt, used to create quintessential Tuscan recipes such as pappa al pomodoro, panzanella, and ribollita. Dried pasta, legumes, and vegetables are staples in the Southern diet: for example, pasta e fagioli in Naples and lagane e ceci in Basilicata. In big cities where butchering traditions have always had a significant role, the cucina povera revolves around the "quinto quarto," the affordable cuts of meat left after the slaughtering, including heads, tails, and all the innards. So in traditional trattorias, you still find hearty, gutsy dishes such as rigatoni alla vaccinara in Rome, along with trippa—a fixture also in Milan and in Florence—and liver stewed with onions in Venice.

MY TUSCAN ROOTS

Tuscany's cucina povera is in my blood. I was born in the Tuscan countryside and raised in a traditional tight-knit family, with a mother and a grandmother who applied the principles of the cuisine to our everyday meals. My mother, Anna, and my grandmother Marcella informed the way I now cook for my family.

My grandma, who was also born and raised in the Tuscan countryside and grew up during World War II, taught me that a well-stocked pantry is not only the starting point of almost every meal but also a source of pride and security. In her home, any leftover pieces of stale bread were religiously collected in a cotton bag that hung behind the kitchen door, to become the basis of a stuffing for green peppers, a topping for roasted vegetables, or, in summer, panzanella.

My mom, who worked outside the home, taught me not how to cook (that was Grandma) but how to feed and nurture your loved ones with food. She can assemble a satisfying meal in less than half an hour, with humble, affordable

ingredients. The sound of a fork beating an egg in a ceramic bowl to make a frittata for dinner is the sound of home to me, as is the hiss of frozen garden vegetables (preserved in summer) thrown into a hot pot with sautéed onions as the foundation of a quick minestrone.

I also inherited my mom and grandma's love of canning. When I was growing up, late-summer afternoons were devoted to preserving the abundant seasonal produce: there were bottles of tomato puree that could be turned into a quick sauce for pasta or a topping for my mom's pizza, jars of blackberry or plum jam to spread on bread for breakfast or use in a crostata on Sundays, and pickled vegetables that could stretch a meal on a weeknight. My mother and grandmother didn't set out to instill a passion for food in me, nor did they push me to pursue a career in cooking. That happened quite naturally, the result of witnessing daily their respect for honest, uncomplicated fare and realizing that my happiest place has always been the kitchen.

I love writing as much as I love food. After getting a degree in communications, I spent a few years working in marketing and event planning. In 2009, I started a food blog, JulsKitchen.com, as an outlet for these two passions. It started as a personal project and soon turned into a journey of discovery into my culinary roots. I began looking at my family's foodways, something I had almost taken for granted, with a fresh, new appreciation. I realized that the recipes I had always thought of as quite commonplace were in fact special and important, and the foods of my heritage became an ongoing source of curiosity and inspiration for me. That is when I started connecting the dots between cucina povera and its traditional but contemporary approach to food and life.

I began teaching cooking classes, where I slowly developed a personal culinary repertoire based on my family traditions, with that cucina povera approach. I start each class with a market tour, and the students and I decide on the lunch menu based on what looks good at the market that day. These meals revolve around vegetables and homemade fresh pasta. Just a handful of fresh ingredients from the market and some pantry staples like stale bread, flour, eggs, and homemade preserves, along with a couple of hours of convivial cooking, result in a seasonal Tuscan feast that we enjoy together in the garden. What I want to pass on to my students is not just a set of recipes but also a deep respect for seasonality, a new consideration for humble pantry staples, clever ideas for repurposing leftovers, and the belief that everyone can be an excellent cook, especially when provided with the right ingredients.

My best travel memories are, unsurprisingly, related to food (after all, I'm Italian): feasting on cicchetti in a Venetian *bacaro*, indulging myself with saffron risotto and ossobuco made by the book in an old-school trattoria in a hot Milanese August, devouring arancine in Sicily as a midafternoon snack after a day spent at the beach, or smiling with joy at the sight of a platter of the local salumi in Umbria. Most of our family weekend trips and holidays are planned with a precise goal: learning new recipes, discovering unfamiliar regional ingredients, or reconnecting with our roots through food. Baking pizza and talking about the local bread and salami with my grandfather's family in Basilicata, or spending an afternoon shaping orecchiette with my husband's aunt in Salento, create memories that will last and reinforce family traditions I can pass on to my daughter, Livia.

Everything I've learned from cooking with my mom and grandmother, exploring Italy and its variegated food scene, teaching cooking classes for more than ten years, and feeding my own family has now come together in this book.

HOW TO USE THIS BOOK

You don't need to be an accomplished cook to make the recipes of cucina povera. Start with excellent ingredients, and your food is almost guaranteed to turn out well. Whenever possible, shop seasonally and locally—that way, you will be buying ingredients that are at their peak, have a better flavor, and are a better value.

With cucina povera, you want to keep things uncomplicated and let each ingredient shine: a simple garlicky tomato sauce is often the best way to dress a bowl of fresh pasta.

The recipes in this book are ones that I love to make with my cooking students and that I rely on to feed my family and to serve at gatherings for friends. All of these have been tested in American kitchens using American ingredients, as well as Italian ingredients. You'll also find ideas and tips on how to make substitutions if needed, along with variations for many of the recipes.

The recipes come from all the regions of Italy. Some are common to the entire peninsula, such as fresh pasta, bread soups, tripe stews, and chicken cacciatora. Others embody the unique spirit of a single region, such as cassoeula and ossobuco from Lombardy, orecchiette with broccoli rabe and pancotto from Apulia, and agnello cacio e ova from Abruzzo. You will see how cooks from different regions of Italy draw on the same basic cucina povera principles of creativity and resourcefulness: cacio e pepe and supplì in Rome, ribollita and pappa al pomodoro in Tuscany, calf's liver and sarde in saor in Veneto, and spaghetti frittata and pasta e fagioli in Naples.

Here you will find an authentic and sustainable approach to food, along with recipes to make the most of less-expensive cuts of meat and ideas for cooking simple ingredients and seasonal produce with Italian flair. You will discover the cucina povera approach to cheese, which is often paired with bread or vegetables to make a hearty meal, as in zuppa valpellinese, the Savoy cabbage, rye bread, and Fontina casserole from Val d'Aosta. The book will also guide you to a new appreciation of local, environmentally friendly fish, as even the small, bony catch of the day can give you a comforting soup like brodetto, the fish stew from Marche.

And here you will find new ways with staples such as potatoes, corn, and chestnuts: the first will give you not only pillowy gnocchi but also a delicious crispy frico from Friuli–Venezia Giulia, while chestnuts and chestnut flour may become your new favorite ingredients for gnocchi, soups, fresh pasta, or cakes. You'll learn about endless variations on polenta, from cheesy polenta concia to irresistible fried polenta wedges. And because of traditions ranging from the Florentine reliance on beans to the use of chickpea flour in Liguria and dried fava beans in the South of Italy, many of cucina povera's traditional recipes are naturally gluten-free, dairy-free, and vegetarian or vegan, making them suitable for everyone around your dinner table.

And the basic principles of cucina povera can also be applied to baking: respect for local and seasonal ingredients, the use of leftovers—every breadcrumb counts—and an inventiveness that leads to celebratory though simple desserts.

Cucina povera doesn't rely on complicated techniques: imagine instead slow, forgiving stews; easy baked casseroles and other dishes; breads based on a long, slow unattended rise thanks to an overnight pre-fermented dough; and fresh pasta dough, the making of which is one of my favorite stress-reducing activities.

Learning about Italian cucina povera is a timeless and delicious way to inform your own way of cooking, adding simple and nutritious recipes to your cooking repertoire.

THE ITALIAN PANTRY

A well-stocked pantry is the starting point for many easy, affordable recipes in Italian cucina povera. Improvising a meal with ingredients from the pantry is simple, satisfying, liberating, and creative. In fact, a pantry-driven approach to cooking teaches you to focus on what you have, rather than on what you are missing. Stock your pantry with the ingredients listed below, and your cooking will immediately take on an Italian flair.

OLIVE OIL AND OTHER VEGETABLE OILS

Extra-Virgin Olive Oil

A bottle of top-quality extra-virgin olive oil is one of the best gifts you can receive (or give). Keep at least one bottle of extra-virgin oil in your pantry: aim for one of average quality, 100 percent Italian, and organic, if possible. You can cook, braise, bake, and even fry with extra-virgin olive oil.

In addition, have a bottle of excellent extra-virgin olive oil to use for final seasoning. In my pantry, that might be one of the few bottles of extra-virgin olive oil we press every year from the olives of our own grove or a local one, an oil from a producer I love, or maybe a PDO (Protected Designation of Origin) or PGI (Protected Geographical Indication) oil, from Tuscany or another region.

Remember that extra-virgin olive oil is not like wine: it won't age gracefully, so don't save it for special occasions; instead, use it daily, and freely. Think of olive oil as the juice of olives. Look at the harvest date on the bottle's label: it should be late in the previous year, from October to December. The shelf life is usually 18 months, if stored correctly: in a dark bottle (pour it into a different bottle after you buy it, if necessary) in a cool, dark cupboard, never next to the stove. Light and heat are the enemies of olive oil. A bad oil—for example, one that smells rancid—can ruin a dish.

Vegetable Oil

I keep organic vegetable oil—usually peanut—on hand for frying when I need a neutral-tasting oil, such as for supplì (page 236), arancine (page 242), or elderflower fritters (page 296).

SALT

Italy is surrounded by the sea, so we have always had plenty of salt to preserve our food: prosciutto, pork cheeks, the aged pecorino cheeses, and even tomato paste or olives are all cured and preserved with salt and time. Smoke-cured salumi, like Alpine speck, belong to northeastern Italy, where the influence of the German countries and their cuisines is still strong.

Thanks to Italy's geographical proximity to Mediterranean saltworks, fine and coarse sea salt are my go-to salts. I use coarse sea salt mainly for seasoning pasta water; I use fine sea salt for cooking.

HERBS AND SPICES

Italian cucina povera is generally not heavy on spices, because these used to be extremely expensive and reserved for the wealthier classes. However, there are exceptions, such as Venetian cuisine, because of the city's central role in the spice trades.

Black pepper is the most commonly used spice in Italy, from curing prosciutto to sprinkling over cannellini beans or chickpeas to the now-world-famous cacio e pepe (page 153). Nutmeg, one of the most loved spices in the Renaissance times, when it was worth more than gold, is still used, primarily for gnocchi (pages 225 and 229), besciamella, and fresh ricotta. I often use juniper berries for game meats, and fennel seeds for pork, as in the pork liver spiedini (page 78). Chili peppers, most often dried, are used in many Southern recipes, especially those from Calabria.

Italian cuisine relies heavily on fresh herbs. Consequently, you won't find dried herbs in our spice racks; rather, we often pick fresh herbs directly from a pot or the garden when in season. Sturdy herbs that can flourish year-round, such as rosemary and sage, are a constant in many dishes throughout the year, from roasted meats to baked fish. Other herbs appear in our cooking only during peak season: think of, for example, summertime basil and wild fennel, which marry beautifully with other ingredients that share the same season, such as ripe tomatoes or new potatoes.

There is only one exception to our preference for fresh herbs: oregano, which is always used in its dried form. Southern Italian cooking uses it in many recipes, not only for pizza: see also salmoriglio (page 138).

DRIED LEGUMES

I always have bags of dried cannellini beans, borlotti beans, chickpeas, fava beans, and lentils. Experiment with local varieties from your own region too, to provide you with many affordable, wholesome, plant-based meals. Along with dried beans, I keep cans of beans and chickpeas on hand. They can be turned into an impromptu pasta e fagioli (page 185) or a summery tuna and bean salad (page 172).

FLOUR

An Italian pantry stocks several varieties of wheat flour, more and less refined: bread flour (with a high protein percentage) and all-purpose, to make fresh pasta, along with semolina flour, that is also used to make bread (page 303). I keep chickpea flour in my pantry to make torta di ceci (page 179) and pane e panelle (page 176), as well as chestnut flour, which I store in the freezer, as it is very perishable. I use it for castagnaccio (page 273) and fresh pasta. All over the country, but especially in pantries in northeastern Italy, you will also find corn flour, used to make polenta (see page 224).

BREAD

Bread at various stages is one of the most important staples in the Italian pantry. Fresh, it plays a central role in many frugal meals; stale, it's the secret ingredient of many soups, meatballs, dumplings, and cakes; and whatever is left over can be turned into breadcrumbs.

CANNED OR PRESERVED TOMATOES

Tomatoes are a relatively recent part of Italian food history, but they play an important role. Tomato sauce and tomato puree, canned peeled tomatoes (pelati), and tomato paste are among the most common ingredients in the Italian pantry.

A can or jar of tomato puree can be turned into a quick dinner of pasta al pomodoro with a shower of grated Parmigiano-Reggiano, or, if you also have a couple of eggs, frittata trippata (page 101). A tablespoon of tomato paste was always my grandma's secret ingredient to impart an umami kick to soups and stews.

DRY PASTA AND RICE

There's a myth that Italians eat only fresh pasta made from scratch. In our family tradition, fresh pasta is made when there is something to celebrate, such as a Sunday gathering with relatives and friends or a holiday like Christmas. At other times, we buy dried pasta, choosing the shape that best suits a certain sauce or seasoning. I keep a variety of dried pastas on hand.

Rice is a staple grain of Italian cuisine, along with barley and farro; for more on Italian rice, see Rice for Any Recipe, page 33.

OTHER INGREDIENTS

A well-stocked Italian pantry will also include nuts, anchovies preserved in salt or oil, tiny capers, canned tuna, sun-dried tomatoes, raisins, dried mushrooms (especially porcini), jams, and preserved vegetables. These basic ingredients make improvising in the kitchen easy and fun.

VEGETABLES

COOKING FROM THE GARDEN

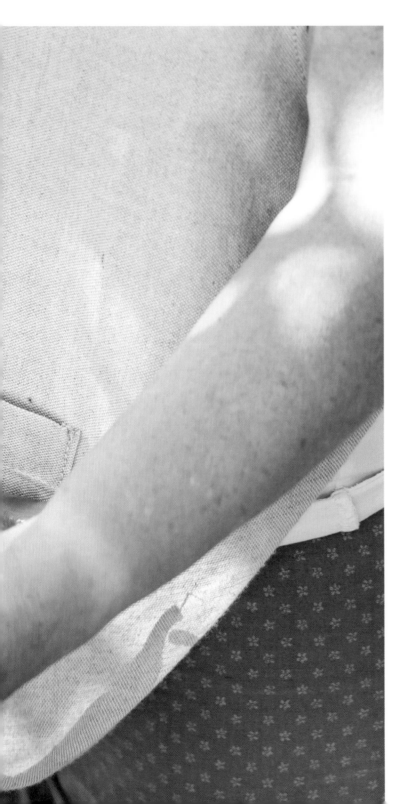

Involtini di peperoni alla piemontese
**Roasted Pepper Rolls
Stuffed with Tuna and Capers 22**

Minestrone di verdure
Vegetable Soup 24

Licurdia
Onion Soup from Calabria 27

Risi e bisi
Rice and Pea Soup 28

Risotto alla zucca
Roasted Squash Risotto 31

Orecchiette con le cime di rapa
Orecchiette with Broccoli Rabe 35

Pansoti con salsa di noci
Foraged-Herb Tortelli with Walnut Pesto 38

Pomodori ripieni di riso alla romana
Rice-Stuffed Tomatoes 43

Zucchini ripieni alla ligure
Potato-and-Mushroom–Stuffed Zucchini 44

Melanzane ripiene alla calabrese
Bread-and-Cheese–Stuffed Eggplant 46

Peperoni ripieni alla lucana
**Bread-and-Anchovy–Stuffed
Sweet Green Peppers 48**

Vignarola
**Artichoke, Fava Bean,
Pea, and Lettuce Stew 50**

Ciambotta
Summer Vegetable Stew 54

LONG BEFORE THE FARM-TO-TABLE MOVEMENT BECAME TRENDY ON restaurant menus, it was the only way Italian peasants and farmers ate. Seasonal vegetables have always had a central role in cucina povera. Having a small patch to grow vegetables was a blessing and a lifesaving asset. The garden bounty, supplemented with ingredients gathered by foraging, could sustain people during meager times. Anything edible, whether grown in a vegetable garden or in the wild, would be artfully used. Even today, when it's possible to get any ingredient you desire in a grocery store, focusing on seasonal vegetables and making them the main part of your meal is the most sustainable way of eating.

Your food will be fresher, tastier, and more nutritious, and a better value too. Buying locally also means supporting the local economy and knowing where your food comes from.

Eating seasonally results in a deeper connection with nature and a profound sense of expectation for the seasons. After a long, cold winter, the bounty of spring tastes green and fresh. Tender peas, a triumph of spring firstlings, can be used in Venetian risi e bisi (page 28) or Roman vignarola (page 50).

Summer is the season when cooking from the vegetable garden is the most satisfying and effortless, and when shopping at your local farmers' market is more affordable. Sliced sun-kissed tomatoes can become a meal with a drizzle of olive oil and some crusty bread. And when you have more tomatoes than you know what to do with, try stuffing them with cheese, rice, and breadcrumbs (page 43) or stew them for ciambotta (page 54). Knowing that eggplants will soon be out of season will make you enjoy them more lavishly, frying them, grilling them (page 179), or stuffing them with cheese and breadcrumbs (page 46).

When autumn squashes and pumpkins arrive in the market, it's time to make creamy risotto alla zucca (page 31). Winter is the time for bitter green leaves and sturdy brassicas, perfect for making orecchiette con le cime di rapa (page 35).

And just when you feel that you cannot eat yet another broccoli floret, you realize that spring is just around the corner, and the never-ending carousel of seasons, fruit, and vegetables is about to start anew.

Follow the seasonal, local approach to guide your ingredient pairings. Ingredients that grow together go together: think delicate spring peas and asparagus in a fresh salad with a shower of pungent pecorino, or grilled zucchini and eggplant with goat cheese in a summery tart.

Whether you are tending your own vegetable garden or shopping at the weekend farmers' market, if you choose to cook seasonally, you'll be following the cucina povera approach, with pleasure in the sense of expectation that every season brings.

Involtini di peperoni alla piemontese

ROASTED PEPPER ROLLS STUFFED WITH TUNA AND CAPERS

**SERVES 4
AS A STARTER**

4 red bell peppers or
4 jarred roasted red
peppers (see Note)
Two 5-ounce/142 g
cans tuna packed in
olive oil, drained
2 tablespoons brined
capers, rinsed
6 oil-packed anchovy
fillets
¼ cup/60 ml extra-
virgin olive oil
1 tablespoon red wine
vinegar
2 tablespoons minced
fresh flat-leaf
parsley
Flaky sea salt and
freshly ground
black pepper

NOTE: *If you don't have
time to make roasted
peppers, check your
pantry for a jar of good-
quality roasted red
peppers in oil. You'll
have a tasty starter
made with cupboard
staples in no time.*

These Piedmontese involtini made with seasonal vegetables and pantry staples show off a perfect balance of flavors: on one hand, the smoky sweetness of roasted bell peppers, and on the other, briny tuna, blended with capers and anchovies into a smooth, velvety filling.

These are an ideal starter to serve at a summer garden party, as you can prepare them in advance and also easily scale up the recipe to make enough to fill a large platter. Or double the recipe to make a main course for two.

––––

If using fresh peppers, preheat the oven to 450°F/230°C.

Wash the peppers and place on a parchment paper–lined baking sheet. Transfer to the oven and roast the peppers, turning them frequently, until the skin is charred all over, about 25 minutes. If you want to further blacken the skin, pop them under the broiler for 5 more minutes.

Remove the peppers from the oven and, using tongs, carefully transfer them to a bowl. Cover the bowl with plastic wrap and let the peppers cool completely. The steam trapped in the bowl will make it easy to peel the peppers.

Peel the peppers, remove the cores and seeds, and cut each pepper into 4 wide strips. Transfer to a bowl, cover with plastic wrap, and store in the refrigerator for up to 3 days.

Prepare the pepper rolls: In a food processor, combine the tuna, capers, anchovies, and 2 tablespoons of the olive oil and process until smooth.

If using jarred roasted peppers, drain well and cut each one into 4 wide strips.

Arrange the pepper strips on a work surface. Spoon some of the filling across the bottom of each strip and press it down gently, then roll up the pepper and place on a serving plate. Drizzle with the remaining 2 tablespoons olive oil and the vinegar, sprinkle with the parsley, and season with salt and black pepper.

Serve the involtini at room temperature. Any leftovers can be stored in the fridge for 2 days.

Minestrone di verdure

VEGETABLE SOUP

SERVES 8
AS A FIRST COURSE

FOR THE CROUTONS

¼ cup/60 ml extra-
virgin olive oil

1 clove garlic, crushed
and peeled

4 slices day-old bread,
such as Tuscan
Bread (page 302)
or Semolina Bread
(page 303), cut
into ½-inch/1.5 cm
cubes

Fine sea salt and
freshly ground
black pepper

FOR THE SOUP

¼ cup/60 ml extra-
virgin olive oil, plus
more for drizzling

½ red onion, thinly
sliced

Fine sea salt

2 medium zucchini,
diced

4 ounces/115 g green
beans, trimmed and
cut into ¾-inch/
2 cm lengths

2 medium carrots,
peeled and diced

2 cups/130 g thinly
sliced Savoy
cabbage

4 ounces/115 g baby
spinach (about
4 cups), rinsed

1 medium potato,
peeled and diced

Minestrone is not just any vegetable soup. The endless variations throughout Italy all have in common an array of seasonal vegetables that are slowly simmered in water or stock. After long, patient cooking, the vegetables become soft and release all their flavors into the broth but still retain their shape. Depending on where you are in Italy, beans (fresh or dried), pasta or rice, or even boiled and mashed potatoes are added to the pot to make a thicker, creamier, more fortifying soup. In Liguria, minestrone is typically finished with basil pesto.

In Italy, you can often find bags of already cut vegetables at the market; these are a shortcut to preparing a minestrone and encourage customers to avoid buying frozen or canned soup. When you have time, though, nothing beats a minestrone made with vegetables that are in season, picked at the right moment, and bursting with flavor. In time, you will develop your own favorite combination of vegetables. Use the following recipe as an inspiration, but change it up as you like: add fresh peas in spring, for example, or strips of kale in winter.

You can cook the minestrone in advance and refrigerate it for a day or so, then reheat before serving, or even serve it at room temperature during summer.

_____

Make the croutons: Pour the olive oil into a large frying pan set over low heat, add the crushed garlic, and cook until fragrant, 3 to 5 minutes. Add the bread cubes, tossing them with the oil, then increase the heat to medium and cook, stirring often with a wooden spoon, until crisp and golden, about 5 minutes. Season with salt and pepper and set aside.

Make the soup: Pour the olive oil into a large pot set over low heat, add the onion, and season with a generous pinch of salt. Cook, stirring, for 5 to 8 minutes, until the onions are soft and translucent.

Add the remaining vegetables and stir them into the onions, then increase the heat to medium and cook, stirring occasionally, for 10 minutes, or until the vegetables start to soften.

Put 1 cup/200 g of the beans into a bowl and, with a potato masher or the back of a fork, mash with 1 cup/240 ml of the reserved cooking water (or

½ leek, trimmed and
  thinly sliced
3 cups/600 g cooked
  or canned cannellini
  beans
3 cups/720 ml
  reserved bean
  cooking water or
  hot water, or as
  needed
A handful of fresh
  basil leaves
Freshly ground black
  pepper
½ cup/110 g prepared
  basil pesto

hot water). Pour into the pot, add the remaining whole beans, along with the remaining bean cooking liquid (or hot water), and stir well. Bring to a boil, then lower the heat and cook, covered, for 20 to 25 minutes, stirring occasionally, adding the basil leaves halfway through the cooking time. You can cook the soup for a bit longer if you like your minestrone thicker, or add some more bean liquid (or hot water) if you prefer a soup on the brothier side. Taste and season with additional salt as necessary and with pepper.

Add the pesto to the minestrone and stir to dissolve. Ladle into warmed bowls, scatter the croutons on top, and drizzle each serving with olive oil.

VARIATIONS

Minestrone con la pasta: Omit the croutons. Add about 1½ cups/12 ounces/ 340 g short pasta, like tubettini, to the minestrone about 10 minutes before it is ready and cook, stirring occasionally, until the pasta is done. You may need more cooking liquid, so consider adding more hot water along with the pasta.

Passato di verdure con il riso: Once the minestrone is ready, blend it with an immersion blender or pass it through a food mill and return it to the pot. Return it to the heat, add ¾ cup/115 g cooked rice per person, and simmer for 5 minutes before serving. You may need more cooking liquid, so consider adding more hot water along with the rice. Top each serving with some grated Parmigiano-Reggiano and finish with a drizzle of olive oil.

HOW TO PREP MINESTRONE FOR WINTER

If you want to make a stash of soup for winter, toward the end of summer, when vegetables are abundant, fresh, and more affordable, scale up the recipe for minestrone and buy large quantities of everything you want to include. Then spend a few hours rinsing, chopping, slicing, and bagging a supply of vegetables for winter.

Transfer the vegetables to zip-top freezer bags, about 1 pound/ 455 g of mixed vegetables in each one, enough for one batch of soup. Press out the air from the bags, seal, and lay flat on a rimmed baking sheet. Transfer to the freezer and freeze until the vegetables are solid, then stack the bags in the freezer.

Then, when you crave hot soup, all you have to do is throw a bag of the frozen prepared vegetables into a pot and make the minestrone just as you would with fresh vegetables.

Licurdia

ONION SOUP FROM CALABRIA

SERVES 6
AS A FIRST COURSE

6 large Tropea (see
   Note) or Vidalia
   onions (about
   2 pounds/1 kg)
⅓ cup/80 ml extra-
   virgin olive oil
Fine sea salt
Red pepper flakes
4 large Yukon Gold
   potatoes (about
   1¾ pounds /800 g),
   peeled and diced
4 cups/1 L water
6 slices day-old bread,
   toasted
9 ounces/255 g
   caciocavallo or
   provolone, diced
5 tablespoons/30 g
   grated Pecorino
   Romano

NOTE: *Licurdia is
traditionally made
with Tropea onions,
the large sweet onions
typical of Calabria.
Vidalia onions would
be the best substitute.
Otherwise, any firm
sweet onions will do.*

Alliums are the critical elements that build flavor in a dish, the bass notes of an Italian melody, a catalyst of flavor, a quintessential ingredient for soups, sauces, and stews. But during the Middle Ages, garlic, leeks, and onions were associated with the poor. These aromatics served as the spices of the rural masses, the only ingredients they could afford to add flavor to food.

Onion soup is a supreme example of cucina povera. Calabria, a Southern region famous for its large sweet onions and fiery chili peppers, is the home of one of the most rustic onion soups in the Italian tradition. Within the short ingredients list hides a soup bursting with flavor, texture, and character. Onions are simmered in water until almost collapsing: they lose their pungency completely in favor of a mellow sweetness that counterbalances the sharp provolone cheese. Instead of grating the cheese onto toasted slices of bread, as you would for the French soupe à l'oignon, though, you put slices of day-old bread in the bottom of the bowls, so they can soak up the flavorful soup. It makes for a hearty bowl, something to fill your stomach on a cold winter night.

———

Peel and thinly slice the onions; a mandoline or sharp knife will help you with this chore.

Pour the olive oil into a large pot set over medium-low heat and add the onions. Season with a large pinch of salt and red pepper flakes to taste and sauté the onions, stirring often, for 10 minutes, or until soft and translucent.

Add the potatoes to the pot, stir, and pour in the water. Add salt to taste and bring to a boil, then reduce the heat so the liquid is simmering and simmer gently for about 40 minutes, until the potatoes break up easily when mashed against the side of the pot with a wooden spoon. The soup will still be quite brothy, as you want enough flavorful stock to soak the toasted bread. Taste and adjust the seasoning as necessary.

Place a slice of toasted bread in each of six warmed bowls and divide the caciocavallo evenly among the bowls. Ladle the soup over, drizzle each serving with some olive oil, sprinkle with grated pecorino, and serve.

Risi e bisi

RICE AND PEA SOUP

SERVES 4 TO 6
AS A FIRST COURSE

2 pounds/1 kg peas
    in the pod (about
    1⅔ cups/255 g
    shelled peas; see
    headnote)
6 tablespoons/85 g
    unsalted butter
2 tablespoons extra-
    virgin olive oil
1 spring onion or
    6 scallions, finely
    chopped
2 ounces/60 g
    pancetta, diced
2 teaspoons finely
    chopped fresh flat-
    leaf parsley
½ clove garlic, minced
1¼ cups/255 g Vialone
    Nano or Carnaroli
    rice (see page 33)
2 teaspoons fine
    sea salt
¼ teaspoon freshly
    ground black
    pepper
¼ cup/25 g grated
    Parmigiano-
    Reggiano

Risi e bisi, literally "rice and peas," is one of the most representative dishes of Veneto and a perfect example of the nutritious and balanced marriage of carbs and vegetable protein.

Use fresh organic peas in the pod for this dish if you can get them. Make a stock out of the pods, which will infuse the soup with an intense flavor. Then strain the stock and blend the pods into a puree, to add creaminess to the soup. Not precisely a soup or a risotto, risi e bisi should be soft but not too loose, creamy but not too dense.

For a quicker version, use 1½ cups/255 g shelled peas, either fresh or frozen, and 3 cups/720 ml vegetable stock (skipping the pea pod puree). The dish is a warm and delicious welcome to spring.

———

Make the pea stock: Shell the peas into a small bowl and set aside. Transfer the pods to a colander. Remove the tough stems and the strings from the pods.

Transfer the pea pods to a medium pot, add cold water to cover, and bring to a boil over high heat. Reduce the heat to medium-low and simmer for about 45 minutes, until the pods are very tender.

Strain the stock through a fine-mesh strainer into a bowl, then transfer the pods to a food processor and process until smooth. Pass the pea pod puree through a fine-mesh strainer set over a clean bowl, pressing on the solids to release as much puree as possible. You should have about 2 cups/500 g puree and 3½ cups/840 ml stock.

Make the risi e bisi: In a medium saucepan, melt 3 tablespoons/45 g of the butter with the olive oil over medium-low heat. Add the spring onion, pancetta, parsley, and garlic and cook, stirring occasionally, for about 5 minutes, until the onion is softened and golden. Add the peas and cook, stirring, for 2 minutes.

Add the pea stock, stir, and return to a simmer. Add the rice and simmer, stirring often, for about 10 minutes.

Add the pea pod puree and cook for about 10 more minutes, stirring, until most of the liquid has been absorbed and the rice is tender.

Remove from the heat, taste, and season with the salt and pepper. Add the remaining butter and the Parmigiano-Reggiano, stir, and serve immediately.

Risotto alla zucca

ROASTED SQUASH RISOTTO

**SERVES 4
AS A FIRST COURSE**

1 medium butternut
squash (about
2 pounds/1 kg),
halved lengthwise,
seeds and
membranes
removed

2 tablespoons extra-
virgin olive oil

½ teaspoon grated
nutmeg

Fine sea salt and
freshly ground black
pepper

7 tablespoons/100 g
unsalted butter

1 white onion, minced

1½ cups/300 g
Carnaroli, Arborio,
or Vialone Nano rice
(see page 33)

½ cup/120 ml dry
white wine

4 cups/1 L vegetable
stock, heated until
hot

2 ounces/60 g
Parmigiano-
Reggiano, grated

Risotto is often considered a rich and celebratory dish, the star of
Sunday meals, especially in Italy's northern regions, such as Piedmont,
Lombardy, and Veneto, that have traditionally been dedicated to growing
rice. But I think risotto makes an ideal weeknight meal. And if you learn
to make it by heart, you can have a nutritious dinner on the table in no
time.

Once you're confident with the basic recipe, vary it according to the
seasons: Add Tuscan kale or radicchio and walnuts in winter; asparagus,
peas, and fava beans in spring; zucchini, eggplant, and roasted tomatoes
in summer. Autumn has much to offer in terms of risotto comfort:
squash, porcini mushrooms, chestnuts, apples, and pears all represent the
quintessential idea of comfort in a dish. Most vegetables for risotto should
be cooked in advance and stirred in when the risotto is almost ready: for
example, sautéed zucchini, roasted tomatoes, or stewed radicchio. Shelled
fresh peas and fava beans or shaved asparagus are the exception; as they
require just a very brief cooking time, they can simply be stirred into the
risotto shortly before it is done.

——

Prepare the squash: Preheat the oven to 400°F/200°C.

Place the squash cut side up on a baking sheet lined with parchment paper.
Drizzle with the olive oil, sprinkle with the nutmeg and salt and pepper
to taste, and rub the oil and seasonings over the cut surfaces of the squash
with your fingers. Roast for about 1 hour, until the flesh is golden, almost
caramelized on the edges, and the pulp is so soft that it can be scooped out
with a spoon. Remove from the oven and set aside to cool.

When the squash is cool enough to handle, use a spoon to scoop out the
flesh; discard the skin. You should have about 2 cups/450 g squash flesh.

Prepare the risotto: In a large saucepan, melt half of the butter over low heat.
Add the onion and ½ teaspoon salt and cook, stirring with a wooden spoon,
until the onion is translucent and soft but not browned, about 5 minutes.

Add the rice, increase the heat to medium-low, and toast, stirring, for about
5 minutes, until the rice is translucent, almost pearly; if you listen carefully,
you will hear an almost imperceptible crackle. Another tip: Pick up a few

grains of rice; if they are too hot to handle, they are nicely toasted. Pour the wine over the rice and cook, stirring, until it has evaporated.

Add a ladleful of the hot stock and cook, stirring often, until the rice has absorbed most of the stock. Add another ladleful of stock and continue to cook, adding more stock when the rice looks dry, for about 10 minutes. As the rice cooks, it will release starch and the risotto will become creamier.

Add the butternut squash pulp by the spoonful, stirring well; the squash will melt into an orange cream and color the grains of rice. Continue cooking until you've added all the stock and the risotto is creamy but the rice is still slightly al dente; it should take about 18 minutes in all. Depending on the variety of rice you use, the cooking time may vary, and you may not need all the stock.

Remove the pan from the heat, add the Parmigiano-Reggiano and the remaining butter, and stir very well. This technique is what we call *mantecare* in Italian, meaning to cream the butter and cheese into the risotto. Taste and season with additional salt and pepper as necessary.

A traditional test to see if the risotto is properly made is to ladle a small amount of it onto the center of a plate. Tap on the bottom of the plate, and the risotto should easily spread across it; if the risotto is too thick, add some more stock before serving.

Ladle the risotto into warmed bowls and serve immediately.

VARIATION

Riso al salto: If you have leftover risotto, you can make riso al salto. Sprinkle some dry breadcrumbs over a medium platter, then press the risotto onto the breadcrumbs, shaping it into a thick disk. Sprinkle some breadcrumbs on top too. Melt a generous knob of butter in a heavy-bottomed nonstick pan over medium heat, then carefully slide the risotto disk into the pan. Cook until the risotto cake turns a deep golden brown and a crisp crust forms on the bottom. Invert the risotto onto a plate, then slide it back into the pan and brown on the other side. Serve immediately, cut into wedges if necessary.

THE CULTURE OF RICE IN ITALY

Rice is a symbol of Italian regional cuisine, a key ingredient in such iconic recipes as Venetian risi e bisi (page 28) and Sicilian arancine (page 242).

Although it had been used as medicine and a cosmetic since Roman times, during the Middle Ages, rice was an imported product mainly considered a spice or an ingredient for confectionery. Rice cultivation in Italy began because of foreign occupiers, and it occurred in different stages and territories, beginning in Sicily and moving to Lombardy and Veneto, Tuscany, and Naples. It was not until the fifteenth century that rice cultivation began to spread to the Po Valley, the area now universally associated with high-quality rice. Along this path, rice became a peasant food, often given as pay to the *mondine*, the legendary rice weeders who inspired many folk songs as well as literary and cinematographic works, including the 1949 neorealistic *Riso Amaro* (*Bitter Rice*).

The ingenuity of the rice farmers turned marshy, unproductive soils into important resources. The complex biological system of paddy fields became a precious gastronomic landscape that allowed for the cultivation of as many as five different types of crops that, together, provided a balanced diet for peasants. The main one was rice, often eaten with beans and lentils and vegetables.

The other "crops" consisted of fish, mainly carp and tench; ducks and geese; migrant birds; and frogs. They were a key ingredient of the cucina povera of rice-growing areas until after World War II, when, because of changes in rice cultivation techniques, their population declined, but risotto con le rane, made with frog, is still a testament to those times. Today, most of Italy's rice production takes place in two areas: Lombardy/Piedmont and Veneto.

RICE FOR ANY RECIPE

These are the most common varieties of Italian rice, but each person has their own preference, often based on their location or culinary traditions.

Arborio: This is the most popular rice in Italy and the easiest to find in North America. It has very large grains that hold up well to cooking, keeping their shape in soups. Choose Arborio to make risotto.

Carnaroli: Considered by many as the king of Italian rice, Carnaroli has a higher starch content than Arborio, as well as a good balance between its ability to absorb fat and its ability to release starch during cooking, key qualities for making a creamy risotto. It is also good for rice salads.

Originario: This is an ancient round-grain Italian rice. It is good for soups, including minestrone (page 24), as well as fritters, cakes, and puddings.

Ribe: Ribe is suitable for parboiled processing and often sold that way. It's good for incorporating into pilafs, salads, soups, and timbales, as well as for stuffed peppers (page 22) and stuffed tomatoes (page 43).

Roma: With large round grains, Roma is perfect for risotto, or boiled and served with tomato sauce, and for flans.

Vialone nano: From Italy's northeastern Veneto region, Vialone is an especially good choice for risi e bisi (page 28) or risotto with vegetables, such as squash (page 31).

Orecchiette con le cime di rapa

ORECCHIETTE WITH BROCCOLI RABE

**SERVES 4
AS A FIRST COURSE**

FOR THE ORECCHIETTE

2¼ cups/400 g
   semolina flour
¾ cup plus
   2 tablespoons/
   200 ml water

**FOR THE BROCCOLI RABE
DRESSING**

5 tablespoons/75 ml
   extra-virgin olive oil
½ cup/50 g dry
   breadcrumbs
1 pound/455 g broccoli
   rabe, tough stems
   removed
1 clove garlic, crushed
   and peeled
4 oil-packed anchovy
   fillets, chopped
Red pepper flakes

Cime di rapa, known variously as broccoli rabe (or rape) or rapini in English, is the most representative vegetable of the Apulian winter. You'll find it piled high in market stalls in the Southern Italian region as soon as the first cold days arrive.

With its bitter taste, broccoli rabe calls for robust, strong flavor combinations: it is excellent with meats, especially pork chops and sausages; with cheese, from a sharp pecorino to a creamy burrata; and even with fish, especially cod and anchovies. It is also a perfect complement to the Apulian extra-virgin olive oil, which is also usually quite bitter; don't be stingy with the oil when cooking broccoli rabe.

If I had to choose one regional dish that summarizes the Apulian way with broccoli rabe, the best choice by far would be orecchiette con le cime di rapa. The flowers and leaves and tender stems of the greens are boiled together with fresh orecchiette, the ear-shaped pasta, and then tossed in anchovy-and-garlic–infused olive oil spiced with red pepper flakes. The dish is topped with breadcrumbs fried in olive oil to add color, flavor, and a satisfying crunch.

———

The day before, make the orecchiette: Pour the flour onto a work surface and shape it into a mound with a large well in the center. Add the water to the well and, using a fork, stir slowly to incorporate it, starting from the center and gradually picking up more flour from the edges. When the dough turns crumbly, switch to kneading with your hands. You want to knead the dough until it forms a ball and the gluten starts to develop, as this will render the sheets of pasta more elastic. The dough is ready when you have clean hands and a clean board and the dough is smooth, silky, and no longer sticky.

Alternatively, you can make the dough in a stand mixer fitted with the dough hook. Knead for about 5 minutes on low speed, then turn it out and finish kneading by hand for about 5 minutes. (Or use dried orecchiette; see Note.)

Cut off a small piece of the dough and keep the rest covered with an upturned bowl while you shape the orecchiette. Roll the piece of dough under your palms into a rope about ½ inch/1.5 cm thick, then use a blunt knife to cut it into ½-inch/1.5 cm pillows of dough.

One at a time, use the rounded tip of the knife to push each dough pillow down and toward you; pushing the knife hard against the work surface will create the orecchiette's characteristic rough texture. Press it down more in the center to thin the middle of the piece of dough; the dough will curl around and over the knife. Pull it off the knife and flip it over onto your thumb. Arrange the orecchiette on a clean tea towel and repeat with the remaining dough.

Let the orecchiette dry overnight at room temperature.

The next day, prepare the broccoli rabe dressing: In a small frying pan, heat 1 tablespoon of the olive oil over medium heat. Add the breadcrumbs and toast, stirring, for about 5 minutes, until golden brown. Set aside.

Bring a large pot of water to a rolling boil and salt it generously. While the water heats, clean the broccoli rabe: Cut off the toughest stalks and discard. Rinse the rabe under cold running water and rip into large pieces.

Plunge the broccoli rabe into the boiling water. Submerge it with a spoon and cook for 10 minutes, or until soft.

Add the orecchiette, stir, and cook with the broccoli rabe for about 10 minutes, until al dente.

While the pasta cooks, pour the remaining ¼ cup/60 ml olive oil into a large high-sided frying pan and heat over medium heat. Add the garlic, anchovies, and red pepper flakes to taste and cook for about 5 minutes, until the garlic is golden and the anchovies have melted.

Drain the orecchiette and broccoli rabe and toss them into the pan with the garlicky olive oil. Cook for about 2 minutes, tossing well to coat the orecchiette and rabe, then sprinkle with the toasted breadcrumbs. Serve immediately.

NOTE: *You can substitute 1 pound/455 g dried orecchiette for the fresh pasta. If using dried orecchiette, remove the broccoli rabe from the boiling water once it is cooked, then cook the orecchiette in the same water according to the package instructions.*

VARIATION

If you want to go the extra mile, serve the orecchiette with burrata, the decadent cheese with a creamy filling of shredded mozzarella and cream. Cut the burrata open, pull it apart, and place on top of the pasta.

Pansoti con salsa di noci

FORAGED-HERB TORTELLI WITH WALNUT PESTO

SERVES 4 TO 6
AS A FIRST COURSE

FOR THE WALNUT PESTO

2 ounces/60 g day-old
bread
1 cup/240 ml whole
milk
1½ cups/5 ounces/
150 g walnuts
1 clove garlic
Leaves from 3 fresh
marjoram sprigs
¼ cup/25 g grated
Parmigiano-
Reggiano
Fine sea salt and
freshly ground
black pepper

FOR THE PASTA DOUGH

3¼ cups/400 g
all-purpose flour
⅔ cup/160 ml water
1 tablespoon dry white
wine
¼ teaspoon fine
sea salt

FOR THE FILLING

2 pounds/1 kg mixed
foraged greens (see
headnote)
½ clove garlic, minced
3 fresh marjoram
sprigs
Scant ½ cup/
3½ ounces/100 g
fresh ricotta, well
drained
½ cup/50 g grated
Parmigiano-
Reggiano

Ligurian pansoti are traditional stuffed ravioli made for Lent. _Pansoti_ means potbellied, a name that describes their plump round shape. The filling is made of a mixture of foraged herbs known as _preboggiòn_; the pasta is dressed with a traditional walnut pesto.

In Liguria, you can buy verdant bunches of preboggiòn at the market. The greens change according to season, locality, and family tradition, as foragers tend to pass down their knowledge from generation to generation, but the mix usually includes a perfect balance of bitter greens, such as dandelion or chicory, and milder greens, such as nettle, borage, or chard, which makes these pansoti irresistible. If you cannot find some of these, choose more common leafy greens, such as chard, arugula, escarole, and/or Savoy cabbage. Opt for as many varieties as possible to maintain the layered herbal taste of pansoti.

———

Make the pesto: Preheat the oven to 275°F/135°C.

Tear the bread into small pieces. Transfer to a medium bowl, pour the milk over, and set aside for about 15 minutes to soften the bread.

Squeeze the soaked bread over the bowl to remove the excess milk and then crumble it into another bowl. Set the bread aside and reserve the milk.

Spread the walnuts on a rimmed baking sheet and toast for 10 minutes. Let cool completely.

Transfer the walnuts to the bowl of a food processor and add the crumbled bread, garlic, and marjoram and blend to a paste, gradually adding the reserved milk as necessary; you might not need all the milk. Transfer to a medium bowl, add the Parmigiano-Reggiano, and mix well. Taste and adjust the seasoning with salt and pepper. Set aside.

Make the pasta dough: Pour the flour onto a work surface and shape it into a mound with a large well in the center. Add the water, white wine, and salt to the well and, using a fork, stir slowly to incorporate the liquid, starting from the center and gradually picking up more flour from the edges. When the dough turns crumbly, switch to kneading with your hands. You want to knead the dough until it forms a ball and the gluten starts to develop, as this

1 teaspoon fine
    sea salt
1 large/50 g egg,
    lightly beaten

Semolina flour for
    rolling
Grated Parmigiano-
    Reggiano for
    serving
Fresh marjoram
    leaves for garnish

will render the sheets of pasta more elastic. The dough is ready when you have clean hands and a clean board and the dough is smooth, silky, and no longer sticky.

Alternatively, you can make the dough in a stand mixer fitted with the dough hook. Knead for about 5 minutes on low speed, then turn it out and finish kneading by hand for about 5 minutes. Shape the dough into a ball.

Cover the dough with an upturned bowl and let rest for 30 minutes.

While the dough rests, make the filling: Bring a large pot of water to a rolling boil and salt it generously. Add the greens and blanch until wilted and tender, about 10 minutes. Drain and let cool slightly.

When the greens are cool enough to handle, squeeze well with your hands to remove excess water; you should have about 1 pound/450 g greens. Finely chop the greens, then transfer to a medium bowl, add the garlic, marjoram, ricotta, and Parmigiano-Reggiano, and mix well. Season with the salt, then add the egg and mix with a fork to thoroughly incorporate.

Make the pansoti: Lightly flour a work surface with semolina flour.

To roll out the dough by hand: Cut the dough into 2 pieces (or more, if you prefer); work with one piece of dough at a time, keeping the rest covered with a clean towel. On the lightly floured work surface, using a rolling pin, roll one piece of dough into a paper-thin sheet.

To roll out the dough using a pasta machine: Divide the pasta dough into 6 equal portions. On the lightly floured work surface, with a rolling pin, roll out one piece of dough into a ½-inch-thick/1.5 cm rectangle. (Keep the remaining pieces covered with a clean kitchen towel.)

Turn the dial on your pasta machine to the widest setting. Feed the dough through the rollers once, then fold the sheet of pasta in three, as if you were folding a letter. Starting with one of the open sides, feed the pasta dough through the machine again. Repeat 3 times, lightly dusting the sheet of dough with semolina flour each time to prevent it from sticking and tearing.

Turn the dial to the next narrower setting. Roll the pasta through the machine, gently pulling it toward you as it comes out of the machine; hold the pasta sheet with the palm of one hand while you crank the machine with the other hand. Continue to reduce the settings and roll the dough through the machine again, lightly dusting the sheet of dough with semolina flour each time, until the dough is as thin as you'd like; I usually stop at the next to last setting.

(CONTINUED)

Once you've rolled out one sheet of dough (by hand or with the pasta machine), start to shape the pansoti: Cut the sheet of dough into approximately 2-inch/5 cm squares. Place a teaspoon of filling in the center of each square, then fold the edges over to form a triangle. Press the edges together to seal the filling inside, then bring the outer corners at the bottom together, overlapping them, and press them tightly together. You will have potbellied parcels of pasta. Transfer the formed pansoti to a rimmed baking sheet dusted with semolina flour.

Repeat the rolling and shaping process with the remaining dough and filling.

Bring a large pot of water to a rolling boil and salt it generously. Add the pansoti and boil for 2 minutes. Drain, reserving ½ cup/120 ml of the pasta water, and transfer the pansoti to a bowl.

Add the walnut pesto to the pansoti and gently toss to coat, adding a bit of the pasta cooking water as needed to loosen the texture of the pesto so it coats the pansoti well. Divide the pansoti among four to six serving plates and sprinkle each serving with grated Parmigiano-Reggiano and some marjoram leaves. Serve immediately.

ALL THE GREENS

Preboggiòn is the main ingredient of pansoti, but it also has a key role in salads, rice soups, and savory cakes, such as torta pasqualina (page 165). These are the most common greens in preboggiòn, with their given English, Italian, and Latin names.

Borage - Borragine - *Borago officinalis*

Brighteyes - Caccialepre or grattalingua - *Reichardia picroides*

Chard - Bietola - *Beta vulgaris*

Chicory - Cicoria - *Cichorium intybus*

Dandelion - Tarassaco - *Taraxacum officinale*

Nettle - Ortica - *Urtica dioica*

Prickly sow thistle - Cicerbita - *Sonchus asper*

Poppy - Papavero - *Papaver rhoeas*

Salad burnet - Pimpinella or sanguisorba - *Poterium sanguisorba*

Smooth golden fleece - Boccione - *Urospermum dalechampii*

White campion - Silene bianca - *Silene latifolia*

Pomodori ripieni di riso alla romana

RICE-STUFFED TOMATOES

**SERVES 4
AS A MAIN COURSE,
8 AS A FIRST COURSE**

8 ripe but firm
  beefsteak tomatoes
  (about 2 pounds/
  1 kg)
6 tablespoons/90 ml
  extra-virgin olive oil
Fine sea salt and
  freshly ground black
  pepper
1 clove garlic, finely
  minced
1 tablespoon finely
  chopped fresh basil
1 cup/200 g Arborio
  or Ribe rice (see
  page 33)
4 medium potatoes
  (about 1 pound/
  455 g), peeled and
  cut into wedges

If you are searching for an inclusive vegan and gluten-free main course for a summer meal, look no further. Stuff ripe round tomatoes with Arborio rice, plumped with the juices of the hollowed-out tomatoes and flavored with chopped basil and garlic. Bake them along with wedges of potatoes until golden brown, starting to caramelize, and almost collapsing, and serve hot or at room temperature. One bite, and you'll be instantly transported to a trattoria in Trastevere, with rusty red plaster walls and an ivy-covered pergola.

———

Cut off the top of each tomato with a sharp knife; set the tomato tops aside. Gently empty out each tomato with a spoon, collecting the flesh, seeds, and juices in a bowl.

Add 2 tablespoons of the olive oil, 1 teaspoon salt, ¼ teaspoon pepper, the garlic, and the basil to the tomato flesh and juices and blend with an immersion blender (or use a stand blender and then return to the bowl) until smooth. Add the rice and stir to combine. Let the filling stand at room temperature for a few hours, until the rice has absorbed most of the liquid.

Sprinkle the inside of each tomato with salt and place the tomatoes cut side down on a rimmed baking sheet to drain.

Preheat the oven to 400°F/200°C. Choose a baking pan that will hold the tomatoes and potatoes comfortably, without crowding; the potatoes will need space to brown properly.

Arrange the emptied tomatoes cut side up in the baking pan. Fill them with the soaked rice up to one finger's width from the top, then place the tomato tops over the rice, without closing them completely. Scatter the potato wedges around the tomatoes, then drizzle everything with the remaining ¼ cup/60 ml olive oil and season with salt and pepper.

Transfer the baking pan to the oven and bake for 45 to 50 minutes, until the rice is cooked through, the tomatoes are soft and slightly caramelized at the edges, and the potatoes are golden brown.

Serve hot or at room temperature. Any leftovers can be stored in the fridge for 2 days; reheat gently before serving.

Zucchini ripieni alla ligure

POTATO-AND-MUSHROOM–STUFFED ZUCCHINI

**SERVES 4 TO 6
AS A MAIN COURSE**

⅓ cup/½ ounce/
   15 g dried porcini
   mushrooms
12 small zucchini
   (each about
   5 inches/13 cm
   long)
1 pound/455 g Yukon
   Gold potatoes,
   peeled and diced
1 clove garlic, minced
1 tablespoon minced
   fresh marjoram
1 teaspoon fine sea
   salt, or more to
   taste
¼ teaspoon freshly
   ground black
   pepper, or more
   to taste
2 large/100 g eggs,
   lightly beaten
2 tablespoons dry
   breadcrumbs
3 tablespoons extra-
   virgin olive oil

Stuffed vegetables of all sorts are traditionally prepared well in advance for this typical Ligurian summer dish, then served at room temperature. To me, this is a win-win situation: you can relax and enjoy a meal with your guests (and have a clean kitchen by the time they arrive).

Of all the regional cuisines on the Italian peninsula, Ligurian is one of the most inventive with vegetables. Here an aromatic filling of potatoes, marjoram, porcini mushrooms, and garlic is nestled into parboiled zucchini shells: you could also use artichokes, onions, small eggplants, mushrooms, or bell peppers, or even zucchini flowers. The filling, referred to as *ripieno di magro* (lean) because it is made without meat, is based on what is found in Ligurian vegetable gardens nestled in the terraces overlooking the sea as well as what grows wild in its fertile soil.

———

Put the porcini in a small bowl and add hot water to cover. Let stand for 30 minutes.

Meanwhile, bring a large pot of water to a rolling boil and salt it generously. Add the zucchini, reduce the heat to medium, and cook for 10 to 12 minutes, until the zucchini can be easily pierced with the tip of a knife. Using tongs, transfer the zucchini to a colander, rinse under cold water, and let cool completely.

Add the potatoes to the pot and return the water to a boil, then lower the heat and cook until the potatoes can be easily pierced with the tip of a knife. Drain the potatoes in the colander, then return them to the pot and mash with a potato masher, or use a ricer.

Cut the zucchini lengthwise in half and scoop out the flesh with a teaspoon, leaving shells about ¼ inch/6 mm thick. Add the zucchini pulp to the mashed potatoes.

Drain the porcini, squeeze out any excess water, and finely chop. Add the porcini to the potato mixture, along with the garlic, marjoram, salt, and pepper, and mix well. Taste and adjust the seasoning if necessary, then add the eggs and mix thoroughly. Transfer the filling to a pastry bag fitted with a large plain tip, or use a spoon to fill the zucchini shells.

Preheat the oven to 350°F/175°C.

Line a rimmed baking sheet with parchment paper and arrange the zucchini shells on the pan, cut side up. Pipe or spoon the potato filling into the shells, dividing it evenly, then sprinkle the zucchini with the breadcrumbs and drizzle with the olive oil.

Transfer the pan to the oven and bake for 40 minutes, or until the filling is golden brown.

Serve the zucchini hot or at room temperature. Any leftovers can be stored in the fridge for 2 days; reheat gently before serving.

Melanzane ripiene alla calabrese

BREAD-AND-CHEESE–STUFFED EGGPLANT

SERVES 4
AS A MAIN COURSE,
8 AS A FIRST COURSE

4 medium eggplants
9 ounces/255 g day-old bread, crusts removed
2 cups/520 g Garlicky Tomato Sauce (page 308), reheated
1 clove garlic, minced
2 tablespoons minced fresh basil
1¼ cups/120 g grated pecorino
Fine sea salt and freshly ground black pepper
1 large/50 g egg, lightly beaten
7 ounces/200 g provolone, cut into 16 cubes
2 cups/480 ml vegetable or other neutral oil for deep-frying
Extra-virgin olive oil for drizzling

Eggplant parmigiana, eggplant caponata, pasta alla Norma with fried eggplant, ricotta salata, and tomato sauce: all of these recipes tell the story of Southern Italy's love affair with this Mediterranean ingredient. This recipe from Calabria has it all: a punchy tomato sauce blanketing fried eggplant shells filled with a stuffing of day-old bread, minced garlic and basil, sharp pecorino cheese, and melting provolone. It may sound like there's a lot to do to make this summer recipe, but you can tackle one step at a time, and keep in mind that these can be prepared in advance and gently reheated before serving.

———

Bring a large pot of water to a boil. Add the eggplants to the boiling water and boil for about 15 minutes, until you can easily pierce them with a knife. Drain and let them cool completely.

Meanwhile, tear the bread into big chunks, transfer to a bowl, add cold water to cover, and set aside to soak. Check the bread after 5 to 10 minutes; it should have soaked up enough water to become soft. If it's still a bit hard, let it soak a few minutes longer. When the bread is soft, remove it from the water, squeeze to remove the excess water, and transfer to a large bowl.

Cut the cooled eggplants lengthwise in half and scoop out the flesh with a spoon, leaving shells about ¼ inch/6 mm thick. Transfer the eggplant pulp to a colander set over a bowl and let cool until it's easy to handle, then squeeze as much water as possible from the flesh. Set the eggplant shells and pulp aside.

Add the eggplant pulp, 3 tablespoons of the tomato sauce, the garlic, basil, and 1 cup/100 g of the pecorino to the bowl with the bread and mix thoroughly to combine, then season to taste with salt and pepper. Stir in the beaten egg. The filling will be thick and dense.

Divide the filling equally among the eggplant boats. Press 2 cubes of provolone into the filling in each eggplant, making sure the cheese is completely covered.

Pour the oil into a large high-sided pot set over medium-high heat. Set a wire rack on a rimmed baking sheet and place nearby. When the oil registers 350°F/175°C on a deep-frying thermometer, or when a wooden spoon immersed in the oil is immediately surrounded by tiny bubbles, add a few of the eggplant halves to the pan, filling side down, and fry for about 5 minutes to seal the filling; when the filling is golden brown, flip the eggplant using two forks and fry for 1 more minute. Transfer to the wire rack to drain and fry the remaining eggplants in batches, letting the oil return to temperature between batches.

Preheat the oven to 400°F/200°C.

Arrange the eggplants in a single layer in a baking dish, filling side up, and spoon the remaining tomato sauce over. Sprinkle with the remaining ¼ cup/ 20 g pecorino and drizzle with olive oil. Transfer the baking dish to the oven and bake for 35 minutes, or until the eggplant is browned all over.

Serve hot or at room temperature. Any leftovers can be stored in the fridge for 2 days; reheat gently before serving.

Peperoni ripieni alla lucana

BREAD-AND-ANCHOVY–STUFFED SWEET GREEN PEPPERS

**SERVES 4
AS A MAIN COURSE,
8 AS A FIRST COURSE**

18 friggitelli or other
  thin-skinned sweet
  green peppers,
  such as cubanelle
  or Jimmy Nardello,
  or even shishitos
  (see Note)
4 salt-packed
  anchovies
½ cup/120 ml extra-
  virgin olive oil, plus
  more for drizzling
1½ cups/185 g coarse
  breadcrumbs
2 tablespoons
  chopped pitted
  black olives
1 tablespoon brined
  capers, rinsed and
  minced
2 Roma (plum)
  tomatoes, diced
⅓ cup/60 g canned
  tuna packed in olive
  oil, drained
½ teaspoon dried
  oregano
Fine sea salt and
  freshly ground
  black pepper

Every year, my parents plant four rows of sweet green peppers in our garden for one single purpose: making stuffed friggitelli. This traditional recipe belongs to the Southern Italian branch of my family, from the hilltop town of Melfi in the region of Basilicata. The friggitelli peppers are stuffed with pantry ingredients: fried breadcrumbs and anchovies are the filling for the simplest version, a true cucina povera leitmotif. My aunt's version is stuffed with tuna, capers, and olives. The underlying philosophy is to take whatever is found at the back of your pantry or your fridge—cheese, gherkins, pickled onions, you name it—and mix it with breadcrumbs to make a rich and tasty filling.

———

Gently wash and dry the peppers, then remove the stems with a sharp knife and pull out the seeds. Set the peppers aside.

Rinse the anchovies under cold running water. Gently remove and discard the backbones, opening up each anchovy and separating it into 2 fillets. Finely chop the anchovies.

Pour the olive oil into a large frying pan set over low heat. Add the anchovies and cook, stirring, until they have melted into the oil. Increase the heat to medium, add the breadcrumbs, and cook, stirring, until they are golden brown, about 5 minutes.

Transfer the breadcrumb mixture to a bowl and add the olives, capers, tomatoes, tuna, and oregano. Mix well; you should have a moist filling that holds together when you squeeze it.

Preheat the oven to 400°F/200°C. Line a baking pan that will hold the peppers comfortably with parchment paper.

Stuff the peppers to about one finger's width from the top without compressing the filling too much or overfilling the peppers, as the stuffing has a tendency to burst out during baking.

Arrange the stuffed peppers in the baking pan, drizzle with extra-virgin olive oil, and season with salt and black pepper. Transfer to the oven and bake until the peppers are browned all over, 30 to 45 minutes, depending on the size of the peppers.

Serve hot or at room temperature. Any leftovers can be stored in the fridge for 2 days; reheat gently before serving.

NOTE: *You can substitute cubanelle, Jimmy Nardello, or shishito peppers for the friggitelli if necessary. Friggitelli are usually around 4 inches/10 cm long; if substituting a smaller pepper, you might need to increase the amount you use.*

Vignarola

ARTICHOKE, FAVA BEAN, PEA, AND LETTUCE STEW

SERVES 4 TO 6
AS A FIRST COURSE
OR SIDE DISH

4 large artichokes
1 lemon, halved
1⅔ cups/255 g shelled
    fresh peas (from
    about 2 pounds/1 kg
    in the pod), 10 pods
    reserved
1¾ cups/255 g shelled
    fava beans (from
    about 2 pounds/1 kg
    in the pod), 6 pods
    reserved
2 spring onions,
    dark green parts
    removed and
    reserved, bulbs
    and pale green
    parts sliced, or
    12 scallions, thinly
    sliced
4 cups/1 L water
Fine sea salt
¼ cup/60 ml extra-
    virgin olive oil
2 ounces/60 g
    guanciale or
    pancetta, cubed
½ head romaine
    lettuce, shredded
    (about 3 cups)
Leaves from 1 fresh
    mint sprig
Freshly ground black
    pepper
Shaved Pecorino
    Romano for serving

Vignarola is something to look forward to every spring. A staple of Roman trattorias, and a recipe that belongs to the peasant tradition, it is a stew that celebrates spring produce and the arrival of the season. There's just one short period when young fava beans, fresh peas, artichokes, and spring onions are all at their best, and that is when you must make vignarola.

Spring vegetables demand a slow, gentle simmering, so you want to cook them, covered, in their own stock until they turn into a delicate, creamy stew. Add them to the pan according to the order of their cooking time: begin with the artichokes, which will take the longest, and move on to the fava beans, fresh peas, and, finally, romaine lettuce. Taste the mix each time you add a new vegetable and adjust the seasoning and, if necessary, the cooking time accordingly. Finish with fresh mint.

Enjoy vignarola as a starter or as a side dish; it is perfect served with lamb. Or use it to sauce a bowl of pasta. As with any stew, the leftovers are even tastier the following day.

——

Prep the artichokes: To clean the artichokes, remove the tough outer leaves and cut off the stems; reserve 10 of the leaves for the stock. Peel the stems and cut each artichoke into 8 wedges (see the sidebar about cleaning artichokes on page 53). Use a small spoon to remove the hairy chokes, then rub the artichoke wedges with the halved lemon. Set aside.

Make the stock: Put the reserved 10 artichoke leaves, 10 pea pods, 6 fava bean pods, and dark green parts of the spring onions (or half of the scallions) into a medium pot. Add the water and bring to a boil over high heat, then reduce the heat to an active simmer and simmer for 30 minutes, or until the liquid is reduced by half. Remove from the heat. You need about 2 cups/480 ml stock for this recipe; reserve any extra stock for another use.

Strain the stock through a fine-mesh strainer into a bowl and discard the solids. Return the stock to the pot, season to taste with salt, and keep warm over low heat.

Make the vignarola: In a medium saucepan, heat the olive oil over medium-low heat. Add the guanciale and sliced spring onions (or the remaining

scallions), season with salt, and cook, stirring often, until the spring onions (or scallions) have softened, about 5 minutes. Add the artichoke wedges and stems to the pan, stir, and add 1 cup/240 ml of the stock. Cover and cook for about 10 minutes, until the artichokes have softened a bit.

Add the fava beans and ½ cup/120 ml more stock, cover, and cook for about 5 minutes. Add the peas and the remaining stock and cook, covered, for about 10 minutes. Stir in the shredded lettuce and cook for about 5 more minutes, until the lettuce has wilted.

Add the mint leaves and season to taste with salt and pepper. Transfer the vignarola to a serving bowl and top with shaved Pecorino Romano.

VARIATIONS

You can easily make a vegetarian version by omitting the guanciale.

Some cooks add a glass of dry white wine along with the stock when stewing the vegetables.

HOW TO CLEAN ARTICHOKES

You can treat cleaning artichokes as a form of kitchen meditation: while your hands are occupied with the mechanical action, your mind is free to wander. The following method applies to both baby artichokes and regular-size ones.

Start with a large bowl of acidulated water: Halve a lemon and squeeze the juice into a bowl of water. This will prevent the artichokes from turning brown, as they will oxidize quickly once cut. Keep the 2 lemon halves in the water to use to rub the artichokes as you work, and your hands too.

Remove the tougher outer leaves of each artichoke until you reach the pale softer ones. With a sharp knife, remove the spiky tip of the artichoke, then cut off the stem. Set the stem aside. Rub the artichoke all over with a lemon half and plunge it into the bowl of acidulated water.

Then tackle the stems. One at a time, peel them until you reach the whiter, softer interior, then rub them with a lemon half to prevent them from turning brown and add to the bowl of lemon water. Artichoke stems are flavorful, perfect to use in a risotto or pasta sauce, or to stew along with the artichokes.

If you're serving the artichokes raw, cut them in half and use a small spoon to scoop out the furry choke if necessary. If they are very fresh, you may not need to do this step.

Ciambotta

SUMMER VEGETABLE STEW

**SERVES 6
AS A SIDE DISH**

⅓ cup/80 ml extra-
  virgin olive oil
1 yellow onion, thinly
  sliced
Fine sea salt
1 medium eggplant,
  cut into ½-inch/
  1.5 cm cubes
2 bell peppers, cored,
  seeded, and cut into
  strips
3 medium potatoes,
  peeled and cubed
2 medium zucchini,
  cubed
2 Roma (plum)
  tomatoes, cubed
⅓ cup/80 ml tomato
  puree (passata)
⅓ cup/80 ml hot water
Freshly ground black
  pepper
A few fresh basil
  leaves
Crusty bread for
  serving

Think of ciambotta as the Southern Italian cousin of France's ratatouille. It's a vegetable stew of peasant origins that puts summer bounty to good use. Zucchini, bell peppers, tomatoes, onions, eggplants, and potatoes: one by one, you add the cut-up vegetables to the pot according to their cooking time and simmer until they're all tender but still hold their shape.

Ciambotta was first made to feed farmers and shepherds, when it would be prepared early in the day and poured into a bread bowl, made from a sturdy round loaf of bread from which the crumb was removed. Wrapped in a napkin, it would be left to mellow and blend the flavors until lunchtime.

——

Pour the olive oil into a large pot set over low heat and add the onion. Season with a generous pinch of salt. Cook, stirring, for 5 minutes, or until the onion is soft and translucent.

Add the eggplant, stir well, increase the heat to medium, and cook, stirring occasionally, for 5 minutes, until slightly softened. Add the bell peppers and potatoes and cook, stirring, for 5 minutes, then stir in the zucchini and tomatoes and cook, stirring occasionally, for 5 minutes more.

Stir in the tomato puree, add the hot water, and stir well. Lower the heat and cook, covered, for about 25 minutes, checking from time to time. The ciambotta is ready when all the vegetables are cooked through but still hold their shape; there should still be some liquid left in the pot. Taste and adjust the seasoning with more salt as necessary and black pepper, then stir in the basil leaves.

Serve hot or at room temperature, with crusty bread. Any leftovers can be stored in the fridge for 2 days; reheat gently before serving.

VARIATION

Cook the ciambotta in a large sauté pan and keep it on the brothier side, adding a bit more water when you make it. Break one egg per person into the ciambotta, leaving space between them, and poach until the whites are set but the yolks are still runny. Serve with plenty of crusty bread.

BEEF, PORK, AND LAMB

OFFAL AND AFFORDABLE CUTS OF MEAT

Lingua con salsa verde
Veal Tongue with Parsley Sauce   60

Ossobuco alla milanese con risotto allo zafferano
Milanese-Style Braised Veal Shank with
Saffron Risotto   63

Rigatoni alla vaccinara
Oxtail Stew with Rigatoni   65

Trippa al sugo
Stewed Tripe   68

Stracotto di manzo alla fiorentina
Florentine Beef Stew   70

Fegato alla veneziana
Onion-Stewed Calf's Liver   73

Cassoeula
Pork Stew with Savoy Cabbage   74

Maiale ciffe e ciaffe
Pork Braised in White Wine   77

Spiedini di fegatelli di maiale
Roasted Pork Liver Skewers   78

Agnello cacio e ova
Stewed Lamb with Eggs and Cheese   80

Erbazzone reggiano
Savory Swiss Chard and
Parmigiano-Reggiano Pie   83

THE NOSE-TO-TAIL APPROACH TO COOKING HAS BROUGHT CUCINA povera to the menus of contemporary trattorias and fine-dining restaurants, as well as back to home cooking. Ingredients such as offal, or innards, that were once considered by-products are now viewed as interesting choices, full of taste, flavor, and potential, at an affordable price.

Cucina povera is not limited to offal, though. It also makes use of "second-choice" cuts that require long, diligent, and patient cooking to bring out their best. As my butcher always says, "There's more than just one fillet in a cow." Meaning that it is more sustainable, and respectful, to explore other less familiar cuts that are often even tastier, and more affordable, than a steak.

Those are also the cuts novices in the kitchen should approach first. Stews such stracotto (page 70) are much more versatile dishes than, for example, a grilled or pan-seared steak. And, unlike a steak, which requires perfect time management, a slow-cooked stew is forgiving: ten minutes more or less will usually not make much of a difference in the final result.

In Italian cities, the modern culture of meat eating developed in neighborhoods around the slaughterhouses, where the "quinto quarto" was born—or, better, invented. A beef carcass would traditionally be divided into quarters. The first quarter was intended for the nobles, the second for the clergy, the third for the bourgeoisie, and, finally, the last quarter for the soldiers. The head, tail, and all the offcuts (offal), making up a fifth quarter, were left to butchers and poor people. And that is where the Italian cucina povera found a fertile soil for inventive and nutritious dishes.

The quinto quarto, or frattaglie, includes the innards of slaughtered quadrupeds, a lively, gutsy list people are usually squeamish about: tripe, kidneys, heart, lungs, liver, spleen, sweetbreads, testicles, udder, uterus, brain, tongue, tail, hooves, ligaments, and cartilage, as well as bone marrow. Offal was, therefore, often the only choice for poor households and for the traditional osterias born at the edges of slaughterhouses to feed the local workers; it was also the main ingredient of much street food (see page 85). And nowadays warming dishes such as trippa al sugo (page 68), or a plate of boiled veal tongue draped with a vinegary salsa verde (page 60) are still fixtures of traditional trattorias throughout Italy.

If meat, especially beef and offal, was mainly consumed in the cities, in the countryside, it was really all about pigs and poultry.

The slaughtering of a pig was a ritual, whether pagan or religious, for the peasant people. Although it was a necessity for sustenance, it was also a moment of social aggregation, bringing together family and neighbors.

Slaughtering took place in the early morning, just after dawn, from December to February, when a pig raised by a family or a village was ready to be killed and butchered. The cold months were optimal, so the fresh meat would be better preserved thanks to the biting temperatures. Such rituals were more common fifty or sixty years ago, but today there are still families and groups of friends who raise or buy a pig to butcher and share the meat for the year to come.

There are many dishes to celebrate the annual slaughter, and many of them are linked to the Feast of Saint Anthony the Great, the patron saint of domestic animals and butchers, on the seventeenth of January. In Lombardy, the slaughter is celebrated with a large casserole of steaming-hot cassoeula (page 74), a pork stew with Savoy cabbage, while in Abruzzo, the dish of choice is maiale ciffe e ciaffe (page 77), a pork stew with olive oil, white wine, and rosemary. These, among other typical dishes, are generous and filling, made to feed a crowd.

Lingua con salsa verde

VEAL TONGUE WITH PARSLEY SAUCE

**SERVES 8 TO 12
AS A STARTER**

FOR THE VEAL TONGUE

3 quarts/3 L water
2 whole cloves
1 yellow onion, halved
1 carrot, peeled and
   cut into thirds
1 celery stalk, halved
One 2½-pound/1.1 kg
   veal tongue
1 tablespoon coarse
   sea salt

FOR THE SALSA VERDE

1 slice stale bread
   (about 2 ounces/
   60 g), crusts
   removed
2 tablespoons white
   wine vinegar
2 tablespoons water
1 small bunch fresh
   flat-leaf parsley
   (about 1 ounce/
   30 g), leaves
   removed
1½ tablespoons brined
   capers, drained
1 hard-boiled egg,
   peeled and finely
   chopped
1 clove garlic, minced
1 cup/240 ml extra-
   virgin olive oil
¼ teaspoon fine
   sea salt
¼ teaspoon freshly
   ground black
   pepper

Veal tongue is a typical Piedmontese starter, but it is also often part of bollito misto (see page 305). Serve it with a traditional salsa verde, a thick egg and parsley sauce characterized by a slightly acidic and refreshing taste, thanks to capers and stale bread soaked in vinegar. A glass of robust red wine served alongside is mandatory.

———

Make the veal: Fill a large pot with the water. Stick the cloves into one onion half and add the onion halves to the pot, along with the carrot and celery. Bring the water to a boil over medium-high heat.

Add the tongue and salt and reduce the heat until the liquid is simmering gently. Simmer until the tongue is very tender (the tip of a sharp knife should slide in easily), 2 to 3 hours.

Turn off the heat and leave the tongue in the stock until ready to serve. Or, if you won't be eating the tongue within an hour or so, let cool completely in the stock, then transfer the tongue to an airtight container, pour the stock over it, and refrigerate.

Make the salsa verde: Break the stale bread into chunks, transfer to a bowl, and add the vinegar and water. Let stand for 10 minutes.

Squeeze the bread to remove the excess liquid and crumble into a medium bowl.

Finely chop the parsley and capers together and add to the bowl with the bread. Add the chopped hard-boiled egg and garlic. Pour in the olive oil and stir to combine, then season with the salt and pepper. Let stand for at least an hour before serving so the flavors can mingle. The sauce will keep, refrigerated, for up to 4 days; stir well before serving.

To serve the tongue, peel off the skin and thinly slice. Serve with the salsa verde.

Ossobuco alla milanese con risotto allo zafferano

MILANESE-STYLE BRAISED VEAL SHANK WITH SAFFRON RISOTTO

**SERVES 4
AS A MAIN COURSE**

FOR THE OSSOBUCO

4 veal shanks (about 9 ounces/255 g each)

Fine sea salt and freshly ground black pepper

¼ cup/30 g all-purpose flour

About ½ cup/120 ml extra-virgin olive oil

4 tablespoons/60 g unsalted butter

1 white onion, thinly sliced

1 carrot, peeled and diced

1 celery stalk, diced

2 cups/480 ml dry white wine

2 cups/480 ml Beef Stock (page 305)

FOR THE GREMOLATA

2 tablespoons finely chopped fresh flat-leaf parsley

Grated zest of ½ lemon

½ clove garlic, minced

Saffron Risotto (recipe follows)

Bone marrow lends a deep roasted meat flavor to any dish and makes any sauce silky and rich. It's the bone marrow that makes ossobuco and risotto alla milanese world famous. For ossobuco, veal shanks are braised in tomato sauce and topped with gremolata, a condiment made by mincing lemon zest, parsley, and garlic together. The marrow from the veal shanks becomes the most exquisite part of the dish, meant to be scooped out with a spoon and eaten with a piece of crusty bread.

The classic accompaniment to ossobuco is risotto allo zafferano, milanese saffron risotto, the only risotto other than risotto in bianco that is served as a side dish rather than a first course. You could add a spoonful of bone marrow to flavor the risotto, along with the butter and perhaps rendered fat from a roast.

If you don't have time to make the risotto, serve the ossobuco with braised carrots and peas and mashed potatoes.

———

Make the ossobuco: Season the veal shanks all over with salt and pepper and dredge in the flour to coat. In a large Dutch oven, heat a few tablespoons of olive oil over medium-high heat. When the oil is hot, add the shanks in a single layer (work in two batches, adding more oil to the pot, if necessary) and cook, turning once, until well browned on both sides, about 10 minutes. Transfer the shanks to a plate.

Preheat the oven to 325°F/165°C.

Pour out and discard the oil from the Dutch oven, wipe out with paper towels, and return it to medium-low heat. Add 3 tablespoons oil and the butter to the pot and heat until the butter has melted. Add the onion, carrot, and celery and cook, stirring, until the onion is soft and the carrot is beginning to brown, 8 minutes.

Pour in the wine and beef stock and return the shanks to the Dutch oven. Bring to a boil, then cover, transfer to the oven, and cook for 30 minutes. Uncover the pot; the liquid should be bubbling gently. If it is bubbling vigorously, reduce the oven temperature to 300°F/150°C. Cover the pot again and continue cooking until the meat is fork-tender, 3 to 3½ hours total.

(CONTINUED)

While the ossobuco cooks, make the gremolata: In a small bowl, combine the parsley, lemon zest, and garlic. Set aside.

When the ossobuco is done, the sauce should cloak the meat; if it is still somewhat thin, transfer the shanks to a plate, cover loosely to keep warm, and set the Dutch oven over medium-high heat. Bring the liquid to a boil and boil until reduced enough to coat a spoon. Taste the sauce and season with salt and pepper.

Transfer the veal shanks to a serving platter, spoon some sauce over, and sprinkle with the gremolata. Serve with the risotto.

Risotto allo zafferano

SAFFRON RISOTTO

**SERVES 4 AS A SIDE
DISH OR FIRST COURSE**

3 cups/720 ml Beef
    Stock (page 305)
Pinch of saffron
    threads
8 tablespoons/1 stick/
    115 g unsalted
    butter
1 white onion, minced
Fine sea salt
1½ cups/300 g
    Arborio, Carnaroli,
    or Vialone Nano rice
    (see page 33)
½ cup/120 ml dry
    white wine
2 ounces/60 g
    Parmigiano-
    Reggiano, grated

Pour the stock into a saucepan, add the saffron, and bring to a simmer over medium heat. Reduce the heat and keep warm.

Meanwhile, in a large saucepan, melt half of the butter over low heat. Add the onion and ½ teaspoon salt and cook, stirring with a wooden spoon, until the onion is translucent and soft but not browned, about 5 minutes.

Add the rice to the pan, increase the heat to medium-low, and toast the rice for about 5 minutes, until it is translucent, almost pearly; if you listen carefully, you will hear an almost imperceptible crackle. Another tip: Pick up a few grains of rice; if they are too hot to handle, they are nicely toasted. Pour the wine over the rice and cook, stirring, until it has evaporated.

Add a ladleful of the hot stock and cook, stirring often, until the rice has absorbed most of the stock. Add another ladleful of stock and cook, continuing to add more stock whenever the rice looks dry, for about 10 minutes. As the rice cooks, it will release starch and the risotto will become creamier. Continue cooking until you've added all the stock and the risotto is creamy but the rice is still slightly al dente; this should take about 18 minutes in all. Depending on the variety of rice you use, the cooking time may vary, and you may not need all the stock.

Remove the pan from the heat, add the Parmigiano-Reggiano and the remaining butter, and stir well. This technique is what we call *mantecare* in Italian, meaning to cream the butter and cheese into the risotto. Taste and season with more salt if necessary. Serve immediately.

Rigatoni alla vaccinara

OXTAIL STEW WITH RIGATONI

SERVES 6 TO 8
AS A FIRST COURSE

3 pounds/1.4 kg
    oxtails
Fine sea salt and
    freshly ground black
    pepper
½ cup/120 ml extra-
    virgin olive oil
2 carrots, peeled and
    finely diced
1 celery stalk, finely
    diced
1 red onion, finely
    diced
1 clove garlic, crushed
    and peeled
1 cup/240 ml dry red
    wine
½ cup/100 g tomato
    paste
3 cups/720 ml hot
    water
1 pound/455 g rigatoni
Grated Pecorino
    Romano for serving

Coda alla vaccinara, an oxtail stew made with celery, pine nuts, and cocoa powder, is an iconic quinto quarto Roman recipe, born at the edges of the Testaccio Market. Once popular with the slaughterhouse workers and manual laborers who appreciated a filling and cheap dish, it is now enjoyed by tourists and locals alike, who love nothing more than getting their hands and chins greasy stripping the meat off the bones.

This recipe is a simplified version of the traditional dish, a hearty stew that can double as a rich sauce for pasta. I use rigatoni because its ridges and holes will hold the chunky sauce.

———

Season the oxtails all over with salt and pepper. In a large Dutch oven, heat ¼ cup/60 ml of the olive oil over medium-high heat. When the oil is hot, working in batches if necessary, add the oxtail pieces in a single layer and cook, turning with tongs, until browned on all sides, about 20 minutes. Transfer the oxtails to a plate as they are browned.

Pour out any excess oil and wipe out the pot with paper towels. Return the pot to medium-low heat and add the remaining ¼ cup/60 ml oil. When the oil is hot, add the carrots, celery, onion, garlic, and a generous pinch of salt. Cook, stirring occasionally, until the vegetables are soft and beginning to brown, about 10 minutes.

Return the browned oxtails to the pot and stir thoroughly to coat with the sautéed vegetables. Pour in the wine, bring to a boil, and boil until reduced by half, about 10 minutes.

In a large measuring cup, stir together the tomato paste and hot water, then pour into the Dutch oven. Bring to a boil, then reduce the heat until the liquid is simmering gently, cover, and simmer, stirring from time to time, until almost all the liquid has evaporated and the meat is falling from the bone, about 2 hours. Remove from the heat and let cool to room temperature.

With tongs, transfer the oxtails to a bowl. Using two forks or your fingers, pull the meat from the bones, discarding the bones and membranes, and shred the meat into bite-size pieces.

(CONTINUED)

Return the shredded meat to the Dutch oven, stir to coat, and reheat gently over low heat, stirring occasionally.

Meanwhile, bring a large pot of salted water to a boil. Cook the rigatoni according to the package instructions until al dente, then drain, reserving some of the pasta cooking liquid.

Add the pasta to the oxtail mixture and toss to coat, adding a bit of the pasta cooking liquid as needed to help the sauce cling to the noodles. Transfer to plates or bowls and serve with a generous dusting of grated Pecorino Romano.

TESTACCIO MARKET IN ROME

Rome's Testaccio Market was built in 1890 as a modern slaughterhouse. It had a monumental entrance, and a separate department where the butchering followed kosher ritual. The market was always crowded with customers and workers—butchers, vendors, tanners, wholesalers. Surrounding the slaughterhouse were osterias and trattorias, along with fraschette, holes-in-the-wall pouring local wines. Quinto quarto (see page 10) was the main attraction of any menu, and you could find peasant dishes such as trippa, pajata (the intestines of unweaned calves still containing creamy, curdled milk), coratella (offal from small animals such as rabbits and poultry, as well as lamb) coi carciofi, lamb offal, sweetbreads and brains with artichokes, and the ubiquitous coda alla vaccinara. The market itself moved to a new location in 2012, but the area remains a culinary destination.

Trippa al sugo

STEWED TRIPE

**SERVES 4
AS A MAIN COURSE**

2 pounds/1 kg
   honeycomb tripe,
   rinsed
¼ cup/60 ml apple
   cider vinegar
Fine sea salt
¼ cup/60 ml extra-
   virgin olive oil
1 medium yellow
   onion, thinly sliced
Red pepper flakes
One 15-ounce/425 g
   can whole peeled
   tomatoes, crushed
   by hand, juices
   reserved
1 cup/240 ml hot water
1 tablespoon tomato
   paste, diluted in
   ½ cup/120 ml hot
   water
A loaf of crusty bread
Grated Parmigiano-
   Reggiano (optional)

Every Italian region, or even every town, has its own recipe for tripe, one of the most nutritious foods of cucina povera. Tripe can be prepared in brodo, in a brothy soup with vegetables; as a soup, over slices of toasted bread; with beans, as in Liguria and Lombardy; as a cold summertime salad, in a refreshing vinaigrette; or in umido, stewed in tomato sauce.

Although it was once considered only a peasant dish, or found as street food sold outside big, crowded markets, you can now spot trippa on the menus of modern restaurants that follow the nose-to-tail approach, as well as in traditional osterias. This hearty stew has been a family favorite for as long as I can remember; we eat it with a loaf of good bread to mop up the sauce.

———

Put the tripe in a large nonreactive pot and add 6 cups/1.4 L water, the vinegar, and 2 teaspoons salt. Bring to a boil over high heat, then reduce the heat to a simmer and simmer for 1½ hours, adding water as necessary so the tripe remains covered. Drain and let cool, then thinly slice the tripe.

In a large high-sided frying pan, heat the olive oil over medium-low heat. When it is hot, add the onion, a generous pinch of salt, and a small pinch of red pepper flakes and cook, stirring often, until the onion is translucent and golden, 15 minutes. Add the crushed tomatoes, with their juices, and the hot water, increase the heat to medium, and cook, stirring occasionally, until the tomatoes have broken down and thickened to the consistency of a sauce, about 15 minutes. Taste and season with additional salt and red pepper flakes as necessary.

Add the tripe and diluted tomato paste, reduce the heat to low, and cook, stirring from time to time, until the tripe is very tender and the tomato sauce thickly coats it, 1 to 1½ hours.

Transfer to a serving bowl and serve with crusty bread and grated Parmigiano-Reggiano, if you like.

VARIATIONS

In Rome, stewed tripe is topped with grated Pecorino Romano and mint. In Siena, they add a few ladlefuls of meat ragù to the tomato sauce for a rich, hearty winter stew.

Stracotto di manzo alla fiorentina

FLORENTINE BEEF STEW

SERVES 6 TO 8
AS A MAIN COURSE

1 fresh rosemary sprig
3 fresh sage leaves
1 clove garlic
Fine sea salt
½ teaspoon freshly ground black pepper
3 pounds/1.4 kg beef rump or brisket
1½ ounces/40 g thinly sliced pancetta
½ cup/120 ml extra-virgin olive oil
2 carrots, peeled and diced
2 celery stalks, diced
4 yellow onions, thinly sliced
2 bay leaves
½ cup/120 ml dry red wine
One 15-ounce/425 g can whole peeled tomatoes, crushed by hand, juices reserved
2 cups/480 ml Beef Stock (page 305)

The best cuts of beef to use for stracotto are lean cuts that are rich in connective tissue. The collagen breaks down through long, gentle cooking and melts into soft gelatin, giving the beef a moist, tender texture and adding flavor to the meat juices.

I like to serve stracotto when I have friends over for dinner. I make the stew a day ahead and just reheat it shortly before serving. The day after, any leftover gravy is a perfect sauce for fresh tagliatelle or even rigatoni.

———

Pull the needles from the rosemary sprig and discard the stem. Finely chop the rosemary leaves, sage, and garlic together, then transfer to a bowl and add 1 teaspoon salt and the pepper.

Rub the beef all over with the herb mixture, then lay the pancetta slices across the meat, spacing them evenly, and tie the meat with butcher's twine at 1-inch/3 cm intervals.

In a large Dutch oven, heat ¼ cup/60 ml of the olive oil over medium-high heat. Add the beef and cook, turning with tongs, until browned all over, about 10 minutes. Transfer to a rimmed plate or baking sheet.

Wipe out the Dutch oven with paper towels, return to medium-low heat, and add the remaining ¼ cup/60 ml olive oil. Add the carrots, celery, onions, bay leaves, and a generous pinch of salt and cook, stirring, until the vegetables are soft and beginning to brown, 15 to 20 minutes.

Return the beef to the Dutch oven, pour in the wine, and bring to a simmer over medium heat. Simmer until the wine has almost completely evaporated, about 10 minutes.

Add the tomatoes, with their juices, then rinse out the tomato can with ½ cup/120 ml water and pour it into the Dutch oven, along with the stock. Bring to a boil, reduce the heat until the liquid is simmering, cover, and simmer gently for about 2 hours, checking from time to time, until the meat is so tender that it falls apart when tested with a fork but the sauce is still abundant and quite thick.

To serve, remove the beef from the Dutch oven, cut off and discard the butcher's twine, and slice. Arrange the slices on a warm serving plate and spoon the juices and vegetables over them.

Fegato alla veneziana

ONION-STEWED CALF'S LIVER

**SERVES 4
AS A MAIN COURSE**

3½ tablespoons/50 g
unsalted butter

2 tablespoons extra-
virgin olive oil

3 large white onions
(about 1½ pounds/
700 g total), thinly
sliced

Fine sea salt

2 tablespoons white
wine vinegar

1 pound/455 g calf's
liver, cut crosswise
into 1-inch-wide/
3 cm slices

Freshly ground black
pepper

1 tablespoon chopped
fresh flat-leaf
parsley

On a bacari crawl in Venice, you will undoubtedly encounter this beloved dish made with two staple ingredients: liver and onions. The charm of the dish comes from the contrast between the sweet, mellow slow-cooked onions and the bitter, savory flavor of the liver. It is a classic cross-cultural combination that extends from India to Poland and England. It finds its origins in the Ancient Roman pairing of liver with figs (hence the Italian name for liver, *fegato*) to cover the pungent taste of liver that was not always fresh.

The onions require a long, gentle stewing to release their sweetness; the liver, on the other hand, demands just a quick browning over high heat to prevent it from becoming rubbery and tough. Adding a splash of white wine vinegar (or lemon juice) softens the liver-y taste. Serve with soft polenta (see page 224) or mashed potatoes to mop up the onion gravy.

———

In a large nonstick frying pan, heat the butter and olive oil over low heat. When the butter has melted and begun to sizzle, add the onions and 1 teaspoon salt and cook, stirring, until the onions are very soft and translucent, about 30 minutes.

Add the vinegar and cook for about 10 minutes, until it has completely evaporated.

Add the liver and stir to combine, then increase the heat to medium and cook until the liver is browned on the outside but still slightly pink inside, about 5 minutes (cut into one strip to test). Taste and season with salt and pepper.

Transfer to a platter, sprinkle with the chopped parsley, and serve.

Cassoeula

PORK STEW WITH SAVOY CABBAGE

**SERVES 4 TO 6
AS A MAIN COURSE**

5 ounces/140 g pork
    rind (or substitute
    half a pig's trotter;
    see Note)
1 Savoy cabbage
    (about 2 pounds/
    1 kg)
1 pound/455 g
    fresh Italian pork
    sausages
1 pound/455 g
    country-style
    pork ribs, cut into
    2-inch/5 cm riblets
    (see Note)
Fine sea salt and
    freshly ground
    black pepper
2 tablespoons extra-
    virgin olive oil
1½ tablespoons/20 g
    unsalted butter
1 carrot, peeled and
    finely chopped
1 celery stalk, finely
    chopped
1 small yellow onion,
    finely chopped
1 teaspoon tomato
    paste
Polenta (see page 224)
    for serving

An old Italian saying, *"Del maiale non si butta via niente"* ("No part of the pig should be discarded"), is the first thing that comes to mind with cassoeula, a traditional winter stew from Lombardy. Ribs, rind, head, trotters, tail, offal: all of the less noble parts of the pig end up in this seasonal dish.

Every province in Lombardy has its own version of cassoeula, but they all have in common a sheer simplicity and a long, gentle braising. The cassoeula you find in Milan is slightly brothier than the others, and there a pig's head is essential. In Novara, they also add goose meat. In Brianza, the stew is traditionally served over steaming-hot polenta.

For the best results, make the cassoeula a day in advance and let it sit overnight in the fridge. Reheat it thoroughly before serving.

———

Put the pork rind (or trotter) in a medium saucepan, add cold water to cover, and bring to a boil over medium-high heat. Reduce the heat so the water is gently bubbling and simmer for 45 minutes. Drain and, if using pork rind, cut it into strips (if using a trotter, leave it as is).

While the pork rind is simmering, prepare the cabbage: Separate the leaves and transfer them to a large pot. Add 1 cup/240 ml water, cover the pot, and steam the leaves over medium-low heat for 15 minutes, or until wilted. Remove from the heat and set aside.

Pierce the sausages with a fork. In a large Dutch oven, sear the sausages over medium-high heat, turning frequently, until browned all over, 10 to 15 minutes. With tongs, transfer the sausages to a large plate; set aside.

Season the pork riblets all over with salt and pepper, add to the Dutch oven, and cook, turning frequently, until browned on all sides, 10 to 15 minutes. Add to the plate with the sausages.

Wipe out the Dutch oven with paper towels and return it to medium-low heat. Add the olive oil and butter, then add the carrot, celery, and onion, season with a generous pinch of salt and a few grinds of pepper, and cook, stirring frequently, until the vegetables are soft, about 10 minutes. Stir in the tomato paste, then transfer the vegetables to a bowl.

Return the ribs to the pan, arranging them in an even layer. Top with the vegetable mixture and arrange the sausages and pork rind strips (or trotter)

NOTES: *If you cannot get pork rind, substitute half a pig's trotter and proceed as directed.*

Ask your butcher to cut the ribs into 2-inch/5 cm riblets for you.

on top. Cover with the steamed cabbage leaves. Season with salt and pepper and add 2 cups/480 ml hot water, pouring it around the edges of the pot.

Cover and bring to a simmer over medium heat. Reduce the heat to maintain a gentle simmer and cook for about 1 hour, until the ribs are tender and the stew is thick.

You can serve the cassoeula immediately, but it is even better the next day. Reheat thoroughly if necessary before serving over the polenta.

Maiale ciffe e ciaffe

PORK BRAISED IN WHITE WINE

SERVES 6 TO 8
AS A MAIN COURSE

1 fresh rosemary sprig
6 fresh sage leaves
4 bay leaves
1 pound/455 g
    country-style
    pork ribs, cut into
    2-inch/5 cm pieces
    (see Note)
About 1⅓ pounds/
    600 g pork jowl or
    pork belly, cut into
    big chunks
12 ounces/340 g pork
    collar or boneless
    pork shoulder, cut
    into big chunks
Fine sea salt and
    freshly ground
    black pepper
½ cup/120 ml extra-
    virgin olive oil
6 cloves garlic, not
    peeled
2 cups/480 ml dry
    white wine
1 dried árbol chili
2 dried sweet peppers,
    such as peperoni
    cruschi (see
    headnote), torn
    into pieces
4½ cups/800 g
    cooked cannellini
    beans (see page
    174), warmed, for
    serving

Some people say that the Italian name of this dish refers to the simplicity and straightforwardness of the recipe, but according to others, it's named after the sounds the pork makes when turned in the pan. The stew is full of flavor, thanks in part to the bouquet of fresh herbs and to the dried sweet peppers added at the end of the cooking. Dried sweet peppers are a common ingredient in Abruzzo. A Slow Food product from the town of Altino, they lend an unmistakable sweet and smoky note to the dish. The abruzzese peppers are very similar to peperoni cruschi from Basilicata, which you can find in specialty stores or online.

Serve the stew with a side of warm cannellini beans, drizzled with the flavorful oil left in the bottom of the pan.

_____

With kitchen twine, tie the rosemary, sage leaves, and bay leaves together in a bundle. Season all the cuts of pork with salt and pepper.

In a 12-inch/30 cm heavy-bottomed frying pan or Dutch oven, heat the olive oil over medium-high heat. When the oil is hot, add the garlic and fry, stirring, for about 1 minute. When the garlic is golden, scoop it out with a slotted spoon and reserve.

Working in batches, add the pork chunks in a single layer and cook, turning occasionally with tongs, until browned on all sides, 15 to 20 minutes. Transfer the pork to a large plate as it is browned.

Return all the meat to the pan now. Add the herb bundle and the reserved garlic and pour in the wine. Bring to a simmer, then reduce the heat to low, cover, and cook, stirring occasionally, for about 1 hour, until the pork is tender and all the wine has evaporated.

Taste a piece of the meat and season the braise with salt and pepper, then add the dried sweet peppers and stir well. Cook for 2 minutes, then transfer to a platter and serve with the cannellini beans alongside.

NOTE: *Ask your butcher to cut the ribs into 2-inch/5 cm riblets for you.*

Spiedini di fegatelli di maiale

ROASTED PORK LIVER SKEWERS

SERVES 4
AS A MAIN COURSE

FOR THE SKEWERS

3½ ounces/100 g pork caul fat (see Note) or 8 paper-thin slices pork belly, each about 3 inches/8 cm long

12 ounces/340 g pork or calf's liver (see Note)

8 ounces/225 g fresh Italian pork sausages (about 2 sausages)

12 slices baguette

8 bay leaves

Extra-virgin olive oil for drizzling

FOR THE RUB

¼ cup/50 g dry breadcrumbs

½ tablespoon crushed fennel seeds

½ teaspoon fine sea salt

½ teaspoon freshly ground black pepper

EQUIPMENT

Four 10-inch/25 cm wooden or metal skewers (see Note)

Calf's liver is prized and delicate, but pork liver is popular in Italy as well. As with other seasonal recipes related to pig slaughtering, it was commonly associated with the Feast of Saint Anthony the Great on the seventeenth of January.

Pork liver is available at many butcher shops; it's often already wrapped in caul fat, the lacy fatty membrane that encases the internal organs of the pig. Wrapping the liver in fat is essential to keep it moist and prevent it from drying out during roasting. The caul fat melts in the oven, creating a delicious crust. Like any fat, it also gives a deeper, rich flavor to the liver.

––––

Soak the caul fat, if using, in hot water for about 15 minutes.

Meanwhile, make the rub: Combine the breadcrumbs, fennel, salt, and pepper on a plate and mix well.

Preheat the oven to 400°F/200°C.

Cut the liver into 8 equal pieces. Cut each sausage into 4 pieces. Drain the caul fat, lay it out on a cutting board, and cut into 8 equal pieces. (If using pork belly, lay it out on a cutting board or tray.)

Roll each piece of liver in the seasoned breadcrumbs to coat, transfer to a piece of caul fat (or pork belly), and tightly wrap in the fat, enclosing it completely.

Assemble the skewers: Slide a slice of baguette onto a skewer, then add a piece of pork liver, a bay leaf, and a piece of sausage. Add another slice of bread and repeat with a second piece of pork liver, another bay leaf, and a second piece of sausage. Finish with a slice of baguette. Repeat with the remaining ingredients to make a total of 4 skewers.

Set the skewers over an 8-inch/20 cm square baking dish, balancing the ends of the skewers on the sides of the dish so the skewers are suspended; this will allow the fat to drip off the skewers and down into the dish. Drizzle the skewers with olive oil and roast them for about 45 minutes, turning them after about 25 minutes. It is important not to overcook the liver: To check it, pierce a piece with a toothpick. If the liquid that comes out is clear, the skewers are ready; if the juice is still pinkish, roast the skewers a little longer.

Serve the skewers as soon as they are done.

NOTES: *If you cannot find caul fat, you can substitute 8 thin slices of fresh pork belly.*

If pork liver is challenging to locate, substitute the same amount of calf's liver and cook it as directed.

You will need four 10-inch/25 cm wooden or metal skewers for this dish; if using wooden skewers, soak them in water for 30 minutes and drain before using.

VARIATION

You could also cook the skewers on a grill, over indirect heat so that the dripping fat doesn't cause flare-ups. In this case, the bread should be in large cubes.

Agnello cacio e ova

STEWED LAMB WITH EGGS AND CHEESE

**SERVES 6
AS A MAIN COURSE**

1 fresh rosemary sprig
6 fresh sage leaves
4 bay leaves
3 pounds/1.4 kg
    boneless lamb
    shoulder, cut into
    1-inch/3 cm pieces
Fine sea salt and
    freshly ground
    black pepper
⅓ cup/80 ml extra-
    virgin olive oil
4 cloves garlic, not
    peeled
1 cup/240 ml dry white
    wine
3 large/150 g eggs
¼ cup/25 g grated
    Pecorino Romano

In Abruzzo, a lamb shoulder stew finished with a cheese and egg sauce is typically prepared for Easter. The shoulder has more fat than leg of lamb; the fat melts into the pan as it roasts, giving the dish flavor and richness. If you want to prepare this in advance, cook the lamb until almost all of the wine has evaporated, then remove from the heat and set aside. When ready to serve, reheat the lamb thoroughly, add the cheese and egg sauce, and proceed as directed.

———

Remove the needles from the rosemary and reserve for another use, if desired. With a piece of kitchen twine, tie the rosemary stem, sage leaves, and bay leaves together into a bundle; set aside. Season the lamb all over with salt and pepper.

In a large Dutch oven, heat the olive oil over medium-high heat. Add the garlic and cook until fragrant, about a minute. Working in batches to avoid crowding the pot, add the lamb pieces in a single layer and sear, turning with tongs, until browned on all sides, about 10 minutes. Transfer the lamb to a plate as it is browned.

When all the meat has been browned, return it all to the pot and add the herb bundle and wine. Cover, reduce the heat to low, and cook for about 45 minutes, stirring occasionally, until almost all of the liquid has evaporated.

In a medium bowl, whisk together the eggs and cheese with a couple of tablespoons of the warm lamb broth to temper the eggs, so they won't curdle when you add them to the pot. Uncover the pot, remove and discard the herb bouquet, and pour the egg and cheese mixture over the lamb. Cook over low heat, stirring constantly to prevent the eggs from scrambling, until the egg and cheese sauce has thickened and coats the meat, 2 to 3 minutes. Remove from the heat, taste, and season with additional salt and pepper if necessary.

Transfer to a platter and serve immediately.

Erbazzone reggiano

SAVORY SWISS CHARD AND PARMIGIANO-REGGIANO PIE

SERVES 6 TO 8
AS A MAIN COURSE,
12 AS A STARTER

FOR THE DOUGH

2¼ cups plus
    2 tablespoons/
    300 g all-purpose
    flour, plus more for
    rolling
1 teaspoon fine
    sea salt
¼ cup/60 g cold
    lard, cut into small
    pieces
½ cup/120 ml warm
    water

FOR THE FILLING

3 pounds/1.4 kg
    Swiss chard (about
    6 bunches)
¼ cup/50 g lard
4 spring onions or
    1 bunch scallions,
    finely chopped
½ clove garlic, minced
3½ ounces/100 g
    Parmigiano-
    Reggiano, grated
Fine sea salt and
    freshly ground
    black pepper
Flaky sea salt

3 tablespoons lard,
    melted, for brushing

Emilia-Romagna, renowned for its fresh pasta and its superb salumi, is one of the Italian regions where the pig-raising culture is most entrenched. Lard is, therefore, a key ingredient in some of its most typical foods, from piadina romagnola (the local flatbread) to erbazzone reggiano, a savory pie stuffed with chard, onion, garlic, and a generous amount of grated Parmigiano-Reggiano. Erbazzone is a simple dish, made from a short list of humble ingredients, and its delectable taste is mainly due to the lard used in the rich, flaky dough and in the chard filling, and brushed on top of the pie as well, to give an additional flavor boost.

Erbazzone reggiano is usually served as a starter, along with a salumi and cheese board, but it can also be served as a main course or as a midmorning snack. And in its hometown, Reggio Emilia, erbazzone is a favorite breakfast, enjoyed in local cafés with a cappuccino.

———

Make the dough: Put the flour in a large bowl, add the salt, and stir to combine. Add the lard and use your fingertips to rub the lard into the flour until the mixture resembles grated Parmigiano-Reggiano. Add the water and knead the dough into a ball. Wrap in plastic wrap and let rest at room temperature for about 1 hour.

While the dough rests, prepare the filling: Remove the thick ribs from the Swiss chard and rinse it under cold running water.

Bring a large pot of water to a boil, add the chard, and blanch for 5 minutes. Drain, and when the chard is cool enough to handle, squeeze well to remove excess water. Roughly chop the chard and set it aside.

Add the lard to a large frying pan set over low heat. When it has melted, add the spring onions and garlic and cook, stirring, until golden. Add the chard and toss to coat, then turn the heat up to medium and cook for about 10 minutes, tossing every 5 minutes or so, until all the liquid has evaporated and the chard is tender. Transfer to a bowl and set aside to cool completely.

Add the grated Parmigiano-Reggiano to the chard, mixing well, and season to taste with salt and pepper.

(CONTINUED)

Preheat the oven to 400°F/200°C. Generously grease a 10-inch/25 cm springform pan or 3-inch-deep (8 cm) round cake pan with butter or lard.

Divide the dough into 2 pieces, one slightly larger than the other.

On a lightly floured surface, with a lightly floured rolling pin, roll the larger piece of dough into a 14-inch/36 cm round, then transfer it to the prepared pan, fitting it into the bottom and up the sides. Add the Swiss chard mixture, spreading it into an even layer.

Roll out the remaining piece of dough into a 12-inch/30 cm round and drape it loosely over the filling. Press the edges to seal and trim the excess dough. Brush the surface of the dough with the melted lard, then pierce the dough all over with a fork. Sprinkle with flaky sea salt.

Bake the erbazzone until golden brown, 45 to 50 minutes. Serve warm or at room temperature.

Leftover erbazzone keeps well on the kitchen counter for several days.

LARD AND LARDO

In those regions of Italy where the culture of pig raising is deeply rooted, lard is a common and beloved ingredient. Lard is pork fat, rendered and clarified. In Italy, it is known as *strutto*, which means melted. Traditionally it was one of the most common cooking fats, used since medieval times, when it was readily available and affordable, even for poor people.

Today, lard is still used in some areas of Italy as a cooking fat for roasting and frying, in bread dough, and to preserve salumi and meats, as for fegatelli di maiale (page 78). Do not mistake lard, or strutto, for lardo, which is, instead, a cured pork product. Lardo, the fat of the back of the pig, is traditionally cured for months in marble basins with salt, pepper, and a mixture of herbs and aromatics. Once a food reserved for poor people, given as part of a salary or as a donation, lardo is now a delicacy. You can thinly slice it as you would prosciutto and serve it on toasted bread as a starter. Lardo is also used to wrap lean meats before cooking to add moisture and flavor.

ITALIAN STREET FOOD

In the past, street food was the lunch, or even breakfast, of laborers and the poor. It is now appreciated by locals of all social classes and tourists alike, who search for the authentic taste of a city through that most democratic experience: street food. For less than five euros, you can enjoy a quick, filling meal. Offal and other less noble parts of the animal are often the basis of Italian street foods. You devour these standing up, slightly hunched over—the ergonomic body position developed over the centuries as the way to eat greasy, dripping, juicy foods.

Trippa is one of the most common street foods throughout Italy, as almost every region has a recipe for it. From busecca in Milan to trippe in Liguria, this affordable, filling dish has been a fixture for centuries. Veneto is famous for its cicchetti, the savory finger food served in local bacari, traditional osterias, during the aperitivo hour. Along with sarde in saor (page 119), baccalà, and folpetti (boiled small octopus), you can help yourself to nervetti (the boiled ligaments, sinew, and cartilage of calf's hock and shin served in a salad with onion and beans), spienza (boiled spleen dressed with olive oil and spices), and rumegal (morsels of boiled calf's stomach).

Lampredotto is the most typical street food of Florence, sold by trippai, tripe vendors, inside and nearby the local markets, in the busiest squares, and in strategic locations such as outside offices and schools. The fourth stomach of the cow, lampredotto has a chewy texture, just like tripe. It is commonly served sandwiched into a crusty bun that has been soaked in a hot meat stock. The trippaio will ask you how you want your lampredotto: seasoned just with a shake of black pepper, topped with a generous spoonful of salsa verde, or with a fiery hot sauce. Along with lampredotto, the trippai also sell trippe, in a stew or in a refreshing salad in summer; lingua, boiled tongue; poppa, boiled cow's udder; and matrice, boiled cow's uterus.

Rome is the fried food capital of Italy, and that is reflected in its street food. In a classical fritto misto alla romana, you may find lamb's or calf's brain, bone marrow, and sweetbreads along with the artichokes, zucchini, and cauliflower florets.

In the center and southern parts of Italy, where pastoralism still plays a significant role, especially in Abruzzo, Molise, Basilicata, and Puglia, lamb's entrails are rolled up in the intestines and roasted on a spit over a flame. These are known by different names, depending on the region: torcinelli, gnummareddi, turcinieddhri, mazzarelle. In Puglia, where there is a tradition of fornelli pronti, small wood-burning ovens set outside butcher shops where meat is cooked and often eaten on the spot, torcinelli are often joined by bombette (rolls of pork meat from the capocollo stuffed with pecorino) and zampine (minced pork pressed into lamb's intestines, coiled into a spiral, and barbecued).

Sicily has a wide variety of street food, from arancine (page 242) to pane e panelle (page 176), but what makes the local food scene so remarkable and fascinating is the ingenuity that has turned offal and entrails into filling, mouthwatering dishes. The best place to experience gutsy Sicilian street food is the Vucciria in Palermo, a historical market located where the slaughterhouse once was, next to the Jewish ghetto. According to kosher law, Jewish workers could not accept money for butchering animals, so they would be paid with the entrails left behind, which they would then sell to the local Christians—the only ones who could eat them, as these were forbidden for Jews and Muslims. Pani ca' miusa, a sesame seed bun stuffed with chopped veal lung and spleen, boiled, and fried in lard, is still one of the favorite street foods in Palermo, served as it is, or topped with fried ricotta and caciocavallo for the version known as maritata, which means married.

Local street food vendors also offer quarume (a tripe stew served hot with olive oil, salt, pepper, and lemon juice), insalata di mussu e carcagnola (just as in Naples, a salad made of boiled bones, calf's head, pig's trotters, and snout, dressed with olive oil, parsley, and lemon juice), stigghiole (barbecued bundles of calf's offal secured inside knotted intestines), and frittula, small pieces of meat, fat, and calf cartilage, boiled and then freeze-dried to preserve them. At the market, the frittularu fries the frittule in lard, seasons it with black pepper and bay leaf, and places it in a large wicker basket. You can have your frittula as the stuffing for a sandwich or in a paper cone.

POULTRY AND RABBIT

RECIPES FROM THE FARMYARD

Patè di fegatini
Chicken Liver Spread   90

Tonno di coniglio
Rabbit Preserved in Olive Oil   93

Stracciatella in brodo
Roman Egg Drop Soup   94

Insalata di pollo lesso
Boiled Chicken Salad   97

Pollo alla cacciatora
Chicken Cacciatore   98

Frittata trippata
Frittata Cooked in Tomato Sauce   101

Pane frattau
Flatbread with Tomato Sauce
and Poached Eggs   102

Vincisgrassi marchigiani
Chicken and Pork Lasagne   104

Petto di tacchino ripieno
Stuffed Turkey Breast Roulade   109

WHY BUY AN OVERPRICED CHICKEN BREAST WHEN YOU CAN GET A better-quality whole chicken for much less? A good-quality free-range chicken from the local farmers' market or your trusted butcher is an investment in your meals for the entire week. You can use it to make a golden cure-all stock (page 306); a fortifying stracciatella (page 94), the Italian egg-drop soup, gently flavored with lemon zest and nutmeg; and a colorful shredded chicken salad (page 97). Or stew the chicken with tomato sauce, as in chicken cacciatore (page 98), and it will feed a crowd—then use the leftover sauce to dress a bowl of tagliatelle.

Italian cucina povera has always favored poultry, making the farmyard the center of the household economy, just as the hearth was the center of family life. In a romanticized vision of Italian country life, the farmyard was the place where people would gather after the harvest, holding feasts to celebrate the threshing, the grape harvest, or weddings.

The farmyard was also a tangible image of the peasant food culture, as this was where they raised chickens, rabbits, guinea fowl, and turkeys, fed with kitchen scraps and agricultural by-products in a perfect example of a circular, sustainable economy. Like the vegetable garden, the farmyard was traditionally the women's domain. The dishes that resulted were simple, humble, and seasonal, making meals that were far greater than those eaten by poor city dwellers.

Historically, chickens were raised mainly for their eggs, to barter with or sell at the market, and as an essential source of protein. In the Italian tradition, eggs are not a breakfast item but rather the main ingredient for a meal, as in rich vegetable omelets (page 101), fresh pasta, or stracciatella.

Well-fed meaty, tasty cappone was once the centerpiece of celebratory meals, the perfect way of feeding a large family, or even given as gifts to the notable people of the time, such as landowners, doctors, and lawyers. Today, a roasted capon is a glorious Sunday roast, its melting fat making the meat juicy as it cooks. It can become both a main course and a sauce for pasta if cooked "in umido," stewed with tomato sauce.

Rabbits were appreciated in cucina povera not only because they were incredibly prolific but also because they took up very little space in the farmyard and could be fed on scraps, hay, and grass. Rabbit meat is delicate and lean, so rather than being roasted, it should be gently poached in an aromatic stock, as in tonno di coniglio (page 93), stewed in tomato sauce, or battered and fried.

Goose has been a popular meat in Italy since classical times, and it was traditionally substituted for pork in Jewish gastronomy all over Europe. In Italy, goose was once mainly raised in northern regions such as Piedmont, Lombardy, Veneto, and Friuli. Like pork, goose meat can be cured to make salame and prosciutto, and its fat can stand in for lard. Goose lard can be used not only as a cooking fat—potatoes roasted in goose fat are phenomenal—but also to preserve the meat, as in oca in onto (goose confit) from Veneto. Even goose skin can be enjoyed, fried until hot and crisp.

Patè di fegatini

CHICKEN LIVER SPREAD

**SERVES 8
AS A STARTER**

¼ cup/60 ml extra-virgin olive oil

1 celery stalk, finely minced

1 carrot, peeled and finely minced

1 small onion, finely minced

1 bay leaf

2 juniper berries

Fine sea salt

10½ ounces/300 g chicken livers and hearts, rinsed and patted dry

¼ cup/60 ml vin santo

1 tablespoon tomato paste

2 tablespoons salt-packed capers, rinsed and squeezed dry

1 ounce/30 g oil-packed anchovy fillets

4 tablespoons/60 g unsalted butter, plus more if needed

1½ teaspoons red wine vinegar

Tuscany's crostini neri, or black crostini, topped with a chicken liver pâté or spread, are a classic starter found at family gatherings and on trattoria menus. The pâté is traditionally made with chicken livers and hearts, onions, celery, carrots, capers, fresh herbs, and butter. Capers and anchovies add savoriness to the slightly sweet liver, butter lends richness, and red wine vinegar balances the flavors with its acidity. (If you are using capers pickled in brine instead of salted capers for this recipe, omit the vinegar.)

For crostini, simply slather the creamy chicken liver pâté on buttered toasted bread. If you're serving a meal that includes a broth, you can dip the bread slices into the stock—just on one side—before topping with the spread.

———

Pour the olive oil into a medium saucepan set over medium heat and add the minced vegetables, along with the bay leaf and juniper berries. Add a pinch of salt (this will help cook down the vegetables, releasing their moisture and preventing them from burning) and sauté for about 10 minutes, until softened and beginning to brown.

Add the chicken livers and hearts to the saucepan and cook, stirring with a wooden spoon, until nicely browned, about 10 minutes. Add the vin santo and tomato paste, reduce the heat to medium-low, and cook for about 10 minutes, stirring from time to time, until the livers are cooked through, but still slightly pinkish inside.

Add the capers, anchovies, butter, and vinegar to the pan and stir until the butter melts. Remove the bay leaf and pass the mixture through a food mill for a spread with a smooth yet rustic texture. Alternatively, use an immersion blender to blend it into a creamy, velvety paste. Check the seasoning and add more salt if necessary and/or more butter to round out its taste. Let cool to room temperature.

The spread can be prepared in advance and kept in the fridge for up to 3 days. Any leftovers can be gently reheated in a saucepan with a knob of butter, stirring until smooth and soft again.

Tonno di coniglio

RABBIT PRESERVED IN OLIVE OIL

**SERVES 8
AS A STARTER,
4 AS A MAIN COURSE**

12 fresh sage leaves
5 fresh basil leaves
2 bay leaves
2 fresh thyme sprigs
1 fresh parsley sprig
1 carrot, cut into thirds
1 celery stalk, cut in
   half
1 yellow onion, halved
4 whole cloves
2 tablespoons coarse
   sea salt
1 rabbit (about
   2½ pounds/1.1 kg),
   cut into 6 pieces
Fine sea salt and
   freshly ground
   black pepper
2 cloves garlic,
   slivered
2 tablespoons whole
   black peppercorns
1 cup/240 ml extra-
   virgin olive oil, plus
   more if needed

This traditional recipe uses oil as a way to preserve meat without refrigeration. Cook the rabbit in a stock full of aromatics, shred the meat, and cover it with extra-virgin olive oil. The texture will be very similar to that of canned tuna, hence the name *tonno di coniglio*. This is a typical Piedmontese dish, belonging to the culinary traditions of Monferrato.

Serve tonno di coniglio with toasted bread and pickled vegetables. It makes a perfect starter for an alfresco dinner.

———

Prepare the aromatic bouquet: Using kitchen twine, tie half of the sage leaves, the basil, bay leaves, thyme, and parsley into a bundle.

Fill a large pot with 8 cups/2 L of water and add the carrot and celery. Push 2 cloves into each onion half and add to the pot, along with the herb bouquet. Bring the water to a boil over medium heat.

Add the coarse salt to the boiling water, then plunge the rabbit pieces into the water and reduce the heat so the water is simmering gently. Simmer the rabbit for at least 1 hour, until the meat is so tender that it comes away from the bones when prodded with a fork. Remove from the heat and let the rabbit cool in the stock until cool enough to handle.

Remove the rabbit pieces from the pot with tongs and, using a fork, shred the meat from the bones, discarding the bones. (Discard the stock.)

Line a tray with paper towels and spread the shredded rabbit meat on top. Season with fine salt and ground pepper and leave to drain away the excess liquid.

When the rabbit meat is dry, transfer one-quarter of it to a 4-cup/17 cm oval terrine mold or a ceramic bowl. Press it into an even layer with a fork, then top with 2 of the remaining sage leaves, one-third of the garlic, and 2 teaspoons of the peppercorns. Drizzle with some of the olive oil. Repeat the layering with the remaining rabbit and herbs, drizzling the layers with olive oil and finishing with a layer of meat. Cover the final layer with olive oil, cover, and refrigerate for at least 1 day before serving.

The rabbit tends to absorb the olive oil, so check to see if it needs to be topped up if you plan to store it for longer than a day; the meat should be completely covered with oil so it doesn't spoil. The rabbit will keep in the fridge for 3 to 4 days. Bring to room temperature before serving.

Stracciatella in brodo

ROMAN EGG DROP SOUP

SERVES 4
AS A FIRST COURSE

6 cups/1.4 L Chicken
    Stock (page 306)
4 large/200 g eggs
5 tablespoons/30 g
    grated Parmigiano-
    Reggiano, plus
    more for serving
Grated zest of
    ½ lemon
Pinch of grated
    nutmeg

Stracciatella is a simple, fortifying soup belonging to the Roman tradition, although there are similar recipes from Emilia-Romagna and Marche. It was devised as a way to recycle leftover chicken stock, often prepared during the Christmas festivities. Stracciatella owes its name to the light, delicate shreds—*stracci*—that the beaten eggs produce when dropped into the hot stock. Make it whenever you have some good homemade chicken stock on hand, or when you crave a simple, comforting soup on a chilly day. If you make this soup in early spring, drop some fresh peas or asparagus tips into it at the last minute.

———

Bring the chicken stock to a simmer in a large saucepan over medium-high heat. In a medium bowl, whisk the eggs until well beaten, then whisk in the Parmigiano-Reggiano, lemon zest, and nutmeg.

Gradually pour the beaten eggs into the hot chicken stock, gently whisking. Reduce the heat to medium and simmer, stirring constantly, until the eggs thicken into light, delicate shreds.

Immediately ladle the soup into warmed bowls and serve with more grated Parmigiano-Reggiano alongside.

THE OTHER STRACCIATELLA

Curiously enough, the name *stracciatella* also refers to an Apulian cheese from Andria, the land of burrata. Stracciatella is the ancestor of burrata, created at the beginning of the twentieth century to upcycle the remains of mozzarella production. Every last shred of mozzarella left in the water it was made in would be mixed with cream to make stracciatella. When stracciatella is wrapped in a casing of stringy cheese like mozzarella, you get burrata.

Insalata di pollo lesso

BOILED CHICKEN SALAD

**SERVES 4 TO 6
AS A MAIN COURSE**

2 tablespoons raisins
1 pound/455 g
shredded boiled
chicken (about
4 cups; reserved
from making
Chicken Stock,
page 306)
1 head radicchio
tardivo or endive
(about 200 g), thinly
sliced
1 celery heart, finely
sliced
1½ cups/200 g drained
giardiniera, coarsely
chopped
2 tablespoons pine
nuts, toasted
6 tablespoons/90 ml
extra-virgin olive oil
Fine sea salt and
freshly ground
black pepper

A farmyard chicken lends itself to more than one meal: a savory broth with seasonal vegetables from the garden, a soup with shredded meat, and this colorful chicken salad with bitter greens like radicchio and endive, celery, and some giardiniera for flavor.

Giardiniera, pickled mixed vegetables, adds a fresh vinegary note to the chicken salad, also providing a nice crunch. If you want to skip the giardiniera, add 1 tablespoon of white wine vinegar to the salad dressing. Add a handful of fresh herbs like thyme, parsley, mint, or basil for a refreshing, herbaceous note.

———

Put the raisins in a small bowl and add warm water to just cover. Let stand for 10 minutes, then drain the raisins and squeeze them dry.

In a large bowl, combine the chicken, radicchio, celery, giardiniera, pine nuts, and raisins. Add the oil and mix well, then season to taste with salt and pepper. Let the salad stand at room temperature for about an hour (30 minutes if it's very warm where you live) to bring out the flavors before serving.

Pollo alla cacciatora

CHICKEN CACCIATORE

SERVES 4
AS A MAIN COURSE

1 chicken (2½ to
   3 pounds/1.1 to
   1.4 kg)
Fine sea salt and
   freshly ground
   black pepper
⅓ cup/80 ml extra-
   virgin olive oil
1 red onion, diced
1 clove garlic, finely
   chopped
3 fresh sage leaves
1 fresh rosemary sprig
A glass of dry white
   wine
One 14-ounce/397 g
   can peeled whole
   tomatoes, crushed
   by hand, juices
   reserved
½ cup/120 ml water
⅓ cup/60 g pitted
   brined black olives

Pollo alla cacciatora is a dish with a distinctly rustic appeal. It is one of those recipes that you find throughout Italy. All you need is a good farm-raised chicken, aromatics and fresh herbs from the garden, a handful of juicy tomatoes, and a glug of wine, white or red. Chicken cacciatore can vary according to the season and tradition: some cooks add luscious black olives, other foraged mushrooms or vegetables like carrots, celery, and peppers. Serve it with crusty fresh bread to mop up the sauce, or spoon it over soft polenta (see page 224).

Use any leftover tomato sauce from the cacciatore to make a second meal, serving it over tagliatelle.

————

Cut the chicken into pieces: 2 thighs, 2 legs, 2 wings, and 2 breasts; cut the breasts crosswise into 2 pieces each. Then cut the backbone into 4 pieces. Season the chicken pieces all over with salt and pepper and set aside.

In a 12-inch/30 cm heavy-bottomed frying pan with a lid, heat the olive oil over medium heat. Add the onion, garlic, sage, rosemary, and a generous pinch of salt and cook, stirring frequently, until the onion begins to brown, about 5 minutes.

Add the chicken pieces skin side down to the pan, increase the heat to medium-high, and cook, stirring and turning frequently, until browned all over, about 10 minutes. Don't worry if the skin tears or falls off the meat; after the meat is braised, it won't matter. If the onion starts to brown too much as you cook the chicken, reduce the heat slightly.

Pour in the wine, reduce the heat to medium, and cook until the wine has almost completely evaporated, about 10 minutes. Add the tomatoes, with their juices, and the water, cover, reduce the heat to low, and simmer gently for about 30 minutes, stirring from time to time, until almost all the liquid has evaporated.

Uncover the pan, stir in the black olives, and cook, uncovered, for a few more minutes, until the sauce cloaks the chicken. Taste the sauce and season with additional salt and/or pepper if necessary.

Transfer to a platter and serve.

Frittata trippata

FRITTATA COOKED IN TOMATO SAUCE

**SERVES 4
AS A MAIN COURSE**

6 large/300 g eggs
Fine sea salt and
    freshly ground
    black pepper
¼ cup/60 ml extra-
    virgin olive oil
2 cups/520 g
    Garlicky Tomato
    Sauce (page 308),
    reheated
¼ cup/25 g grated
    Pecorino Romano
A handful of fresh
    basil leaves, torn
Crusty bread for
    serving

Frittata, a sort of rustic, substantial omelet cooked in olive oil or butter, can change with the seasons. Make it with bitter greens, potatoes, or onions in winter, and with fava beans, wild asparagus, or artichoke hearts in spring. It reaches its peak in summer made with zucchini or red peppers, or when the last green tomatoes, fried for this dish, meet the first grapes. In fall, the eggs are bound together with thick slices of pumpkin coated in flour and fried in olive oil, or foraged mushrooms, with a few leaves of fresh calamint.

The ingenuity of peasant cooking goes the extra mile when a frittata is cut into strips and cooked in tomato sauce. Known as *frittata trippata* in Tuscany, or *busecca matta* in Lombardy, the dish has a close resemblance to stewed tripe, including the final shower of grated Pecorino Romano or Grana Padano. Cooking the sliced frittata in tomato sauce satisfies two needs: it gives flavor to the eggs, and it allows the frittata to soak up the tomato sauce like a sponge, so that what would've been a dish for two turns into a meal to feed a family if served along with some bread to mop up the sauce.

Preheat the oven to 400°F/200°C.

In a small bowl, beat the eggs with a pinch each of salt and pepper. Heat a 9-inch/23 cm nonstick frying pan over medium heat and add 2 tablespoons of the olive oil. Pour in the beaten eggs and cook for a few minutes, until barely set. Invert a large plate over the pan and, in one quick motion, flip the frittata onto the plate. Return the pan to the stove, slide the frittata back into the pan, and cook on the second side for a few more minutes, just until set. Transfer the frittata to a cutting board, roll it up, and cut it into thin strips, about ¾ inch/2 cm wide.

Pour the tomato sauce into a bowl, add the frittata strips, and stir gently to coat, then transfer to a baking dish. Sprinkle with the grated Pecorino Romano, drizzle with the remaining 2 tablespoons olive oil, and bake for 20 to 25 minutes, until golden.

Remove from the oven, scatter the torn basil leaves over the top, and serve immediately.

Pane frattau

FLATBREAD WITH TOMATO SAUCE AND POACHED EGGS

**SERVES 4
AS A MAIN COURSE**

6 cups/1.4 L beef or vegetable stock

4 large/200 g eggs, at room temperature

4 sheets pane carasau (see Note), quartered

4 cups/1 kg Garlicky Tomato Sauce (page 308), reheated

A generous handful of fresh basil leaves, torn

3 ounces/90 g aged pecorino sardo or Pecorino Romano, grated

Fine sea salt and freshly ground black pepper

Pane carasau, also known as *carta da musica,* or music paper, has the texture of the old parchment on which sacred music was written. It is a traditional paper-thin crispy flatbread from Sardinia. A double rise and a double baking in a scorching-hot wood-burning oven ensure light, brittle, golden disks with a long shelf life if kept in a dry place. When you then moisten pane carasau in hot broth, it behaves like lasagne sheets. Layer it with tomato sauce and pecorino cheese, then crown it with poached eggs for pane frattau, a thrifty, nutritious dish.

———

Pour the stock into a large high-sided frying pan and bring to a simmer over medium-high heat.

One at a time, crack each egg into a small bowl, then gently pour it into the simmering stock. Poach the eggs until the whites are firm but the yolks are still soft, 2 to 3 minutes. With a slotted spoon, transfer the poached eggs to a plate lined with paper towels (remove them in the order you added them to the pan). Turn off the heat.

Quickly moisten one of the quartered sheets of pane carasau in the hot stock. Don't leave it to soak for too long, or it will become floppy; a few seconds will be enough. With tongs, remove the moistened pane carasau and place one-quarter on each of four dinner plates. Top with a thin layer of the tomato sauce, scatter over a few basil leaves, and sprinkle with some grated pecorino. Repeat to make three more layers on each plate, quickly moistening the pane carasau quarters and topping with tomato sauce, basil, and pecorino (reserve some of the pecorino and basil for finishing).

Transfer the poached eggs to the plates, setting them on top of the pane frattau. Season with salt and pepper, sprinkle with the remaining pecorino and basil, and serve immediately.

NOTE: *Pane carasau can be found in specialty stores and online markets, such as Eataly.*

Vincisgrassi marchigiani

CHICKEN AND PORK LASAGNE

SERVES 8 TO 10 AS
A FIRST COURSE,
4 TO 6 AS A MAIN
COURSE

FOR THE MEAT SAUCE

About 3 tablespoons extra-virgin olive oil

8 ounces/225 g chicken livers

1 thick slice prosciutto (about 5 ounces/ 140 g), finely diced

1 celery stalk, minced

1 carrot, peeled and minced

1 medium yellow onion, minced

Fine sea salt

1 pound/455 g boneless pork sirloin, finely diced

12 ounces/340 g boneless, skinless chicken thighs, finely diced

1 rabbit leg (about 8 ounces/225 g), boned and finely diced (if you cannot find rabbit, increase the amount of chicken to 1¼ pounds/565 g)

½ cup/120 ml dry white wine

One 28-ounce/794 g can whole peeled tomatoes, crushed by hand, juices reserved

⅓ cup/100 g tomato paste

4 cups/1 L Beef Stock (page 305), heated

The Marche region is known for vincisgrassi, an interesting twist on lasagne and the local festive Sunday dish. Although most of the time vincisgrassi differs little from traditional lasagne, the original version used a meat sauce made from a selection of poultry, including chicken, goose, and duck, as well as rabbit, pork, prosciutto, and chicken innards.

The recipe might seem quite daunting, but if you tackle it in stages, you'll realize it is just a matter of organization. Make the beef stock, the besciamella, and meat sauce one or two days ahead so you'll have them ready to go (or make the sauce well in advance and freeze it; see the Note on page 108). The sauce recipe calls for finely diced meat. It might take some time to cut up all the meat by hand, but this is what makes the difference, giving the sauce a chunky texture befitting the rustic nature of the dish. (If you have a meat grinder, though, you can instead grind all the meats together.) The base of the sauce is a mixture of finely chopped vegetables—celery, carrot, and onion—that is known as *battuto* (literally, beaten down) in Italian, and is used as a starting point for a wide range of dishes, from soups to stews.

——

Make the meat sauce: Pour 2 tablespoons of the olive oil into a large Dutch oven set over medium heat. When the oil is hot, add the chicken livers and cook, stirring often, for about 10 minutes, until nicely browned. Transfer to a cutting board and let cool, then finely chop and transfer to a bowl.

Wipe out the pot, set over low heat, and cover the bottom of the pot with a film of olive oil. Add the prosciutto, celery, carrot, onion, and a generous pinch of salt and cook for about 10 minutes, stirring often with a wooden spoon. The "battuto" should be happily sizzling, but do not let it darken too much.

Increase the heat to medium, add the pork, chicken, and rabbit, if using, and stir to coat the meat with the vegetables. The meat will release some liquid as it cooks, so stir it often and cook until all the liquid has evaporated and the meat is nicely browned, 30 to 35 minutes.

Add the diced chicken liver and cook for 5 minutes. Gradually pour in the wine and cook, stirring occasionally, until it has cooked off. Add the tomatoes, with their juices, the tomato paste, and stock and season with salt and pepper. The sauce will begin to sputter; cover the pot and simmer over the lowest heat for at least 2½ hours, stirring from time to time. Eventually

Freshly ground black
  pepper

FOR THE FRESH LASAGNE
SHEETS

1 cup plus
  2 tablespoons/
  140 g all-purpose
  flour
7 tablespoons/80 g
  semolina flour
2 large/100 g eggs
1 tablespoon vin cotto
  or Marsala

FOR THE BESCIAMELLA

5 tablespoons/70 g
  unsalted butter
½ cup/60 g all-
  purpose flour
4 cups/1 L whole milk
½ teaspoon grated
  nutmeg
Fine sea salt

FOR ASSEMBLY

Butter for greasing
  the pan
4 ounces/115 g
  Parmigiano-
  Reggiano, grated
Extra-virgin olive oil
  for drizzling

you will notice puddles of olive oil forming on the surface of the sauce, colored red by the long cooking time with the tomato sauce and paste; this means the sauce is ready. Taste, adjust the seasoning with additional salt and pepper as necessary, and set aside. (*You can prepare the meat sauce in advance, let it cool, and refrigerate in an airtight container for up to 2 days. Gently reheat it before proceeding.*)

While the sauce cooks, make the lasagne sheets: Pour the two flours onto a work surface and shape into a mound with a large well in the center. Crack the eggs into the well and add the vin cotto. Using a fork, stir slowly to incorporate the eggs, starting from the center and gradually picking up more flour from the edges, then whisking with the fork as if you are beating eggs for an omelet. When the dough turns crumbly, switch to kneading with your hands. You want to knead the dough until it forms a ball and the gluten starts to develop, as this will render the sheets of pasta more elastic. The dough is ready when you have clean hands and a clean board and the dough is smooth, silky, and no longer sticky.

Alternatively, you can make the dough in a stand mixer fitted with the dough hook. Knead for about 5 minutes on low speed, then turn it out and finish kneading by hand for about 5 minutes. Shape the dough into a ball.

Cover the dough with an upturned bowl and let rest for 30 minutes.

While the dough rests, make the besciamella: In a large saucepan, melt the butter over medium heat. Add the flour and whisk for a few minutes, until golden and toasted. Pour in the milk in a thin stream, whisking constantly to prevent lumps. Cook the besciamella for a few minutes, stirring constantly, until thickened; your whisk should leave visible trails in the sauce. Season with the nutmeg and salt to taste. (*You can prepare the besciamella in advance, let it cool, and refrigerate it in an airtight container for up to 2 days. Gently reheat it before using.*)

Form the pasta sheets: Preheat the oven to 400°F/200°C. Lightly flour a work surface with semolina flour.

To roll out the dough by hand: Cut the dough into 2 pieces (or more, if you prefer); work with one piece of dough at a time, keeping the rest covered with a clean towel. On the floured work surface, with a rolling pin, roll out one piece of dough into a paper-thin sheet.

To roll out the dough using a pasta machine: Divide the dough into 6 equal portions. On the lightly floured work surface, with a rolling pin, roll out one piece of the dough into a ½-inch-thick/1.5 cm rectangle. (Keep the remaining pieces covered with a clean kitchen towel.)

(CONTINUED)

Turn the dial on your pasta machine to the widest setting. Feed the dough through the rollers once, then fold the sheet of pasta in three, as if you were folding a letter. Starting with one of the open sides, feed the pasta dough through the machine again. Repeat 3 times, lightly dusting the sheet of dough with semolina flour each time to prevent it from sticking and tearing.

Turn the dial to the next narrower setting. Roll the pasta through the machine, gently pulling it toward you as it comes out of the machine; hold the pasta sheet with the palm of one hand while you crank the machine with the other hand. Continue to reduce the settings and roll the dough through the machine again, lightly dusting the sheet of dough with semolina flour each time, until the dough is as thin as you'd like; I usually stop at the next to last setting.

Lay the pasta sheet on a rimmed baking sheet dusted with semolina and repeat with the remaining dough; if you need to stack the sheets, dust each one with more semolina flour so they don't stick together.

When you've rolled out all the dough, cut it into sheets approximately 3 inches by 13 inches/8 cm by 33 cm (the exact dimensions aren't important, as you can overlap and/or trim or patch the sheets as necessary when you assemble the vincisgrassi).

Cook the lasagne sheets: Bring a large pot of water to a rolling boil and salt it generously. Cook the lasagne sheets in batches of 3, boiling them for just a minute and then immediately transferring them to a colander and passing them under cold water. Lay the drained sheets out on a clean cloth to absorb the excess water.

Assemble the vincisgrassi: Have all the ingredients nearby. If the besciamella and meat sauce are cold, gently reheat them until warm.

Butter a 9-by-13-inch/23 by 33 cm baking dish. You want to make 5 layers of pasta, sauce, and cheese: Line the bottom of the dish with enough sheets of pasta to cover it. Spoon some of the meat sauce over the pasta and spread it into a thin, even layer. Spoon some besciamella over the meat sauce and spread into an even layer. Sprinkle with some of the grated Parmigiano-Reggiano. Repeat the layering until you have used all of the pasta, meat sauce, besciamella, and Parmigiano-Reggiano, ending with besciamella and Parmigiano-Reggiano.

Drizzle the top layer with extra-virgin olive oil. Bake the vincisgrassi for about 45 minutes, or until golden brown and bubbling. Remove from the oven and let cool and rest for at least 30 minutes, or up to an hour or two.

When ready to serve, if necessary, reheat the vincisgrassi, covered, in a hot oven until heated through, then cut into squares and serve. Vincisgrassi improves with time; if you'd like, let it cool completely and refrigerate overnight, then reheat the next day, covered, in a hot oven.

NOTES: *The lasagne dough includes a tablespoon of vin cotto, which is cooked grape must, a dark, sweet, syrupy reduction found in many rural areas of Italy. It adds a deeper flavor to the pasta. You can substitute Marsala or skip it altogether and just add a tablespoon of water.*

If you don't want to make the fresh lasagne noodles, you can substitute about 12 ounces/340 g store-bought fresh pasta sheets or lasagne noodles.

The meat sauce can be made well ahead and frozen in an airtight container for up to 6 months. Thaw it overnight in the fridge and gently reheat before using.

Petto di tacchino ripieno

STUFFED TURKEY BREAST ROULADE

**SERVES 8
AS A MAIN COURSE**

One skinless,
 boneless turkey
 breast (about
 3 pounds/1.4 kg),
 preferably
 butterflied by
 the butcher (see
 headnote)
2 large/100 g eggs
Fine sea salt and
 freshly ground
 black pepper
½ cup plus
 1 teaspoon/125 ml
 extra-virgin olive oil
3½ ounces/100 g
 thinly sliced
 prosciutto cotto
 (about 6 slices)
3½ ounces/100 g
 Fontina or
 provolone, thinly
 sliced
2 fresh rosemary
 sprigs
1 cup/240 ml dry white
 wine

A butterflied turkey breast, stuffed with meat, cheese, and fresh herbs, is a special Sunday meal when there is something to celebrate, such as a holiday or visiting friends or family. It is one of the most affordable, versatile, and substantial recipes of cucina povera. When filled with delicious ingredients, a small turkey breast can easily feed a crowd.

First, find a good butcher, one who has high-quality local meat and, preferably, can butterfly the turkey breast for you (alternatively, follow the instructions below to do it yourself). From there, the recipe is easy. The classic filling includes prosciutto cotto (cooked ham), Fontina cheese, and cooked eggs; the eggs give moisture to the filling. If you want to use other cheeses, opt for those that will melt but not release too much liquid, such as Fontina, scamorza, and fresh pecorino; avoid mozzarella, stracchino, and robiola.

———

If the turkey breast has not been butterflied by the butcher, place it on your work surface. Holding the blade of the knife parallel to the board, starting from one of the longer sides, slice into the thickest portion of the breast, about halfway down, and cut along the length of the breast almost but not all the way through.

Open the turkey out like a book. Cover with a piece of plastic wrap and pound with a meat mallet until the meat is of uniform thickness (about ½ inch/1.5 cm). Set aside.

In a small bowl, beat the eggs and season them with a pinch each of salt and pepper. Heat a 9-inch/23 cm nonstick frying pan over medium heat and add the teaspoon of olive oil. Pour the beaten eggs into the pan and cook, swirling the pan occasionally, until the bottom of the omelet is set, 2 minutes. Using your fingers or a wide spatula, flip the omelet and cook on the second side just until set, 1 minute more. Slide onto a plate.

Season the turkey with salt and pepper. Arrange the prosciutto cotto on top of the turkey, cutting the slices to fit and leaving a border of about ½ inch/1.5 cm, then top with the sliced cheese. Lay the omelet on top, trimming as needed to fit. Orient the turkey breast so that a long side is facing you, then roll it up away from you, tucking in any bits of ham, cheese, or egg that slip out, until you have a nice roulade. Using butcher's

twine, tie the roulade at 1-inch/3 cm intervals. Season all over with salt and pepper, then tuck the rosemary sprigs under the butcher's twine.

In a large Dutch oven, heat the remaining ½ cup/120 ml oil over medium heat. When the oil is hot, add the turkey skin side down and cook, turning occasionally, until browned all over, about 10 minutes.

Pour in the wine, cover, reduce the heat to low, and cook, checking occasionally, until most of the liquid has evaporated and an instant-read thermometer inserted into the center of the roulade registers 155°F/68°C, 35 to 40 minutes.

Remove the pot from the heat, cover again, and let stand for about 1 hour before serving, to ensure neat slices. (Alternatively, if you want to serve the turkey cold, let the roulade cool completely, then tightly wrap and refrigerate until ready to serve.)

To serve, transfer the roulade to a cutting board (set the Dutch oven aside) and cut off and discard the butcher's twine and the rosemary sprigs. Cut the roulade into thick slices.

Rewarm the pan juices. Transfer the sliced turkey to a warmed serving platter and spoon the hot juices over.

Any leftovers can be stored in the fridge for up to 3 days. Reheat gently before serving.

VARIATIONS

Here are a few other ideas for stuffing a turkey breast:

- **Fresh pecorino + vegetable omelet**. Choose your favorite seasonal vegetables and add them to the omelet. Spinach, artichokes, asparagus, and peas work well.

- **Grilled eggplants + cooked ham + scamorza cheese**. Grilled eggplants serve the same role as the eggs, making the filling moist and tasty.

- **Sausage + diced apples + dried chestnuts**. With this filling, even a simple turkey breast can be dressed up for a party.

FISH AND SEAFOOD

ITALIAN PESCE POVERO

Bagna caoda
Anchovy and Garlic Dip   116

Sarde in saor
Sweet-and-Sour Sardines with Onions   119

Brandacujun
Potato and Dried Stockfish Puree   122

Bigoli in salsa
**Pasta with Anchovy, Onion,
and Black Pepper Sauce   124**

Riso al nero
Squid Ink Risotto   127

Tiella di patate, riso e cozze
Mussel, Potato, and Rice Gratin   128

Brodetto marchigiano
Fish Soup   131

Orata all'acqua pazza
Sea Bream Stewed with Tomatoes   134

Baccalà al forno con le patate
Baked Salt Cod with Potatoes   137

Sgombro al salmoriglio
Grilled Mackerel with Salmoriglio Sauce   138

WHEN YOU LOOK AT THE OFFERINGS AT THE FISH MARKET, YOUR EYES
are drawn easily to the sea bass, sandy-colored sole, swordfish steaks,
salmon fillets, octopus, and tuna. But if you look past these beauties,
you'll see other fish that are just as remarkable. At an Italian fish market,
you can find crates of anchovies, sardines, mackerel, bonito, herring,
and many more local varieties, well known and appreciated by the
coastal populations. These little fish are considered *pesce povero*, or poor
fish, or even sometimes labeled *pesce dimenticato*, forgotten fish, because
they've been traditionally snubbed in favor of bigger fish. Since the 1960s,
when the Italian government launched a campaign promoting their
consumption for both health and nutritional reasons, these fish have also
been known as *pesce azzurro*, a term that refers to the shimmering blue
skin of the oily fish.

Pesce azzurro have played a key role in the history and culture of Italian
gastronomy since Roman times, when anchovies and sardines were cured
with salt and herbs to make garum. This pungent fish sauce was a powerful
flavor enhancer, a must-have in many a Roman dish. In recent years, pesce
azzurro have been rediscovered thanks to the increasing attention given to
local regional traditions, and to ongoing awareness campaigns. Choosing
lesser-known but equally tasty fish relieves fishing pressure on more
sought-after species and ensures that the biodiversity of fish species in our
seas is maintained. Pesce azzurro are, therefore, low-impact fish, usually
sustainable and less expensive as well.

Pesce povero, compared to other types of fish, spoil easily: the meat, rich
in polyunsaturated fatty acids, is nutritious and easy to digest but highly
perishable. That is the reason these fish have long been preserved in salt, oil,
or vinegar, as for the Venetian sarde in saor (page 119).

Salted anchovies hold an important place in cucina povera. These
small, humble fish brim with flavor; you can eat them on their own,
especially if paired with excellent butter and crusty bread. Drape one over
half a hard-boiled egg, and you'll elevate it to the status of cicchetti, the
Venetian version of tapas. And anchovies can become a secret ingredient
in your kitchen when slowly melted in warm olive oil. The fish add
an umami boost not only to seafood dishes and soups but also to meat
stews and braises, to vinaigrettes, and to vegetable stir-fries, as when you
are making orecchiette con le cime di rapa (page 35). Keep salt-packed
anchovies in your pantry, and you'll be able to improvise a dinner with
just a handful of other basic ingredients, making, for example, bigoli in
salsa (page 124) with just a box of spaghetti, some onions, black pepper,
and those anchovies.

The no-waste approach of cucina povera also applies to the coastal seafood cuisine, where the innards of squid and cuttlefish turn into a delicacy, as in squid ink risotto (page 127). Likewise, a hearty fish soup, such as the Adriatic brodetto (page 131), is a forgiving dish that can be made with any seafood you can find, emblematic, once again, of the resourcefulness of cucina povera.

For regions located far from the sea, sourcing fish has always been a challenge. Fish and seafood preserved through strategies like salting, drying, fermenting, and smoking became the solution. Baccalà, dried salted cod, and stoccafisso, air-dried cod, were once cheap, staple foods, strongly connected to tradition, politics, and religion. But if they were merely the perfect food to store for long sea journeys or to eat for lean days then, now they are beloved by home cooks and chefs alike for the endless possibilities they offer. Stock your pantry with baccalà and bake it with potatoes, breadcrumbs, and cheese (page 137), or opt for stoccafisso, and make brandacujun (page 122) for a starter.

Bagna caoda

ANCHOVY AND GARLIC DIP

**SERVES 4
AS A STARTER**

18 cloves garlic
12 salt-packed
    anchovies (about
    5 ounces/140 g)
½ cup/120 ml extra-
    virgin olive oil
2 cups/480 ml whole
    milk
3½ tablespoons/50 g
    unsalted butter

FOR SERVING

4 boiled potatoes, cut
    into sticks
4 steamed Jerusalem
    artichokes, cut into
    sticks
4 carrots, cut into
    sticks
2 roasted beets, cut
    into wedges
2 celery stalks, cut
    into sticks
2 bell peppers, cored,
    seeded, and cut into
    strips
1 fennel bulb, trimmed
    and cut into wedges
Savoy cabbage leaves

Bagna caoda, a traditional garlic and anchovy dip, is a peasant dish of the Piedmontese autumn. It is more than a recipe, though; it is a ritual, designed to be shared. It is a way to celebrate the grape harvest and the new wine, when you can enjoy the dip around a table where everyone is provided with a small clay bowl, known as a *fojot*, set over a candle to keep the bagna caoda warm. The dip is eaten with an array of seasonal vegetables, both raw and cooked: Savoy cabbage leaves; boiled potatoes, carrots, and beets; celery stalks and fennel wedges; and artichokes and bell peppers. You can also serve it with slices of grilled polenta (see page 224) and some fresh eggs, to be individually fried in the remnants of bagna caoda in each guest's fojot.

The traditional recipe calls for a head of garlic per person, salt-packed anchovies, and extra-virgin olive oil. No butter, milk, or cream to mellow its taste. To reinforce the no-waste approach, even the anchovy backbones would be saved, finely minced and added to the sauce. The recipe below takes a more modern approach, with whole milk and butter to round out the flavor and make it more approachable, and a preliminary blanching of the garlic to soften its pungent smell.

Cook the bagna caoda on the lowest heat; think of it as mindfulness meditation, and you'll be rewarded with an impossibly creamy, savory warm dip.

———

Peel the garlic cloves, cut them in half, and discard their inner sprouts (in Italian these are known as *anima*, or soul). Transfer the garlic to a bowl of cold water and soak for about 30 minutes.

Rinse the anchovies under cold running water. Gently remove and discard the backbones, opening each anchovy and separating it into 2 fillets. Lay the fillets on a paper towel to drain.

Drain the garlic cloves, transfer to a small saucepan, cover them with fresh water, and bring to a boil. Cook the garlic for 5 minutes, then drain; repeat 2 more times, until the garlic is so soft it can be easily mashed with a fork.

Pour ¼ cup/60 ml of the olive oil into a medium saucepan set over the lowest possible heat, add the anchovies and garlic, and, using a wooden spoon, mash the anchovies and garlic to a paste. Gradually add the milk, in ½-cup/120 ml increments, and simmer for about 1 hour, stirring

occasionally. The bagna caoda will gradually thicken and become creamy. Don't worry if at the beginning the milk curdles unappealingly; it will smooth out when you blend it.

Add the butter to the bagna caoda and stir to melt it. Using an immersion blender, blend the bagna caoda into a smooth, creamy sauce (or blend it in a regular blender and return to the pan). Pour in the remaining ¼ cup/60 ml olive oil and simmer over the lowest possible heat for about 20 minutes.

Meanwhile, arrange the vegetables on a large platter.

To serve, divide the bagna caoda among individual bowls, or transfer to a fondue pot with a can of Sterno or a candle beneath it to keep the sauce warm. Serve with the platter of vegetables in the center of the table for dipping.

Leftovers can be kept in the fridge for a day, tightly covered with plastic wrap. Reheat before serving.

SALT-PACKED OR OIL-PACKED ANCHOVIES?

Salt-packed anchovies are sold whole, gutted but with bones and tail intact, covered with coarse sea salt. You can find them in glass jars or tins. They offer a high-quality and intense anchovy experience: the preserving process captures the briny taste of the sea and concentrates their flavor. Use these anchovies in pasta sauces or vinaigrettes, or in bagna caoda.

If you are an anchovy novice and want to acclimate to them gradually, choose anchovies packed in oil instead. These are salt-packed anchovies that have been rinsed, filleted, and preserved in oil. Just fish out a fillet or two from the tin or jar with a fork and lay it on your buttered bread, or melt it in warm olive oil to add an umami boost to any dish.

Sarde in saor

SWEET-AND-SOUR SARDINES WITH ONIONS

**SERVES 8
AS A STARTER,
4 AS A MAIN COURSE**

2 pounds/1 kg fresh
    sardines (see Note)
1 cup/125 g all-
    purpose flour
4 cups/1 L vegetable
    or other neutral oil
    for deep-frying
½ cup/120 ml extra-
    virgin olive oil
3 bay leaves
2 pounds/1 kg white
    onions, thinly sliced
2 cups/480 ml white
    wine vinegar
Fine sea salt
¼ teaspoon freshly
    ground black
    pepper
3 tablespoons raisins
2 tablespoons dry
    white wine
2 tablespoons pine
    nuts
Toasted bread for
    serving

What was born as a way to preserve small fish for long sea voyages has become a quintessential Venetian dish. Sardines are fried and then layered in a pot with a generous amount of white onions that have been cooked in olive oil and then simmered in vinegar. The dish is dotted with pine nuts and raisins, reflecting the city's history as a trading center on the Silk Road. The sardines gain flavor (*saor* in Venetian dialect) while sitting in their curing juices.

Sarde in saor are a fixture of bacari, Venetian wine bars, especially during the intense summer heat. They can be served cold, as a refreshing starter, or as a main course with polenta (see page 224). As they need time to cure, sarde in saor work extremely well as party food—make them 2 days ahead and then take them out of the refrigerator just before serving.

———

Using your fingers, remove the head and guts from each fish and discard them, then rinse the sardines well. Pat dry with paper towels.

Pour the flour onto a plate and dredge the sardines in the flour, shaking off the excess.

Pour the frying oil into a large deep frying pan set over medium-high heat. Place a large plate lined with paper towels nearby. When the oil registers 350°F/175°C on a deep-frying thermometer, start frying the floured sardines in batches; if you crowd the oil, the temperature will drop and the sardines will absorb too much oil. Fry the first batch, turning the sardines once with two forks, until golden brown, a few minutes per side. Transfer to the paper towel–lined plate and fry the remaining sardines, allowing the oil to return to temperature between batches. Set aside.

Pour the olive oil into a large frying pan set over medium-low heat. Add the bay leaves and onions and cook, stirring often, for about 30 minutes, until the onions are softened and golden.

Pour the vinegar into the pan and bring to a boil, then reduce the heat to a simmer and cook for 10 minutes. Turn off the heat and season with salt to taste and the pepper.

(CONTINUED)

Meanwhile, put the raisins in a small bowl, add the wine, and let stand for 10 minutes. Drain, squeezing out the excess liquid.

Arrange half of the fried sardines in the bottom of a large shallow bowl. Top with half of the stewed onions. Add half of the pine nuts and raisins. Top with the remaining sardines, then finish with the remaining onions, pine nuts, and raisins. Pour any vinegar remaining in the pan over the onions.

Cover the bowl with plastic wrap and transfer to the refrigerator. Refrigerate for 2 days before serving the sardines so that all the flavors can mingle and mature.

Serve the sardines cold from the fridge, with slices of toasted bread.

NOTES: *This method for cooking and preserving fish, vegetables, or meat is known as* saor *in Veneto,* carpione *in Piedmont, and* scapece *in Liguria, Campania, and Apulia, a term derived from the Spanish word* escabeche.

If you cannot find fresh sardines, you can use fresh anchovies, small cod, mackerel fillets, or fillet of sole instead.

VARIATIONS

The same cooking technique can be used for shrimp or chicken, or even radicchio. I especially like zucca in saor, made with pumpkin, whose sweet, delicate taste is complemented by the sweet-and-sour dressing.

Brandacujun

POTATO AND DRIED STOCKFISH PUREE

SERVES 6
AS A STARTER

1 pound/455 g dried
  cod, soaked and
  ready for cooking
  (see Note)
12 ounces/340 g
  Yukon Gold
  potatoes (about
  2 large potatoes)
1 tablespoon minced
  fresh flat-leaf
  parsley
1 clove garlic, minced
Fine sea salt
¼ teaspoon freshly
  ground black
  pepper
¼ cup/60 ml extra-
  virgin olive oil

FOR SERVING

⅓ cup/65 g pitted
  Taggiasca or
  Kalamata olives
Toasted bread

Dried stockfish and potatoes were two ingredients essential for sustaining sailors during their long sea journeys. That is where the western Ligurian brandacujun, a potato and dried stockfish puree, was born. These mundane ingredients become a delicacy when combined and beaten with a good pour of extra-virgin olive oil until creamy.

Traditionally brandacujun was prepared by vigorously shaking the covered pot after the potatoes and cod were cooked, getting your pelvis into the movement—the source of its name, brandacujun—or by creaming them together with a wooden spoon. Now you can get the same result far more easily by using a stand mixer with the paddle attachment. The result is a soft, fluffy puree, with still-recognizable flakes of cod.

You can prepare brandacujun in advance and store it in the fridge for a couple of days. Serve as a starter with toasted bread and olives.

———

Cut the cod into 1½-inch-thick/4 cm slices and set aside. Peel and rinse the potatoes, then cut into ¾-inch-thick/2 cm slices.

Put the cod pieces and sliced potatoes in a large pot, add water to cover, and bring to a boil over high heat. Reduce the heat and, with a slotted spoon, remove and discard any scum from the surface of the water. Continue to cook, uncovered, for about 30 minutes, until the potatoes are soft and the cod is starting to flake apart.

Remove from the heat and drain in a colander, reserving about a cup of the cooking water. Remove the cod from the colander, remove any remaining skin, bones, and cartilage and discard, and transfer the fish to the bowl of a stand mixer fitted with the paddle attachment. Add the potatoes to the cod.

Add the parsley, garlic, a generous pinch of salt, and the pepper to the potatoes and fish and mix on medium speed for a few minutes, gradually drizzling in the olive oil. The brandacujun is ready when it is creamy, soft, and fluffy, with flakes of cod still visible. If the mixture is very thick, thin with some of the reserved cooking water, a tablespoon at a time.

Transfer the brandacujun to a serving bowl, garnish with the olives, and serve with toasted bread.

Any leftovers can be stored in a lidded container in the fridge for a couple of days. Bring to room temperature before serving.

NOTE: *To prepare stoccafisso, soak the dried cod in a large bowl of water for 3 to 4 days. Cover the bowl with plastic wrap and store in the fridge, replacing the water at least twice a day. Drain and remove any bones, cartilage, or skin before using. If you can't get stoccafisso, you can substitute salt cod here, soaking it in the same manner.*

Bigoli in salsa

PASTA WITH ANCHOVY, ONION, AND BLACK PEPPER SAUCE

**SERVES 4
AS A FIRST COURSE**

6 salt-packed
   anchovies (about
   2½ ounces/70 g)
6 tablespoons/90 ml
   extra-virgin olive oil
2 small white onions,
   thinly sliced (about
   3 cups)
½ cup/120 ml dry
   white wine
1 pound/455 g dried
   bigoli or thick whole
   wheat spaghetti
1 teaspoon freshly
   ground black
   pepper

In much of Italy, the word *salsa* refers to tomato sauce, but in Veneto when you order bigoli in salsa, you get a bowl of rustic pasta dressed with a punchy onion, anchovy, and black pepper sauce. The dish is a staple of Venetian trattoria menus, but it was traditionally eaten by peasant people on lean (meatless) days, like Fridays, or on the days before big celebrations, like Christmas Eve.

Bigoli is a thick spaghetti-like pasta that has a rough surface, making it ideal for holding a sauce like this. It can be purchased fresh, sometimes made with duck eggs, or dried. For this recipe, you can use either dried bigoli or whole wheat spaghetti—the thicker, the better.

Bigoli in salsa makes for a quick, affordable weeknight meal, something you can improvise with pantry staples. Given the short ingredients list, do not compromise on the quality of the anchovies.

——

Rinse the anchovies under cold running water. Gently remove and discard the backbones, opening each anchovy and separating it into 2 fillets. Finely chop the fillets.

Pour the olive oil into a large frying pan set over medium-low heat. Add the onions and cook, stirring occasionally, for 5 to 8 minutes, until they start to sizzle and turn golden. Add the anchovies and stir to melt, gently cooking them in the oil for a few minutes.

Pour in the wine and cook, stirring from time to time, until the mixture reduces to the consistency of a sauce. Set aside.

Bring a large pot of water to a boil and add some salt; keep in mind that the sauce is salty, so you won't need much salt in the pasta water. Add the bigoli (or spaghetti) and cook according to the package instructions until al dente.

Drain the bigoli, reserving ½ cup/120 ml of the pasta cooking water, and add to the anchovy sauce. Add the reserved cooking water and toss the bigoli over low heat for a couple of minutes, until well coated with sauce. Sprinkle with the pepper and serve immediately.

SQUID INK

All members of the cephalopod family, including squid and cuttlefish, have ink as a defense mechanism. The ink used to be an important ingredient of maritime cucina povera, the only condiment available to sailors and fishermen to dress cuttlefish. Now it is considered an elegant, umami-packed ingredient that adds complexity to various dishes, infusing them with the taste of the ocean. You can use the ink to add a black color and a salty marine flavor to fresh pasta, risotto (opposite), buns, crackers, or gnocchi (page 225).

Riso al nero

SQUID INK RISOTTO

**SERVES 4
AS A FIRST COURSE**

1 pound/455 g squid
⅓ cup/80 ml extra-virgin olive oil
1 clove garlic, finely minced
Fine sea salt
Red pepper flakes
½ cup/120 ml dry white wine
1½ cups/300 g Carnaroli, Arborio, or Vialone Nano rice (see page 33)
3½ cups/840 ml fish stock, heated, or lightly salted hot water
2 teaspoons squid ink (see Note)
2 tablespoons/30 g unsalted butter
2 tablespoons finely chopped fresh flat-leaf parsley

NOTE: *You can use the ink that sometimes comes in tiny sacs with fresh squid or cuttlefish or buy it in jars or individual packets.*

Squid ink is thick and intense, with a salty taste and a hint of iodine, and a brininess similar to that of oysters and sea urchins. Add a couple of squid ink sachets to risotto, and you'll have a showstopping dish.

The use of squid ink is common throughout the Mediterranean, from Venice to the coast of Tuscany, from Croatia to Sicily, and on to Spain, with its traditional arroz negro. Riso al nero, a Venetian dish, was spread all over the Mediterranean by Venetian merchants. Its striking appearance—pitch-black, thanks to the ink—makes it unforgettable. Its intense flavor reduces the need for other seasoning, so a small knob of butter and a pinch of salt are all that is necessary to finish the risotto.

——

To clean the squid, carefully separate the heads from the tentacles and remove the beak and the guts. Wash the squid and remove the outer membrane, then dice the bodies and chop the tentacles.

In a large saucepan, combine the oil, garlic, and a pinch each of salt and red pepper flakes and cook over medium heat until the garlic is fragrant, about 1 minute. Add the squid and cook until it is tender and the liquid it releases has evaporated, about 10 minutes.

Pour in the wine and cook for about 1 minute to let it start to evaporate, then add the rice and use a wooden spoon to stir it into the squid. When all the wine has evaporated, pour in about one-quarter of the hot fish stock and cook, stirring very often, until the rice has absorbed all the liquid. Add another quarter of the stock and cook, stirring, until it has been absorbed. Add the squid ink and stir to dissolve, then continue cooking, stirring and adding more stock as each addition is completely absorbed, until the risotto is creamy but the rice is still slightly al dente. The whole process will take 18 minutes or so. Depending on the variety of rice you use, the cooking time may vary, and you may not need all of the stock. When the risotto is done, add the butter and stir well. This technique is what we call *mantecare* in Italian, meaning to cream the butter into the risotto. Taste and adjust the seasoning.

Top the risotto with the chopped parsley and serve immediately.

VARIATIONS

You can use any leftover risotto to make arancine (page 242); or make a double batch of risotto specifically to have leftovers for this purpose.

Tiella di patate, riso, e cozze

MUSSEL, POTATO, AND RICE GRATIN

**SERVES 8
AS A MAIN COURSE**

3½ pounds/1.6 kg
  mussels
1 cup/240 ml extra-
  virgin olive oil
2 white onions, thinly
  sliced
2 pounds/1 kg Yukon
  Gold potatoes,
  peeled and cut into
  2-inch-thick/5 cm
  slices
1 pound/455 g cherry
  or grape tomatoes,
  halved
2 tablespoons minced
  fresh flat-leaf
  parsley
2 cloves garlic, minced
3½ ounces/100 g
  Pecorino Romano,
  grated
Fine sea salt and
  freshly ground
  black pepper
1 cup/200 g Arborio
  rice

This Apulian gratin of mussels, potatoes, and rice breaks an unwritten rule of Italian gastronomy: never mix cheese and seafood. The two might sound like a clashing of flavors, but here they combine to create a well-orchestrated symphony, a hearty, filling dish that is perfect for big families or large gatherings with friends.

The tiella, which originated during the sixteenth-century Spanish domination, reveals its Iberian influence. It also bears a resemblance to paella, as the ingredients lists of both dishes include rice, brought to Europe by the Arabs and introduced to Apulia by the Spaniards, along with mussels, onions, and tomatoes.

———

Rinse the mussels and scrub them under cold running water. Remove the beard from each one by grabbing it with your fingers and pulling it toward the hinge of the shell, then discard. Discard any open mussels. Using an oyster shucking knife or a dull thin, short knife, open the mussels: Working over a bowl, hold each mussel firmly, using a towel to protect your hand, and slide a knife in between the two halves of the shell. Run the knife around the inside of the shell to cut through the hinge muscle. Once you hear a clack, the mussel can be easily opened; let the mussel liquor drain into the bowl. Remove and discard the empty top shell and leave the mussel in the bottom shell. As you go, arrange the open mussels, still in their bottom shells, on a rimmed baking sheet.

Drizzle ¼ cup/60 ml of the olive oil over the bottom of a 12-inch/30 cm round casserole. Scatter half of the onions over the bottom of the pan, then top with half of the potatoes. Distribute half of the cherry tomatoes on top and sprinkle them with half of the parsley and garlic. Sprinkle one-third of the grated Pecorino Romano over, season with salt and pepper, and drizzle with another ¼ cup/60 ml oil.

Arrange the mussels, in their shells, on top of the cherry tomatoes in an even layer; reserve a dozen mussels for the final layer. Scatter the rice over the mussels, making sure to fill their shells. Sprinkle with half of the remaining pecorino, season with salt and pepper, and drizzle with another ¼ cup/60 ml oil.

(CONTINUED)

Top the rice with the remaining potatoes, then arrange the remaining cherry tomatoes and the reserved mussels on top. Scatter the onions over the tomatoes and sprinkle with the remaining parsley and garlic. Finish with the remaining pecorino and drizzle with the remaining ¼ cup/60 ml oil.

Preheat the oven to 400°F/200°C.

Strain the mussel liquor through a fine-mesh sieve and pour it into the pan. Then add as much salted water as needed to just reach the top layer of potatoes. Use this proportion for the salted water: 1 teaspoon/5 g fine sea salt per 4 cups/1 L water. Do not add too much water, or it will create a watery gratin. There is enough if when you gently press the last layer of onions, you see liquid surfacing.

Place the pan over medium heat and bring the liquid to a boil. Remove from the heat, cover the pan with aluminum foil, transfer to the oven, and bake for 40 minutes. Remove the foil and bake for 30 more minutes, or until all the liquid has been absorbed and the potatoes are golden brown.

Remove from the oven and let stand for at least 2 hours before serving, so that all the flavors can mingle. Reheat gently in a low oven before serving, or enjoy at room temperature.

Any leftovers can be kept in the fridge for a day.

NOTE: *The original recipe for tiella calls for opening the raw mussels and reserving their liquid to cook the gratin. If you do not feel confident with a shucking knife, steam the mussels with a teaspoon of olive oil in a covered pot over medium heat just until they open; a couple of minutes will be enough; you don't want to overcook them. Remove the mussels from the pot and pull off and discard the top shells; pass the liquid that has collected in the pot through a fine-mesh strainer and use as directed.*

Brodetto marchigiano

FISH SOUP

SERVES 6
AS A MAIN COURSE

1 pound/455 g small
    clams
1 tablespoon plus
    2 teaspoons fine
    sea salt, plus more
    to taste
1 pound/455 g
    mussels
1 pound/455 g squid
    or cuttlefish
½ cup/120 ml extra-
    virgin olive oil
1 white onion, minced
2 cloves garlic, minced
2 tablespoons minced
    fresh flat-leaf
    parsley
Red pepper flakes
Two 15-ounce/425 g
    cans whole peeled
    tomatoes, crushed
    by hand, juices
    reserved
8 ounces/225 g cherry
    tomatoes
1 green bell pepper,
    cored, seeded, and
    cut into strips
4½ pounds/2 kg
    whole small fish,
    such as John Dory
    or mackerel, or
    monkfish tail (see
    headnote), or
    1½ pounds/700 g
    fish fillets
1 pound/455 g
    jumbo shrimp
    (U 16/20), peeled
    and deveined
½ cup/120 ml white
    wine vinegar
6 slices country bread
1 clove garlic

The many fish soups of the Italian tradition were originally created to make good use of the unsold fish left after the market closed. Therefore, almost every Italian sea town has its own version, emblematic of coastal cucina povera. In Tuscany, you can order cacciucco in Livorno and caldaro in Maremma. In Liguria, you can find buridda and ciuppin on the local osteria menus. The main Italian islands boast two such recipes: cassòla in Sardinia and cuscusu trapanese in Sicily, an Italian interpretation of Arab couscous made with a flavorful fish soup. The Adriatic coast, from Trieste down to Abruzzo and Molise, has endless variations of brodetto. All of the soups have in common peasant origins, an indissoluble connection with the local fish, the presence of vegetables (especially tomatoes), and the accompaniment of bread, pasta, or polenta, used to thicken the soup and make it more filling.

It is impossible to spell out a precise list of ingredients to make fish soup, as traditionally you would use whatever fish was left over from the daily catch. So talk to your fishmonger, and choose what is local and in season. In Italy, we use pesce povero, small fish full of bones. The only downside is that these fish require an extra dose of patience when you eat them (all those tiny bones to remove), but they reward you with a flavorful, affordable soup. At the market, go for John Dory, scorpionfish, gurnard, small hake, mackerel, or monkfish tail. But if you prefer, you can make the soup with fish fillets instead.

Serve with plenty of crusty bread to mop up the flavorful stock left in the bottom of the bowls.

———

About 2 hours before you cook the soup, put the clams in a colander and set the colander in a larger bowl. Add 4 cups/1 L cold water and the sea salt and set aside to soak, shaking the clams once in a while to rid them of grit.

Rinse the mussels and scrub them under cold running water. Remove and discard the beards and discard any open mussels. Transfer to a bowl and refrigerate.

Clean the squid (or cuttlefish) by carefully separating the heads from the tentacles. Next remove the beak and guts; set aside the ink sacs, if present. Wash the squid and remove the translucent outer skin, then dice the bodies and chop the tentacles. Set aside.

(CONTINUED)

When ready to cook the soup, pour the olive oil into a large shallow pot or a deep frying pan and add the onion, garlic, parsley, and a pinch of red pepper flakes. Cook over low heat for about 5 minutes, until the onion softens and begins to turn translucent, then add the crushed tomatoes, with their juices, the cherry tomatoes, green pepper, and squid, reduce the heat to medium-low, cover, and cook for 15 minutes, stirring every now and then, until the tomatoes start to collapse and the squid starts to soften. Taste and adjust the seasoning with salt as necessary.

Add the whole fish (or fillets), laying them side by side on top of the tomato-squid mixture. Cover and cook for 10 minutes.

Drain and rinse the clams. Arrange the shrimp, mussels, and clams on top of the fish, pour in the vinegar, cover, and simmer for 10 minutes, or until the mussels and clams have opened and the shrimp is cooked through (remove and discard any clams or mussels that have not opened).

While the soup simmers, toast the bread slices, then rub the whole garlic clove over the surface of each slice.

Remove the soup from the heat, taste it again, and adjust the seasoning as necessary. Place a slice of bread in each serving bowl and top with a ladleful of soup, making sure that everyone has some of each type of seafood. Serve immediately.

Any leftover soup can be stored in the fridge for a day. Reheat gently before serving.

NOTES: *Choose a large shallow pot or a deep frying pan so you can arrange the whole fish (or fillets) in a single layer. This will make it easier both to cook the fish evenly and to serve the soup.*

Orata all'acqua pazza

SEA BREAM STEWED WITH TOMATOES

SERVES 4
AS A MAIN COURSE

8 ounces/225 g cherry
  or grape tomatoes
¼ cup/60 ml extra-
  virgin olive oil
1 medium sea
  bream or 2 small
  branzino (about
  1¾ pounds/800 g
  total), cleaned
2 cloves garlic,
  crushed and peeled
A handful of fresh
  basil leaves
A few fresh parsley or
  calamint sprigs
½ cup/120 ml water
¼ cup/65 g pitted
  Taggiasca or
  Kalamata olives
Fine sea salt

Acqua pazza (literally, crazy water) is a poaching liquid for fish with intense Mediterranean flavors, including ripe tomatoes, garlic, fresh herbs, white wine, and olive oil. The recipe belongs to the coastal cucina povera of the Italian South, where the fishermen who could not afford to buy salt would cook the daily catch in seawater, along with whatever aromatics they had on hand.

Acqua pazza is a very simple way of cooking fish—in less than 20 minutes, dinner is served, and you won't even need to turn on the oven. The fish remains juicy, soaked in a bright, aromatic sauce that calls for fresh bread to mop it up.

Although it was originally used for small bony fish, you can apply this same cooking method to any fish with delicate white flesh, such as sea bass, John Dory, perch, haddock, or hake. If you do not feel confident in cooking a whole fish, opt for 4 fish fillets instead and reduce the cooking time accordingly.

———

Halve two-thirds of the tomatoes; leave the rest whole.

Pour the olive oil into a pan large enough to accommodate the whole fish and heat over medium-high heat. When the oil is hot, add the fish to the pan and cook for 2 to 3 minutes, until browned on the first side. With two spatulas, carefully flip the fish and cook until browned on the second side, a few minutes more. Carefully transfer the fish to a rimmed baking sheet and reduce the heat to medium.

Add the garlic, all the tomatoes, the basil, and parsley sprigs to the pan and cook, stirring occasionally, until the tomatoes start to collapse and the olive oil turns reddish, about 4 minutes. Pour in the water and cook for 5 minutes, then add the olives.

Carefully return the fish to the pan, cover, and cook over the lowest possible heat for about 15 minutes for one large fish, or 10 minutes for two smaller fish, until cooked through; the flesh should easily flake when prodded with a fork.

Taste the sauce and add salt if needed, then lift the fish out of the pan and onto a serving platter. Pour the sauce from the pan over the fish and serve immediately.

You can use orata all'acqua pazza to dress a bowl of spaghetti: Cook the sea bream according to the instructions above. Lift it out of the pan, fillet it, and flake the fillets into a bowl; set the pan aside. Cook 12 ounces/340 g spaghetti in a large pot of boiling salted water and drain a couple of minutes before the pasta is done; reserve a ladleful of the cooking water. Add the spaghetti to the pan with the stewed tomatoes and finish cooking the pasta over low heat, tossing it in the pan so that it absorbs the juices; add some of the reserved water if needed. The sauce will cling to the spaghetti, and the starch released by the pasta will create a creamy dressing. Add the flaked fish and serve.

Baccalà al forno con le patate

BAKED SALT COD WITH POTATOES

**SERVES 6 TO 8
AS A MAIN COURSE**

1¾ pounds/800 g
   baccalà, soaked and
   ready for cooking
   (see Notes)
2 pounds/1 kg Yukon
   Gold potatoes
Fine sea salt
4 slices semolina
   bread, crusts
   removed (about
   4 ounces/115 g)
   and crumbled
   (about 2½ cups)
2 ounces/60 g
   Pecorino Romano,
   grated
2 ounces/60 g
   Parmigiano-
   Reggiano, grated
1 tablespoon minced
   fresh flat-leaf
   parsley
1 clove garlic, minced
¼ teaspoon freshly
   ground black
   pepper
½ cup/120 ml extra-
   virgin olive oil
1 scant cup/100 g
   cherry tomatoes,
   halved
2 tablespoons dry
   breadcrumbs

This recipe for salt cod with potatoes belongs to the Southern Italian part of my heritage. It is typical of Basilicata, but it perfectly represents the tradition—common to many regions of the Italian South—of using fresh breadcrumbs as a filling, a seasoning, or simply a way to stretch a meal, as in stuffed green peppers (page 48).

Whether it's artichokes, peppers, or slices of salt cod, the base ingredient is layered with potatoes and a mixture of garlicky breadcrumbs and sharp grated cheese, then baked until crisp. It makes a great summer meal: prepare it in advance, and rewarm it before serving.

——

Preheat the oven to 400°F/200°C.

Cut the baccalà into 1-inch-thick/3 cm slices; set aside.

Peel and rinse the potatoes, cut into ¼-inch-thick/6 mm slices, and transfer to a bowl. Sprinkle with 1 teaspoon salt and set aside.

In a small bowl, combine the crumbled bread, pecorino, Parmigiano-Reggiano, parsley, garlic, a pinch of salt, and the pepper.

Grease a 9-by-11 inch/23 by 28 cm baking dish with half of the olive oil, then arrange half of the potatoes in the pan. Lay the cod slices on top and cover with half of the bread mixture. Top with the remaining potatoes, arranging them in a single layer, and finish with the remaining bread mixture. Scatter the cherry tomatoes over the top, then pour 1 cup/240 ml water around the edges of the pan. Sprinkle the dry breadcrumbs over the top and drizzle over the remaining ¼ cup/60 ml olive oil.

Bake for about 1 hour, or until the potatoes are tender and the breadcrumbs are golden brown. Let stand at room temperature for 10 minutes before serving.

NOTES: *To prepare baccalà, soak it in a large bowl of water for 2 to 3 days. Cover the bowl with plastic wrap and store in the fridge, replacing the water at least twice a day to desalt the cod. Drain and remove any bones, cartilage, or skin before using. Be sure to be careful with the salt you add when cooking with the baccalà, as it may still be quite salty.*

The recipe can also be made with stoccafisso or fresh cod.

Sgombro al salmoriglio

GRILLED MACKEREL WITH SALMORIGLIO SAUCE

**SERVES 4
AS A MAIN COURSE**

4 mackerel (7 ounces/
  200 g each)

FOR THE SALMORIGLIO

½ cup/120 ml extra-
  virgin olive oil
Juice of ½ lemon
2 cloves garlic, finely
  minced
1 tablespoon dried
  oregano
1 teaspoon flaky sea
  salt, or more to
  taste
Red pepper flakes

1 tablespoon coarse
  sea salt
1 dried oregano or
  fresh rosemary
  sprig

Salmoriglio is an ace up your sleeve when it comes to grilling fish or meat. Made with a couple of pantry staples, including extra-virgin olive oil, garlic, dried oregano, and lemon juice, the sauce lends a zingy, bright taste to strong-flavored fish like swordfish, tuna, and mackerel.

The name salmoriglio is similar to the word *salamoia*, or brine; the original Sicilian version has water and salt among the ingredients. There are some who swear by adding a couple of teaspoons of seawater as the sauce's secret ingredient.

Mackerel is one of the most common types of pesce azzurro, the oily fish local to the Mediterranean Sea: affordable, sustainable, and rich in omega-3s, it has an intense flavor that calls for high heat and a good brushing of salmoriglio. Leftover grilled mackerel makes a delicious sandwich filling.

———

Prepare the mackerel: Remove and discard the guts, if present, and rinse well. Pat dry with paper towels and set aside.

Prepare the salmoriglio: Pour the olive oil and lemon juice into a small bowl, add the garlic, oregano, flaky salt, and a pinch of red pepper flakes, and stir thoroughly to mix. Taste and adjust the seasoning.

Sprinkle a cast-iron griddle pan with the coarse sea salt and heat it over high heat. The salt will prevent the mackerel from sticking and help grill the fish to perfection.

When the salt starts to pop almost imperceptibly, place the mackerel on the griddle pan and cook for 5 minutes, or until they easily release from the pan; use the dried oregano sprig to brush them once in a while with the salmoriglio as they cook. Turn the mackerel, lifting them with two spatulas, brush them with more salmoriglio, and cook on the second side for 5 more minutes, or until just cooked through.

Lift the mackerel out of the pan and onto a plate and fillet them. Transfer the fillets to a serving plate, drizzle the remaining salmoriglio over them, and let marinate for 10 minutes before serving.

The mackerel can be served warm or at room temperature.

Any leftovers can be kept in the fridge for a day.

MILK AND CHEESE

DAIRY-BASED MEALS

Pallotte cacio e ova
Cheese-and-Egg Balls Stewed in
Tomato Sauce   144

Mozzarella in carrozza
Fried Mozzarella Sandwiches   147

Frico friulano
Cheese and Potato Cake   148

Gnudi di ricotta e ortiche
Nettle and Ricotta Gnudi   151

Pici cacio e pepe
Hand-Pulled Pici Pasta with Cheese
and Black Pepper   153

Pizzoccheri
Buckwheat Pasta with Cabbage and Cheese   157

*Passatelli asciutti con crema di Parmigiano-
Reggiano*
Passatelli with Parmigiano-Reggiano Sauce   159

Zuppa alla valpellinese
Fontina and Savoy Cabbage Bread
Casserole   162

Torta pasqualina
Ligurian Spinach and Ricotta Pie   165

CHEESE IS ONE OF ITALY'S MOST RENOWNED PRODUCTS, EXPORTED worldwide and a sublime example of what "made in Italy" truly means. But cheese hasn't always had an excellent reputation. Throughout the Middle Ages, cheese had a marginal connotation, both social and geographical: it was the food of poor people, farmers, and pilgrims, and often the only choice for those who lived in isolated Alpine valleys. It was the perfect embodiment of one of the most primitive and essential kinds of companatico—that is, something to eat with bread to make a meal. Cheese was not considered an acceptable part of the diet of the higher classes. That was not just social prejudice. Cheese was looked at with suspicion because of its fermented taste and funky smell, and it was believed to be indigestible.

By the late Middle Ages, though, cheese's reputation had started to change, thanks to abbeys and monasteries. Monks, who dedicated equal time to farming, praying, and studying, laid the foundation of modern dairy farms. Their scientific knowledge meant that they could perfect the aging of cheese. Their interest in cheese was partly dictated by the many dietary restrictions of "lean days" (as opposed to fat days) imposed by the Catholic religion: on those days, meat was not eaten, replaced instead with fish, eggs, and/or cheese. Those rules of abstinence were followed by the entire Christian community, and cheese, once associated with poverty, assumed a new relevance.

That brings us to cheese in modern times. What contributed to the negative reputation of dairy products—the taste and the smell—is what now makes cheese one of the most exquisite Italian foods. Cheese is an element of territorial and cultural identity, be it a rich cow's-milk cheese made in an Alpine *malga* (hut), a sharp pecorino from the countryside outside Rome, or a milky buffalo mozzarella from Campania. It is not just their taste or texture, or how they are consumed: dairy products are a concentration of the culture, traditions, and history of a region in edible form.

Cucina povera makes use of cheese with the same creative, resourceful, and waste-not approach it applies to vegetables and bread. The recipes in this chapter, mainly vegetarian, demonstrate how even the barest fridge and pantry can deliver a generous, delicious meal if dairy is available. Cheese can be a meal on its own, when paired with some crusty bread. Or it can be combined with seasonal vegetables and day-old bread to create substantial, filling dishes, such as the Alpine zuppa alla valpellinese (page 162), a winter casserole of dark bread, Fontina cheese, and braised Savoy cabbage, or the Ligurian torta pasqualina (page 165), a savory torte made with fresh cheese, greens, and eggs.

Even scraps, remnants, and rinds of cheese play an important role in cucina povera. Day-old fresh mozzarella becomes the filling of finger-licking fried sandwiches of Neapolitan origins in mozzarella in carrozza (page 147), and a handful of grated Parmigiano-Reggiano mixed with fine breadcrumbs and eggs can be turned into one of the most comforting dishes of Emilia-Romagna: passatelli (page 159). For the true wonder of cucina povera, think of a Parmigiano-Reggiano rind. When you've used most of your wedge of Parmigiano-Reggiano, don't throw the rind away; wrap it in wax paper and keep it in the fridge. Next time you're making a soup that needs another layer of flavor, as in the pasta, patate, e provola (page 204), or even a stock from vegetable scraps (page 307), throw in the Parmigiano-Reggiano rind to give your dish an umami kick.

Pallotte cacio e ova

CHEESE-AND-EGG BALLS STEWED IN TOMATO SAUCE

SERVES 4 TO 6 AS
A STARTER

FOR THE TOMATO SAUCE

¼ cup/60 ml extra-
    virgin olive oil
2 cloves garlic,
    crushed and peeled
½ celery stalk
¼ red bell pepper,
    seeded
3 cups/720 ml tomato
    puree (passata)
2 cups/480 ml water
Fine sea salt

FOR THE PALLOTTE

7 ounces/200 g
    day-old bread,
    crusts removed
7 ounces/200 g
    Parmigiano-
    Reggiano, grated
3½ ounces/100 g
    Pecorino Romano,
    grated
4 large/200 g eggs,
    lightly beaten
½ clove garlic, minced
2 tablespoons minced
    fresh flat-leaf
    parsley
4 cups/1 L vegetable
    or other neutral oil
    for deep-frying

Crusty bread for
    serving

Pallotte are soft, spongy balls made with day-old bread and grated cheese, simmered in a very smooth tomato sauce. Serve them in small bowls, with plenty of crusty bread to mop up the sauce.

_____

Prepare the sauce: In a large frying pan, heat the olive oil over medium-low heat. Add the garlic, celery, and red pepper and cook, stirring, until the garlic is golden and fragrant, about 2 minutes. Pour in the tomato puree and water and bring to a simmer, then reduce the heat to low and simmer for about 20 minutes, until the sauce is glossy but still quite liquid. Taste and season with salt; set aside.

Make the pallotte: In a medium bowl, soak the bread in cold water to cover for 5 minutes. Check the bread; it should have become soft again. If it's still a bit hard, let it soak for a few minutes longer.

Remove the bread from the water and squeeze it to remove the water. Crumble it into a large bowl. Add the grated Parmigiano-Reggiano and pecorino, then add the eggs, garlic, and parsley. Mix the ingredients together, squeezing them with your hands, until a soft, moist, slightly crumbly dough forms, then continue to mix until it no longer sticks to your hands.

To form the pallotte, scoop up ½ tablespoon of the dough and, with slightly wet hands, roll into a ball. Transfer to a rimmed baking sheet and repeat with the remaining dough; you should end up with about 3 dozen pallotte.

Pour the frying oil into a large high-sided pot set over medium-high heat. Set a wire rack on a rimmed baking sheet and place nearby.

When the oil registers 350°F/175°C on a deep-frying thermometer, add the pallotte to the pot, cooking them in batches; if you crowd the oil, the temperature will drop and the pallotte will absorb too much oil. As you add them, the pallotte should roll over on themselves and dance in the oil; fry until golden brown, about 5 minutes, then transfer to the wire rack. Fry the remaining pallotte in batches, allowing the oil to return to temperature between batches.

Remove the garlic, celery, and pepper from the tomato sauce and heat it until hot. Add the pallotte to the sauce and simmer for 5 minutes. Serve immediately.

NOTES: *The pallotte should be simmered in the tomato sauce just before serving, or they will become soggy. But you can fry the pallotte in advance and store them in the fridge, then cook them in the tomato sauce when ready to serve.*

Use any leftover sauce to dress a bowl of spaghetti: the pallotte infuse the sauce with a cheesy flavor, making it a great choice for a quick meal.

Mozzarella in carrozza

FRIED MOZZARELLA SANDWICHES

SERVES 4 AS A
STARTER, 2 AS
A MAIN COURSE

2 large/100 g eggs
¼ cup/60 ml whole
   milk
Fine sea salt and
   freshly ground
   black pepper
¼ cup/30 g all-
   purpose flour
8 ounces/225 g fresh
   mozzarella, cut into
   4 slices (see Note)
8 slices semolina
   bread (about 2½ by
   2½ inches/6 by
   6 cm), crusts
   removed
4 cups/1 L vegetable
   or other neutral oil
   for deep-frying
Flaky sea salt
   (optional)

NOTE: *Traditionally
prepared with day-
old fresh buffalo
mozzarella, the dish
is now commonly
made with cow's-milk
mozzarella. If the
mozzarella is still very
fresh, slice it and lay
it between some paper
towels to absorb the
excess moisture.*

This dish was born in Naples in the nineteenth century as a clever way to upcycle stale bread and day-old fresh mozzarella. The mozzarella is sliced and sandwiched between two pieces of dense country bread that are then coated in flour, drenched in beaten eggs, and fried until golden. Mozzarella in carrozza is still one of the favorite street foods in Naples, served in local delis, along with other delicacies, such as fried dough. It can also be prepared as a starter or, as it often happened in my family when I was a child, as a quick, filling dinner served with a big salad.

———

In a medium bowl, whisk together the eggs and milk. Season with salt and pepper. Spread the flour in a cake pan or on a rimmed plate.

Sandwich each slice of mozzarella between 2 slices of bread and press together well.

Pour the oil into a large high-sided pot set over medium-high heat. Set a wire rack on a rimmed baking sheet and line a serving platter with paper towels; place nearby.

While the oil heats, dredge the mozzarella sandwiches in the flour, then dip them into the egg mixture, making sure to soak both sides and especially the edges, then press the edges together to seal the mozzarella inside. Return the sandwiches to the baking sheet.

When the oil registers 350°F/175°C on a deep-frying thermometer, or when the handle of a wooden spoon dipped into the oil is immediately surrounded by tiny bubbles, add the sandwiches to the pot. Fry, turning the sandwiches once with two forks, until deep golden brown on both sides, about 6 minutes.

Transfer the sandwiches to the platter, sprinkle with flaky sea salt, if desired, and serve immediately. The mozzarella sandwiches are best while still hot.

VARIATION

Along with the mozzarella, add an anchovy fillet to each sandwich, the way mozzarella in carrozza is usually prepared in Rome, for a boost of flavor that will also cut through the richness of the fried cheese. Or add a slice of prosciutto cotto (cooked ham) to the cheese, as they do in Venice.

Frico friulano

CHEESE AND POTATO CAKE

**SERVES 4 TO 6 AS
A STARTER, 2 AS A
MAIN COURSE**

1 pound/455 g russet
   potatoes
2 tablespoons/30 g
   unsalted butter
1 tablespoon extra-
   virgin olive oil
½ small onion, finely
   minced
Fine sea salt
11 ounces/310 g
   medium-aged
   Montasio or Asiago,
   finely diced
Freshly ground black
   pepper

Frico highlights the resourcefulness of cucina povera in the northeastern Italian border region of Friuli–Venezia Giulia, where the rinds and scraps from wheels of the local cheese are upcycled into this iconic dish. Grated potatoes held together with melted Montasio cheese are served as a main course with a scoop of steaming-hot polenta (see page 224), or as a shared starter along with a few slices of delicate prosciutto. The recipe varies depending on the location; sometimes other ingredients, such as onions or other vegetables, herbs, porcini, speck, or tart apples, are added.

———

Peel the potatoes and grate them using the large holes of a box grater or the grating attachment of your food processor. Transfer the grated potatoes to a bowl.

In a 10-inch/25 cm frying pan, melt the butter over medium-low heat. Add the olive oil, onion, and a pinch of salt and cook, stirring occasionally, until the onion is soft, about 5 minutes.

Add the grated potatoes, season with a generous pinch of salt, and reduce the heat to low. Cook for about 25 minutes, mashing the potatoes against the sides of the pan once they are softened and folding them with a spatula until they come together into a soft, gluey mixture. They should be cooked through but still retain their shape.

Fold the cheese into the potatoes, increase the heat to medium, and cook, stirring, until the cheese is completely melted. Taste and adjust the seasoning with more salt if necessary and with pepper. Press the mixture against the bottom of the pan to shape it into a cake and cook, undisturbed, until a crisp, golden crust forms on the bottom, 8 to 10 minutes.

Remove the pan from the heat, cover it with an inverted plate, and, holding the plate and pan together, invert the cake onto the plate. Return the pan to the stove, slide the potato cake back into the pan, and continue cooking until the second side is golden brown, about 8 minutes.

Slide the potato cake onto a serving plate, sprinkle with salt and pepper, cut into wedges, and serve immediately.

Gnudi di ricotta e ortiche

NETTLE AND RICOTTA GNUDI

SERVES 4 TO 6 AS
A FIRST COURSE

FOR THE GNUDI

1¼ pounds/565 g
stinging nettles (or
substitute Swiss
chard or kale)

1 tablespoon extra-
virgin olive oil

2 cloves garlic,
crushed and peeled

1¼ cups/11 ounces/
310 g best-quality
ricotta, preferably
sheep's milk,
thoroughly drained
(see Note)

5 tablespoons/30 g
grated Parmigiano-
Reggiano

1 teaspoon fine sea
salt, or more to
taste

¼ teaspoon freshly
ground black
pepper, or more
to taste

¼ teaspoon grated
nutmeg

1 large/50 g egg,
slightly beaten

¾ cup plus
1 tablespoon/100 g
all-purpose flour

FOR THE SAUCE

8 tablespoons/1 stick/
115 g unsalted
butter

16 fresh sage leaves

5 tablespoons/30 g
grated Parmigiano-
Reggiano

Gnudi are pillowy dumplings made of ricotta and greens, usually spinach. *Gnudi* is a Tuscan term that means naked, so think of them as nude ravioli, light balls of filling without the fresh pasta envelope. In the area around Siena, they are also known as *malfatti* (literally, badly made).

You can make gnudi with whatever greens you have on hand or are in season: chard, foraged herbs such as nettles, or kale. They are traditionally dressed with brown butter and crisp sage leaves, but during summer, you could serve them with a fresh tomato sauce and a shower of grated Parmigiano-Reggiano. There are two crucial techniques that make a difference when preparing these gnudi: the ricotta must be thoroughly drained, and you must squeeze every last drop of the cooking water from the greens.

——

Make the gnudi: Wearing gloves, wash the nettle leaves and remove any hard stems. Bring a large pot of water to a rolling boil and salt it generously, add the nettle leaves, and push them into the water. Bring back to a boil and blanch the leaves for 5 to 7 minutes, or until tender. Drain and let cool slightly.

When the nettle leaves are cool enough to handle, squeeze well to remove any excess water: To remove all the liquid, work in batches, picking up enough greens to make a ball that you can easily handle and then squeeze it with your hands until you remove all the water; or use a potato ricer (see Note). You should get about 10½ ounces/300 g of squeezed greens. Transfer the greens to a cutting board and finely chop them.

In a medium frying pan, heat the olive oil over medium heat. Add the garlic and cook until fragrant, about 30 seconds, then add the chopped nettles and cook, stirring occasionally, for a few minutes to infuse the greens with the garlicky oil. Transfer to a large bowl and let cool completely.

Add the ricotta, Parmigiano-Reggiano, salt, pepper, and nutmeg to the nettles and stir to combine. Taste and adjust the seasoning if necessary, then add the beaten egg. Mix thoroughly with a fork.

Generously dust a rimmed baking sheet with the flour. To form the gnudi, scoop up 1 tablespoon of the mixture for each one, roll into a ball with slightly wet hands, and transfer to the prepared baking sheet. As you work, shake the baking sheet once in a while to roll the gnudi in the flour to coat.

(CONTINUED)

NOTES: *To drain the ricotta, spoon it into a colander set over a bowl and let it drain for a few hours in the fridge. If the ricotta is very moist, you may want to leave it to drain overnight.*

To thoroughly drain the greens, you can use your hands or a potato ricer, which works magic in squeezing out the excess water.

This will create a film around each one, preventing them from dissolving in the boiling water.

You can cook the gnudi now, but if you refrigerate them for an hour before cooking, the flour will absorb some of the moisture, and you'll have firmer gnudi that are less likely to fall apart in the cooking water.

Just before cooking the gnudi, prepare the sauce: In a medium frying pan, melt the butter over medium-low heat. When the butter stops foaming, add the sage leaves and fry until crisp. With a slotted spoon, transfer the fried sage to a paper towel–lined plate; set the pan of butter aside.

Bring a large pot of salted water to a boil. Cook the gnudi, in batches to avoid crowding, for 3 to 5 minutes, until they float to the top. Remove from the water with a spider or slotted spoon and transfer to a warmed serving dish.

When all of the gnudi have been cooked, drizzle them with the reserved melted butter, sprinkle with the Parmigiano-Reggiano, and garnish with the fried sage leaves. Serve immediately.

Pici cacio e pepe

HAND-PULLED PICI PASTA WITH CHEESE AND BLACK PEPPER

**SERVES 4 AS
A FIRST COURSE**

FOR THE PICI

3¼ cups/400 g all-
   purpose flour
¾ cup plus
   2 tablespoons/
   200 ml water
1 tablespoon extra-
   virgin olive oil
1 teaspoon fine sea
   salt
3 tablespoons
   semolina flour, plus
   more for dusting
¼ cup/35 g cornmeal
Extra-virgin olive oil
   for brushing

FOR THE SAUCE

2 teaspoons whole
   black peppercorns,
   or more to taste
5 ounces/140 g
   Pecorino Romano,
   grated

Cacio e pepe is one of the primary reasons for making a gastronomic pilgrimage to Rome—along with eating carbonara, amatriciana, and gricia, the other hearty pasta dishes that are the main attraction in local trattorias. Cacio e pepe, an iconic pasta dish with a creamy Pecorino Romano and black pepper sauce, is quick to prepare, but don't be fooled by its simplicity: timing and precision make the difference between a perfectly executed dish and a pile of pasta with congealed cheese. The quality of the ingredients is important too, as all you need for the sauce is pecorino cheese and black pepper. A half a cup of the pasta cooking water, rich in starch from the pasta, and energetic stirring give the sauce the proper creamy consistency.

As a variation from the Roman tradition, where cacio e pepe is made with bucatini or rigatoni, I like to make cacio e pepe with pici, a thick hand-pulled pasta typical of Val d'Orcia and Val di Chiana in southern Tuscany.

_____

Make the pici: Pour the flour onto a work surface and shape into a mound with a large well in the center. Add the water, olive oil, and salt to the well and, using a fork, stir slowly to incorporate the water and oil, starting from the center and gradually picking up more flour from the edges. When the dough turns crumbly, switch to kneading with your hands. You want to knead the dough until it forms a ball, the gluten starts to develop, and the dough feels elastic. Continue kneading until you have clean hands and a clean board and the dough is smooth, silky, matte white, and no longer sticky, about 15 minutes. It should spring back when pressed. If it is too stiff, add water a few drops at a time and knead it in.

Alternatively, you can make the dough in a stand mixer fitted with the dough hook. Knead for about 5 minutes on low speed, then turn it out and finish kneading by hand for about 5 minutes.

Cover the dough with an upturned bowl and let rest for 30 minutes.

In a medium bowl, stir together the semolina and cornmeal. Dust a rimmed baking sheet with semolina flour and set nearby.

(CONTINUED)

On a clean work surface, with a rolling pin, roll out the dough into a ¼-inch-thick/6 mm round. Brush the dough with olive oil to keep it from drying out while you make the pici. Using a pizza cutter or a very sharp knife, cut the dough into strips about ¼ inch/6 mm wide. With one hand, hold each strip down on one end and, using the other hand, roll and pull the strip into the pici shape (like thick, chubby spaghetti), drop the pici into the semolina-cornmeal mix, and then coil the noodle around your hand and place on the prepared baking sheet. Repeat with the remaining dough.

Make the cacio e pepe: In a small frying pan, toast the peppercorns over medium heat for a few minutes, until you start smelling their pungent aroma. Transfer the peppercorns to a mortar and pound with the pestle until finely ground.

Transfer the pepper to a large bowl and stir in the pecorino.

Bring a large pot of water to a rolling boil and salt it lightly. Add the pici and cook for 5 to 6 minutes, until just al dente. Pici have a dense, chewy texture; do not overcook them. Just before the pici are done, scoop out ½ cup/120 ml of the pasta water, add it to the bowl with the pecorino and pepper, and stir with a wooden spoon to form a thick paste.

Scoop out another ½ cup/120 ml of the pasta water, then drain the pici, transfer them to the bowl, and toss energetically with the sauce, adding some of the reserved cooking water if needed and tossing to perfectly emulsify the sauce, until it thoroughly coats the pici. Serve immediately, as the cheese tends to cool and set quickly.

NOTES: *Fresh pici should be cooked as soon as they are made, but if you want to prepare them in advance, you can freeze them. Spread the pici on a large rimmed baking sheet dusted with semolina flour and freeze until firm, then transfer to a zip-top freezer bag and freeze for up to 3 months. Pop the pici into the boiling water still frozen, and allow a couple of minutes more to cook them.*

If you don't want to make your own pici, opt for store-bought fresh pasta, such as tonnarelli, or high-quality dried pasta such as bucatini, spaghetti, spaghetti alla chitarra, or rigatoni. Avoid fresh egg pasta like tagliatelle or tagliolini, which would be too heavy for the cacio e pepe sauce.

Pizzoccheri

BUCKWHEAT PASTA WITH CABBAGE AND CHEESE

SERVES 6 AS
A FIRST COURSE

FOR THE PIZZOCCHERI

1½ cups plus
   2 tablespoons/
   200 g buckwheat
   flour
7 tablespoons/50 g
   all-purpose flour,
   plus more for rolling
½ cup plus
   1 tablespoon/
   140 ml water
Fine sea salt

FOR ASSEMBLY

½ Savoy cabbage
   (about 1 pound/
   455 g), cored and
   cut crosswise into
   thin strips
2 medium Yukon Gold
   potatoes (about
   8 ounces/225 g),
   peeled and cut
   into ½-inch/1.5 cm
   cubes
8 tablespoons/1 stick/
   115 g unsalted
   butter
1 clove garlic, crushed
   and peeled
A generous handful of
   fresh sage leaves
5 ounces/140 g
   Parmigiano-
   Reggiano, grated
8 ounces/225 g
   Fontina, diced
Freshly ground black
   pepper

Buckwheat has been grown in Valtellina, an Alpine valley in northern Lombardy on the border between Italy and Switzerland, for at least four centuries. There buckwheat lends its unmistakable aroma and color to recipes such as polenta taragna (see page 224) and to sciàtt and chisciöi, buckwheat fritters with a melted cheese center.

Pizzoccheri was originally a festive peasant dish, made of short buckwheat tagliatelle cooked with potatoes and Savoy cabbage, chard, or chopped green beans, depending on the season. The cooked pasta and vegetables are layered in a baking pan with plenty of cheese and butter and baked briefly until the melting cheese turns the pizzoccheri into a delicious mess of buttery potatoes and soft cabbage. Serve this easy one-pan dish to vegetarian friends for dinner. Hearty, comforting, and rustic, it is one of those dishes that makes everyone happy.

———

Make the pizzoccheri: Pour both the flours onto a work surface and shape into a mound with a large well in the center. Add the water and a pinch of salt and, using a fork, stir slowly to incorporate the water, starting from the center and gradually picking up more flour from the edges. When the dough turns crumbly, switch to kneading with your hands. When the dough is clay-like and moist but not sticking to your hands, it is ready to be rolled out.

Lightly flour a work surface with all-purpose flour and, with a rolling pin, roll out the dough into an ⅛-inch-thick/3 mm sheet. Cut the pasta into 3-inch-wide/8 cm strips. Dust the strips with flour, stack them a few at a time, and cut crosswise into ⅓-by-3-inch/8 mm by 8 cm noodles.

Assemble the pizzoccheri: Bring a large pot of water to a rolling boil and salt it generously. Add the cabbage and potatoes, press down with a wooden spoon to submerge them, and cook for 10 minutes, or until the potatoes are tender.

Add the pizzoccheri and cook until al dente, about 10 more minutes. Drain, reserving ¼ cup/60 ml of the cooking water.

While the pasta cooks, in a medium frying pan, melt the butter with the garlic over medium-low heat. When the butter stops foaming, add the sage and fry until the sage leaves are crisp and the butter is lightly browned and smells nutty.

With a slotted spoon, transfer the fried sage to a paper towel–lined plate. Remove and discard the garlic and set the pan of butter aside.

Preheat the oven to 350°F/175°C.

Arrange half of the pizzoccheri, cabbage, and potato mixture in an 8½-by-11-inch/22 by 28 cm baking dish. Drizzle with half of the brown butter and top with half of the Parmigiano-Reggiano, half of the Fontina, and half of the crisp sage leaves. Season with pepper. Arrange the remaining pizzoccheri mixture on top, drizzle with the remaining brown butter, and finish with the remaining Parmigiano-Reggiano, Fontina, and sage. Drizzle the reserved pasta cooking water over the top.

Transfer to the oven and bake for about 5 minutes, just until the cheese is melted. Stir gently and serve immediately.

Any leftovers can be stored in the fridge for up to 1 day. Reheat gently before serving.

NOTE: *The cheese traditionally used to make pizzoccheri is a mixture of the local bitto—the most precious cheese in the world, as it can be aged for up to fifteen years—and casera, but Fontina can be substituted in this recipe.*

Passatelli asciutti con crema di Parmigiano-Reggiano

PASSATELLI WITH PARMIGIANO-REGGIANO SAUCE

SERVES 4 AS
A FIRST COURSE

FOR THE PASSATELLI

6½ ounces/180 g
    Parmigiano-
    Reggiano or
    Pecorino di Fossa,
    grated
1¼ cups/140 g fine
    dry breadcrumbs
    (see headnote)
¼ cup plus
    1 tablespoon/40 g
    all-purpose flour
Grated zest of
    ½ lemon
½ teaspoon fine
    sea salt
¼ teaspoon grated
    nutmeg
¼ teaspoon freshly
    ground black
    pepper
4 large/200 g eggs,
    slightly beaten

FOR THE CHEESE SAUCE

3½ ounces/100 g
    pancetta, diced
1 teaspoon fresh
    thyme leaves
½ cup plus
    2 tablespoons/
    150 ml heavy
    cream
5 ounces/140 g
    Parmigiano-
    Reggiano, grated

Freshly ground black
    pepper
Grated Parmigiano-
    Reggiano for
    serving

Passatelli are long, thick, rough strands made of breadcrumbs, grated Parmigiano-Reggiano, and eggs, a comfort food born in Romagna to upcycle stale bread and dried-out Parmigiano-Reggiano. Traditionally bone marrow was one of the ingredients; it made the passatelli dough softer and richer, but including it is no longer the norm. The strands are traditionally made with a fer di pasaden, a kitchen tool similar to a potato ricer, with holes of a specific size: no more and no less than 4 mm/about ⅛ inch across. Usually this tool is passed on from one generation the next. If you don't happen to have one, you can use a potato ricer.

This is a fairly simple recipe, so the quality of every ingredient counts, especially the bread. You need fine, sandy breadcrumbs made from dry bread that doesn't contain any salt or fat, neither butter nor oil. A very dry pane toscano (page 302) would work well. To guarantee a perfect result, I add some flour to the passatelli dough: it is not traditional, but it is a foolproof trick.

Usually served in brodo, simmered for a minute in a golden homemade chicken stock, passatelli can also be cooked like fresh pasta in a large pot of boiling water, drained, and served with a sauce of your choice. For this cheese sauce, Parmigiano-Reggiano or pecorino di fossa is generally the most common option, along with some sautéed pancetta.

_____

Make the passatelli: In a medium bowl, combine the Parmigiano-Reggiano, breadcrumbs, and flour. Add the lemon zest, salt, nutmeg, and pepper and stir with a fork to mix well. Add the eggs and continue mixing with the fork. When the dough becomes crumbly, start kneading it with your hands, pressing the mixture against the sides of the bowl. When the dough is thick, smooth, and just slightly sticky, turn it out, wrap it in plastic wrap, and let it rest at room temperature for 1 hour.

Lightly flour a baking sheet. Divide the passatelli dough into 4 equal pieces. Pass one portion through a potato ricer fitted with the large plate and pass the passatelli directly onto the floured baking sheet. Repeat with the remaining dough, then transfer the baking sheet to the refrigerator and let the passatelli rest for 1 hour.

(CONTINUED)

Meanwhile, make the cheese sauce: In a large nonstick frying pan, cook the diced pancetta over medium heat until the fat has rendered and the pancetta is golden brown. Add the thyme, stir, and set aside.

In a small saucepan, heat the cream over medium heat until simmering. Add the grated Parmigiano-Reggiano and stir until the cheese has melted and the sauce is creamy and smooth. Set aside.

When you're ready to cook the passatelli, bring a large pot of salted water to a boil. Gently reheat the Parmigiano-Reggiano sauce if it has cooled.

Cook the passatelli in batches in the boiling water for about 1 minute, or until they float to the top. Remove from the water with a spider or slotted spoon and transfer to the pan with the pancetta.

Heat the passatelli and pancetta over medium heat for a couple of minutes, until the passatelli is coated with the pancetta fat.

Spoon the sauce into four warmed serving bowls. Add the passatelli, sprinkle with pepper and grated Parmigiano-Reggiano, and serve immediately.

VARIATIONS

You could also serve the passatelli with a white clam sauce, with a porcini sauce (see page 219), or with radicchio, sausage, and Taleggio: quickly panfry some shredded radicchio with crumbled Italian sausage, then toss the passatelli into the pan and add some diced Taleggio.

Zuppa alla valpellinese

FONTINA AND SAVOY CABBAGE BREAD CASSEROLE

**SERVES 6 AS
A MAIN COURSE**

1 medium Savoy
   cabbage (about
   2 pounds/1 kg),
   cored and leaves
   separated
8 tablespoons/1 stick/
   115 g unsalted
   butter
½ teaspoon ground
   cinnamon
Fine sea salt and
   freshly ground
   black pepper
11 ounces/310 g rye or
   whole wheat bread,
   cut into ¼-inch-
   thick/6 mm slices
11 ounces/310 g
   Fontina cheese,
   thinly sliced
3½ cups/840 ml beef
   or chicken stock,
   heated

Valle d'Aosta, the tiniest Italian region, nestled between Piedmont, France, and Switzerland, boasts the tallest mountains in Europe, the highest density of cattle per capita in Europe, and the finest dairy production of the whole country. Fontina, a semi-firm, full-fat cheese, has been made in Valle d'Aosta since the thirteenth century. It is the key ingredient in this casserole, a hearty dish made with braised cabbage and dark rye bread, which is fortifying in freezing Alpine winters.

Today, the casserole is so representative of the local gastronomical culture that it is honored with its own food festival every year in July. It is prepared in large trays, following a centuries-old recipe, and served to both locals and tourists who visit the small village in the mountains just to have a taste of the casserole.

———

Bring a large pot of water to a rolling boil and salt it generously. Add the cabbage, press down with a wooden spoon to submerge it, and blanch for about 2 minutes, until wilted. Drain.

In a large frying pan, melt 6 tablespoons/85 g of the butter over medium-low heat. Add the cabbage, cover, and braise it, stirring occasionally, for about 30 minutes. Check on the cabbage and gradually add ½ cup/120 ml water throughout the cooking to help it soften and cook down. When the cabbage is buttery soft, add the cinnamon, taste, and season with salt and pepper. Remove from the heat.

Preheat the oven to 350°F/175°C.

Arrange the sliced bread in a single layer on a baking sheet and toast for about 10 minutes, until crisp.

Arrange one-third of the bread in the bottom of a 10-inch/25 cm oval baking dish. Top with one-third of the braised cabbage and one-third of the cheese. Repeat with the remaining bread, cabbage, and Fontina to make two more layers.

Slowly pour the hot stock around the edges of the baking dish, gently pressing the layers of cabbage and bread down, and let stand for 10 minutes so the bread starts to absorb the stock.

Dot the surface with the remaining 2 tablespoons butter and transfer the pan to the oven. Bake for 40 minutes, or until the Fontina is golden brown and the bread has swelled up, absorbing most of the stock. Serve hot.

Any leftovers can be stored in the fridge for up to 2 days. Reheat the casserole in the oven until it is heated through and the Fontina has melted again.

Torta pasqualina

LIGURIAN SPINACH AND RICOTTA PIE

SERVES 4 TO 6 AS
A MAIN COURSE

FOR THE PASTA MATTA

2¼ cups plus
  2 tablespoons/
  300 g all-purpose
  flour, plus more for
  rolling
2 tablespoons extra-
  virgin olive oil, plus
  more for greasing
  the pan and
  brushing
½ teaspoon fine
  sea salt
½ cup/120 ml water

FOR THE FILLING

2 pounds/1 kg spinach
3 tablespoons extra-
  virgin olive oil
1 small yellow onion,
  minced
1 clove garlic, minced
1⅔ cups/14 ounces/
  400 g fresh ricotta
2 ounces/60 g
  Parmigiano-
  Reggiano, grated
1 tablespoon fresh
  marjoram leaves,
  minced
Fine sea salt and
  freshly ground
  black pepper
6 large/300 g eggs
1½ tablespoons/20 g
  unsalted butter

5 tablespoons/75 ml
  olive oil, plus more
  for the pan and for
  brushing
Flaky sea salt

Torta pasqualina is a savory Ligurian pie traditionally made for Easter. Its seasonality is reflected in the generous use of springtime greens and eggs in the filling. After the fasting time of Lent, eggs are a powerful symbol of rebirth, the return of spring, and the victory of life over death.

The torta is traditionally made with prescinseua, a fresh-curd Ligurian cheese with a delicate tangy taste, similar to ricotta. Prescinseua has been used as a filling for savory pies since medieval times, but it is also served as a snack for children, sprinkled with sugar and cinnamon, like yogurt. It is extremely difficult to find prescinseua outside of Liguria, but you can use ricotta instead. If you want the characteristic slightly sour taste, add a tablespoon of plain yogurt.

The pie shell is made of what is called *pasta matta*, or crazy dough, so named because it is insanely simple to put together. Requiring only flour, water, and olive oil, the dough has a neutral taste and so works equally well for sweet or savory pies, strudels, and tarts. For this torta, it is rolled out into paper-thin layers, stretched, brushed with olive oil, and stacked. You can also use pasta matta as a crust for pumpkin pie (page 281).

Prepare the pasta matta: Dump the flour onto a work surface, make a well in the center, and add the olive oil and salt. Knead the flour and oil together, then gradually add the water, kneading until it has all been incorporated. Continue kneading the dough until it is soft and smooth, about 10 minutes total. It should spring back when pressed. If it is too stiff, add a few drops of water and knead it in.

Alternatively, you can make the dough in a stand mixer fitted with the dough hook. Knead for about 5 minutes on low speed, then turn out and finish kneading by hand for about 5 minutes.

Divide the dough into 6 equal portions. Roll each portion of dough into a ball, cover them with plastic wrap, and let rest for about 1 hour.

While the dough rests, prepare the filling: Remove the thick stems from the spinach, then rinse it in a colander under cold running water. Transfer the still-dripping spinach to a large high-sided frying pan, cover, and cook over medium heat for 7 to 10 minutes, until wilted. Transfer the spinach to a colander to drain and wipe out the pan; set the pan aside.

(CONTINUED)

When the spinach is cool enough to handle, squeeze well to remove any excess water. Roughly chop the spinach and set aside.

Pour the olive oil into the frying pan and heat over medium heat. Add the onion and garlic and cook, stirring, until the onion is soft, about 8 minutes. Add the chopped spinach and stir to combine, then increase the heat to medium-high and cook until the spinach is almost dry, about 10 minutes.

Transfer to a large bowl and add the ricotta, Parmigiano-Reggiano, and marjoram. Stir, then add salt and pepper to taste.

Lightly beat 2 of the eggs and add them to the filling, mixing thoroughly.

Position the racks in the bottom third and middle of the oven and preheat the oven to 350°F/175°C. Grease a 9-inch/23 cm tart pan with olive oil.

On a lightly floured work surface, with a lightly floured rolling pin, roll out one ball of dough as thin as possible. Then drape it over the backs of your hands and start stretching the dough into a round, turning it continuously, until it is about 13 inches/33 cm in diameter, paper-thin, and translucent.

Lay the dough on the floured work surface and gently brush it with 1 tablespoon of the olive oil. Repeat with 2 more balls of dough and stack them on top of the first round, brushing each one with a tablespoon of olive oil.

Fit the three-layer crust into the pan, pressing it over the bottom and up the sides, then place the spinach filling on top, spreading it into an even layer. Using the back of a spoon, make 4 indentations in the filling, as big as an egg, and place a bit of the butter in each indentation. Crack an egg into each indentation and season with salt and pepper.

One at a time, roll out the remaining balls of dough into paper-thin, translucent rounds about 10 inches/25 cm in diameter. Stack 2 of the rounds, brushing each with a tablespoon of olive oil, then arrange the third round on top of the stack. Drape the dough loosely over the filling and press the edges to seal the layers of dough together.

Roll the overhanging dough onto itself all around the edges, then brush the top of the dough generously with olive oil, letting some of it run down the sides of the pie to create a golden crust underneath. Sprinkle the top with flaky sea salt.

Transfer the pie to the lower oven rack and bake for 20 minutes, then move it to the center rack and bake for 30 to 40 minutes longer. The torta is ready when it is golden and puffed. Should it get too dark as it bakes, cover it loosely with a piece of parchment paper.

Let the torta cool for 1 hour before slicing and serving.

Leftover torta pasqualina keeps well on the kitchen counter for a couple of days. Serve it hot, warm, or cold. The leftovers are perfect for your lunch box too.

NOTE: *If you are short on time, you can substitute good-quality store-bought or homemade puff pastry or short-crust dough for the pasta matta (you'll need about 14 ounces/400 g puff pastry or enough dough for a double-crust 9-inch/23 cm pie).*

BEANS AND LENTILS

PLANT PROTEINS

Insalata di tonno e fagioli
Tuna and Bean Salad   172

Pane e panelle
Chickpea Flour Fritters
in Sesame Seed Buns   176

Torta di ceci
Tuscan Chickpea Cake   179

Fave e cicorie
Fava Bean Puree with Chicory   181

Pasta e fagioli
Pasta and Bean Soup   185

Lagane e ceci
Fresh Pasta and Chickpea Soup   186

Zuppa di lenticchie umbra
Umbrian Lentil Stew   190

Ceci in zimino
Chickpea and Chard Stew   193

Ribollita
Bean and Lacinato Kale Soup   195

Farinata con le leghe
Kale and Borlotti Polenta   198

LEGUMES ARE THE OLDEST AND MOST GLOBAL OF OUR FOODS; THEY were fundamental in the development of the world's greatest civilizations because they can stave off famine. Beans, lentils, and peas are dependable when other crops fail. They are also the key ingredients of some of both the most comforting and the richest dishes in the Italian culinary tradition, including Tuscan farinata con le leghe (page 198) and the beloved pasta e fagioli (page 185).

Yet for hundreds of years, legumes suffered the stigma of being the food of the poor. Those who could not afford meat ate beans, chickpeas, and fava beans, and these eventually became a symbol of cucina povera. But highly nutritious legumes can be easily stored throughout the winter months. And, by tradition, pulses are associated with food pairings that create what are universally recognized as perfectly balanced meals. Ribollita (page 195), the bean soup thickened with bread, and risi e bisi (page 28), rice and peas, are filling, healthful, and affordable meals.

In the Italian tradition, beans were a resource for the many meatless days that the Catholic Church imposed throughout the year. The Christian calendar included at least 150 and up to 250 of these lean days: Fridays, sometimes Wednesdays and Saturdays, the eves of major festivities, and all of Lent. Such restrictions didn't concern the peasant class; they were used to eating a pulse-based diet.

Legumes are also a source of pride and regional identity, as in the creamy, thin-skinned fagioli zolfini from Tuscany's Casentino Valley; the green lentils from Castelluccio, in Umbria, that are the key ingredient of the local zuppa di lenticchie (page 190); and the visually dramatic black chickpeas from Le Murge, in Puglia. Legumes are so intertwined with the Tuscan food culture and traditions that Florentines are still known as *mangiafagioli*, bean eaters.

As often happens with traditional ingredients of Italian cucina povera, these eventually moved from the households of the poor to Michelin-starred restaurant kitchens. In 1985, Fulvio Pierangelini started serving a disarmingly simple recipe at his Tuscan restaurant, Il Gambero Rosso, that legitimized the use of pulses in haute cuisine. His passatina di ceci e gamberi, a chickpea puree garnished with raw shrimp and a drizzle of extra-virgin olive oil, is considered one of the greatest dishes of Italian cuisine.

Nowadays both chefs and home cooks alike know how affordable, versatile, sustainable, and good for them and the planet legumes are. Pulses are farmers' friends as well, as they enrich the soil where they are planted, sending nitrogen back into the ground.

Stock your pantry with your favorite legumes, cook them in large batches and stash some of them in your fridge, and use them throughout the week to make warming soups (pages 185, 186, and 195) or a quick, budget-friendly salad (page 172). Having cooked legumes on hand provides you with nourishing, inclusive, plant-based meals. I always keep chickpea flour in my pantry too, as it translates into delicious weeknight meals, such as torta di ceci (page 179) served with fresh, vinegary grilled eggplant.

Insalata di tonno e fagioli

TUNA AND BEAN SALAD

**SERVES 4
AS A MAIN COURSE,
6 AS A STARTER**

1 small red onion,
thinly sliced
½ cup/120 ml red wine
vinegar
4 salt-packed
anchovies or
8 oil-packed
anchovy fillets
4½ cups/800 g
cooked cannellini or
borlotti beans (see
page 174) or one
29-ounce/822 g can
beans, rinsed and
drained
Two 5-ounce/142 g
cans good-quality
tuna, drained (see
headnote)
1 pound/455 g cherry
tomatoes, quartered
1 celery heart, thinly
sliced
Fine sea salt and
freshly ground
black pepper
¼ cup/60 ml extra-
virgin olive oil
A handful of fresh
basil leaves

Eating beans isn't always about hearty stews that simmer for hours on the stovetop. Take this bean salad, for example. Canned tuna is paired with cooked (or canned) cannellini or borlotti beans for a humble weeknight meal. Incorporating other preserved fish adds depth of flavor and character to the salad: you could increase the number of anchovies, or even try smoked herring. Sliced celery lends a pleasant crunch to the salad, while quartered ripe cherry tomatoes provide color and sweetness. Swap them for any other vegetables in season you like.

If you use good-quality tuna packed in olive oil, don't drain it, and omit or reduce the amount of oil you add to the salad. Soaking the thin rounds of onion in red wine vinegar will mellow their pungency and give a refreshing tartness to the beans, making this the perfect salad for sultry summer Italian days.

———

Put the onion slices in a small bowl and pour the vinegar over them. Let stand for 10 minutes; this will tame their pungent taste and infuse the onions with vinegary notes that will complement the salad. Drain the onions before using; if you want an extra boost of flavor, reserve some of the vinegar and drizzle it into the salad when you dress it.

If you are using salt-packed anchovies, rinse them under cold running water. Gently remove the backbones, opening up each anchovy and separating it into 2 fillets. Lay the fillets on a paper towel to dry. If you have oil-packed anchovy fillets, just drain them.

Transfer the beans to a big bowl. Flake the canned tuna with a fork and add it to the beans.

Mince the anchovies and add them to the beans and tuna, along with the onions, cherry tomatoes, and celery. Season with salt and pepper, then drizzle in the olive oil and mix well. Add the basil and stir to mix, then taste again and season with additional salt and pepper if necessary.

Cover the bowl, transfer to the refrigerator, and refrigerate for 30 minutes before serving. The salad can be stored in the fridge for a day.

HOW TO COOK BEANS AND CHICKPEAS

Legumes like beans and chickpeas are usually consumed fresh from June to October, and dried the rest of the year, as they keep well for months. If they are not too old, dried pulses can be cooked without soaking, though most Italian recipes do require you to soak them overnight. Lentils are the exception.

Low and slow is the best way to cook beans and chickpeas. In Tuscany, they were traditionally cooked in old glass wine flasks nestled in the ashes of the fireplace. Elsewhere, as in Puglia, legumes were cooked in a jug-shaped terra-cotta pot that was glazed on the inside. Sometimes beans or other legumes were instead put in a clay pot, seasoned with a few garlic cloves, fresh herbs, and black peppercorns, and taken to the local bakery for a long, slow cooking in the residual heat of the wood-burning oven, after the daily bread had been baked. When I make pizza in our outdoor wood oven in summer, I often cook beans and chickpeas that way too. Simply dressed with fresh olive oil, or "all'olio," it is quite possibly the best way to enjoy them.

Clay pots are traditionally considered the best vessels for cooking beans and pulses, because these pots are slightly alkaline, and alkalinity is what makes legume skins tender. If you do not have a clay pot, add a pinch of baking soda, which is alkaline, to the water when you cook your beans or chickpeas.

Whichever way you cook your legumes, don't throw out the precious cooking water. Beans and chickpeas release nutrients as they cook, making the liquid that surrounds them dense, almost gelatinous, with a concentrated flavor. Save it to use in soups and stews, to thicken them and add creaminess.

VARIATIONS

MAKES ABOUT 6 CUPS/
1.2 KG COOKED BEANS,
6 CUPS/1 KG COOKED
CHICKPEAS

2½ cups/455 g dried
  cannellini or other
  beans or chickpeas
2 fresh sage leaves
  for beans or 1 fresh
  rosemary sprig for
  chickpeas
1 bay leaf
1 clove garlic
A few whole black
  peppercorns
1 tablespoon extra-
  virgin olive oil
Pinch of baking soda
  (optional; see
  sidebar)
Fine sea salt

Extra-virgin olive oil
  and freshly ground
  black pepper for
  serving (optional)

Use the following recipe to cook beans and chickpeas. As for the seasonings, tradition calls for sage leaves and garlic when cooking beans, garlic and rosemary when cooking chickpeas. Remember that you want to aim for soft, buttery, melt-in-your-mouth beans. There's nothing more disappointing than beans that are al dente.

————

Put the dried beans (or chickpeas) in a large bowl, add cold water to cover by several inches, and let soak at room temperature for at least 12 hours, or overnight.

Drain and rinse the beans and put them in a pot. They need enough space to double in volume while cooking, so choose your cooking vessel accordingly. Fill the pot two-thirds full with water, completely covering the beans, and add the sage leaves (or rosemary), bay leaf, garlic, peppercorns, and olive oil. Bring to a simmer over medium-low heat, then reduce the heat to low, cover, and cook, checking occasionally, until the beans are soft, with a buttery texture and thin, transparent skins. They might take as long as 3 hours, depending on their size. If using the baking soda, add it after about an hour of cooking. You may need to add more hot water as the beans cook to keep them covered. When the beans are done, season the cooking liquid generously with salt.

Serve the beans dressed with olive oil and freshly ground black pepper, or use them as directed in one of the recipes in this chapter.

NOTE: *You can make a big batch of beans ahead and store them in their cooking liquid in the fridge for 2 to 3 days. To keep them longer, drain off the cooking liquid and freeze them for up to 8 months.*

Pane e panelle

CHICKPEA FLOUR FRITTERS IN SESAME SEED BUNS

**SERVES 4
AS A STARTER**

2 cups/480 ml water
1¾ cups plus
    1 tablespoon/165 g
    chickpea flour
1 teaspoon fine
    sea salt
¼ teaspoon freshly
    ground black
    pepper
1 tablespoon finely
    chopped wild fennel
    or fresh flat-leaf
    parsley
4 cups/1 L vegetable
    or other neutral oil
    for deep-frying

FOR SERVING

Flaky sea salt
1 lemon, thinly sliced
4 sesame seed buns,
    split

In Sicily, panellari, street food vendors, fry chickpea fritters in enormous cauldrons on the corners of the busiest streets in the city center, close to high schools, offices, and churches. There's always a small crowd of people around the panellaro, who fries throughout the day. His offerings also include crocchè, mashed potato croquettes, and rascatura, made with the scraps of panelle and crocchè.

Pane e panelle can easily be prepared at home, served stuffed into the traditional sesame seed buns or as part of a variety of fried foods on an appetizer board.

———

Pour the water into a saucepan and add the chickpea flour, whisking constantly to prevent lumps. Season with the salt and pepper, set the pan over low heat, and bring to a boil, stirring constantly with a wooden spoon or heatproof spatula (as if you were making polenta; see page 224). As soon as it comes to a boil, lower the heat and simmer, stirring constantly, for about 10 minutes, until the mixture pulls away from the sides of the pan.

Remove from the heat, add the finely chopped fennel (or parsley), and stir well. Pour the chickpea polenta onto a sheet of parchment paper, cover it with a second sheet of parchment, and roll it out with a rolling pin into a ¼-inch-thick/6 mm rectangle. Let cool completely.

Preheat the oven to 400°F/200°C. Pour the oil into a large deep pot set over medium-high heat. Set a wire rack on a rimmed baking sheet and place nearby.

While the oil heats, cut the chickpea polenta into 2½-by-1-inch/6 by 3 cm rectangles. When the oil registers 350°F/175°C on a deep-frying thermometer, add some of the panelle to the pot, cooking them in batches (if you crowd the oil, the temperature will drop and the panelle will absorb too much oil). Fry, turning the panelle once with two forks, until golden brown, about 6 minutes. Transfer to the wire rack set on the baking sheet, then transfer the whole setup to the oven to keep warm. Cook the remaining panelle in batches, allowing the oil to return to temperature between batches and transferring each batch of fried panelle to the oven to keep warm.

When all of the panelle have been fried, sprinkle with flaky sea salt and serve them sandwiched with the thin slices of lemon in the sesame seed buns.

Torta di ceci

TUSCAN CHICKPEA CAKE

SERVES 4
AS A STARTER,
2 AS A MAIN COURSE

FOR THE GRILLED
EGGPLANT

2 eggplants
1 tablespoon finely
    chopped fresh mint
1 tablespoon finely
    chopped fresh
    flat-leaf parsley
1 tablespoon finely
    chopped fresh
    marjoram
1 clove garlic, minced
⅓ cup/80 ml extra-
    virgin olive oil
1 tablespoon red wine
    vinegar
1 teaspoon dried
    oregano
1 teaspoon fine sea salt
¼ teaspoon freshly
    ground black
    pepper

FOR THE CHICKPEA CAKE

1¼ cups/110 g
    chickpea flour
1¼ cups/300 ml water
2 tablespoons extra-
    virgin olive oil
¾ teaspoon fine
    sea salt
¼ cup/60 ml
    vegetable or other
    neutral oil
Freshly ground black
    pepper

4 pieces focaccia,
    split, or 4 soft rolls
    for serving

In Tuscany, it's easy to find torta di ceci, a traditional street food, sprinkled with plenty of black pepper and served on a plate or sandwiched in a soft bun or split focaccia. I often prepare torta di ceci as a starter when I give cooking classes or when we have friends over for dinner. Quick to make, it is both vegan and gluten-free. Cut the torta di ceci into slices and arrange them on a board or platter along with a selection of grilled vegetables, such as eggplant, zucchini, and roasted peppers to serve 4 generously.

──────

Make the grilled eggplant: Slice the eggplants into ¼-inch-thick/6 mm slices. Heat a large nonstick or grill pan over high heat and grill the eggplant slices in batches: Grill them until you see charred marks on the first side, then flip them and grill on the other side until soft and golden. Transfer to a serving platter or bowl.

In a small bowl, combine the chopped herbs, garlic, olive oil, vinegar, oregano, salt, and pepper. Pour over the grilled eggplant while it is still hot and toss so it absorbs the flavors. Cover and refrigerate until ready to use. (*The eggplant keeps well in the fridge for 3 to 4 days if well covered with additional olive oil.*)

Make the batter for the chickpea cake: Put the chickpea flour in a medium bowl and slowly add the water, whisking constantly to prevent lumps. Whisk in the olive oil and salt. Let the batter sit at room temperature for a few hours. If any foam accumulates on the surface, skim it off and discard.

Cook the chickpea cake: Place a 10-inch/25 cm round baking pan or cast-iron skillet in the oven and preheat the oven to 475°F/250°C.

When the oven is hot, carefully remove the pan from the oven, add the vegetable oil to it, and pour in the batter; it will immediately start to sizzle. Return the pan to the oven and bake for 20 to 25 minutes, until the chickpea cake is crunchy and golden on the surface and edges but still soft inside.

Remove the pan from the oven and use a spatula to release the chickpea cake. Slide onto a cutting board and sprinkle with plenty of pepper.

Cut the chickpea cake into 4 slices and sandwich it between the slices of focaccia (or in the rolls), add the grilled eggplant, and eat immediately.

(CONTINUED)

The torta di ceci batter can be used to make an easy vegan baked frittata. Add thinly sliced spring onions, ribbons of kale, strips of roasted pepper, or, my favorite, zucchini blossoms to the batter and bake according to the instructions above.

CHICKPEA FLOUR AND ITALIAN STREET FOOD

Chickpea flour is a staple ingredient in many Mediterranean port towns. They all have in common a version of street food made with this nutritious, affordable flour. In Liguria, you can buy slices of chickpea cake, known there as *farinata*, in the local sciamadde, the traditional fried food shops where they sell it along with fritters, focaccia, and other fried delicacies. In Provence, the cake is known as *socca*, and it is one of the symbols of Niçoise gastronomy.

Tuscany shows its quarrelsome character even when it comes to baking a chickpea cake in a wood-burning oven and bestowing a unique name on it. Ask for cecina in Pisa and Viareggio, but don't dare call it that in Livorno: there you have to ask for torta di ceci, or simply torta. You can also get a version called *cinque e cinque* (literally, five and five); it got its name because in the past, you would buy five cents of torta and five cents of soft bread to go with it.

The Sicilian interpretation of the chickpea cake is pane e panelle (page 176), chickpea flour fritters stuffed into a soft sesame seed bun. The origins of panelle, one of the most beloved street foods of Palermo, date back to the Arab domination of the island, from the ninth to the eleventh century. In the beginning, panelle were made only during a short period of the year, from the Feast of Saint Lucy, on the thirteenth of December, to Christmas Day, as a way to celebrate the abundance of these festive days. But they soon became a cheap and nourishing option for poor people, who would often rely on pane e panelle as their only meal of the day.

Fave e cicorie

FAVA BEAN PUREE WITH CHICORY

SERVES 4
AS A FIRST COURSE,
8 AS A STARTER

FOR THE FAVA BEAN
PUREE

1 pound/4 cups/455 g
dried fava beans
1 small yellow onion,
halved
2 bay leaves
2 medium potatoes
(about 8 ounces/
225 g), peeled and
thinly sliced
Fine sea salt

FOR THE CHICORY

3 pounds/1.4 kg
chicory, such as
escarole, puntarelle,
or Castelfranco or
other radicchio,
separated into
leaves, any tough
stems removed
¼ cup/60 ml extra-
virgin olive oil, plus
more for drizzling
2 cloves garlic,
crushed and peeled
Red pepper flakes

4 slices crusty bread,
toasted, for serving

If Tuscany has a love affair with fresh fava beans—an ideal pairing with the local fresh, milky pecorino cheese—dried fava beans are a staple in the cucina povera of the Italian South, especially in Puglia and Sicily. The fava beans must be soaked overnight, patiently peeled, and then cooked down to a mash. This peasant recipe, known as *incapriata* or *fave e cicoria* in Puglia, or *macco* in Sicily, finds its origins in a classic recipe from ancient Egypt.

The two essential ingredients, fava beans and wild chicory, result in a perfectly balanced dish, with the bitterness of the chicory tamed by the sweet fava bean puree. A drizzle of fruity extra-virgin olive oil seals this marvelous match.

Traditionally served with foraged wild chicory, fava bean puree will work with any other bitter greens, such as broccoli rabe or escarole. Do not chop the cooked chicory; it is placed on top of the fava bean puree in long strands so that you can twirl it with a fork, as if it were spaghetti.

———

Put the fava beans in a large bowl, add cold water to cover by several inches, and let soak overnight at room temperature.

Prepare the fava bean puree: The next day, drain the fava beans and peel them: cut a slit with your thumbnail in the skin of each bean and squeeze the bean between your thumb and forefinger to pop it out of the skin, Discard the skins and transfer the beans to a large pot.

Add the onion and bay leaves to the pot, then arrange the sliced potatoes on top of them. Add cold water to just cover the potatoes, along with 2 teaspoons salt, and bring to a boil over high heat. Reduce the heat so the liquid is gently simmering and simmer for about 1 hour, stirring from time to time and adding a few ladlefuls more water if the mixture gets too thick before the favas are tender; remove the scum from the surface of the beans as it develops. When the fava beans are soft and have absorbed almost all the water, remove the pot from the heat.

Remove and discard the onion and bay leaves, then mash the fava beans and potatoes. If you'd like a chunky, rustic texture, a few energetic stirs with a wooden spoon will do; if you prefer a smoother texture, blend the mixture with an immersion blender until it is the consistency of mashed potatoes. Season to taste with additional salt.

While the fava beans cook, prepare the chicory: Bring a large pot of water to a rolling boil and salt it generously. Add the chicory and cook until wilted and soft, about 15 minutes. Drain in a colander and rinse with cold water; when the chicory is cool enough to handle, squeeze the greens with your hands to remove excess water.

Pour the olive oil into a large pan set over low heat, add the garlic and a pinch of red pepper flakes to taste, and cook, stirring, for about a minute, until the garlic is golden and fragrant. Add the chicory and cook, stirring occasionally, for 10 minutes.

Spoon the warm fava puree into warmed bowls, top with the chicory, and drizzle with olive oil. Serve with the toasted bread.

VARIATIONS

Prepare the fava bean puree as directed, but substitute fronds of fresh wild fennel for the chicory, and you'll have the Sicilian macco di fave. Top it with a drizzle of extra-virgin olive oil and a few turns of black pepper. For an even more filling dish, leave the fava bean puree brothy, and, when the beans are tender, mash them with a spoon, add some dried pasta, and cook until you have a creamy soup. Broken spaghetti would be the most traditional pasta choice. Serve in bowls with a drizzle of extra-virgin olive oil.

Have leftover fava bean puree? Spoon it onto a baking sheet and let it sit at room temperature overnight. It will be thick and dense. Cut it into cubes, toss with flour, and fry in hot oil until golden and crisp. Dress with a squeeze of lemon juice and some black pepper, and enjoy immediately.

PASTA MISTA

For early Neapolitan pasta makers, pasta mista was a way to sell their broken pieces of spaghetti, penne, paccheri, maltagliati, ziti, or other pasta shapes. They would collect these and sell them by weight to those who could not afford to buy the expensive shapes. Now, as it often happens with the ingredients of cucina povera, pasta mista has become a gourmet choice, loved by chefs and home cooks alike. At home, pasta mista is a great use for any leftover dried pastas; cooking them in a forgiving soup ensures a perfect final result, even though the different shapes and sizes might actually have different cooking times.

Use pasta mista to make pasta, patate, e provola (page 204) or to turn lagane e ceci (page 186) into the Neapolitan version of pasta e ceci.

Pasta e fagioli
PASTA AND BEAN SOUP

SERVES 4
AS A FIRST COURSE

¼ cup/60 ml extra-virgin olive oil, plus more for serving

2 cloves garlic, crushed and peeled

6 Roma (plum) tomatoes, quartered

1 tablespoon finely chopped fresh flat-leaf parsley

4½ cups/800 g cooked cannellini beans (see page 174) or one 29-ounce/822 g can cannellini beans, rinsed and drained

3 cups/720 ml reserved bean cooking water or warm water

Fine sea salt and freshly ground black pepper

1¾ cups/7 ounces/200 g short dried pasta, such as ditali

NOTE: *Pasta e fagioli thickens on standing, so if you make it ahead, you might need to adjust the texture with a bit of hot water, and then season to taste again.*

Pasta and beans, pasta and chickpeas, pasta and lentils: Italian cucina povera has always relied upon these well-balanced pairings that, when combined, become more than the sum of their parts. Of the many pasta and legume dishes in the Italian culinary tradition, pasta e fagioli, a comforting bean and pasta soup, is my favorite. It is a dish that unites the whole peninsula, with its many variations mainly related to the type of local beans and the kind of pasta simmered in the thick, flavorful stock. Borlotti are used in the North, often enriched with a pig's trotter or pork rind; cannellini are the beans of choice in Tuscany and Campania. As for the pasta, you can use fresh tagliatelle or tagliolini, as they do in Veneto, or opt for ditali, the favorite shape in Tuscany, or another short dried pasta. I have a soft spot for pasta mista (see the sidebar), a charming collection of different shapes of pasta typical of Naples.

———

Pour the olive oil into a large pot set over low heat, add the garlic, and cook for a minute or so, until golden and fragrant. Add the tomatoes and parsley, stir, and cook for 10 minutes, or until the tomatoes start to collapse. (If you want a creamier and smooth pasta e fagioli, remove the tomatoes and pull off the skins, then return them to the pot.)

Add the beans to the pot along with 1 cup/240 ml of their cooking water, bring to a boil over medium heat, and cook for about 10 minutes. Season with salt and pepper.

Add the pasta and cook over the lowest possible heat, stirring often and gradually adding the remaining 2 cups/480 ml cooking water. As you stir the pasta e fagioli, the beans will fall apart, creating a thick, creamy soup. Pasta e fagioli is ready when the pasta is perfectly al dente; depending on the shape and size of your pasta, this can take from 8 to 16 minutes.

Ladle the pasta e fagioli into warmed bowls, drizzle with olive oil, sprinkle with pepper, and serve.

VARIATION

Sauté some mussels in a large pot, remove, and set aside. Toss the beans into the juices the mussels released, then follow the recipe for pasta e fagioli, adding the cooked mussels to the soup at the end.

Lagane e ceci

FRESH PASTA AND CHICKPEA SOUP

SERVES 6 TO 8
AS A FIRST COURSE

FOR THE FRESH LAGANE

1⅔ cups/300 g
    semolina flour, plus
    more for rolling
½ cup plus
    2 tablespoons/
    150 ml water
¼ teaspoon fine
    sea salt

FOR THE SOUP

6 cups/1 kg cooked
    chickpeas (see
    page 174) or one
    28-ounce/794 g can
    chickpeas, rinsed
    and drained
6 cups/1.4 L reserved
    chickpea cooking
    water or warm water
⅓ cup/80 ml extra-
    virgin olive oil, plus
    more for serving
½ yellow onion, finely
    diced
1 celery stalk, finely
    diced
Fine sea salt
2 fresh rosemary
    sprigs
2 bay leaves
Red pepper flakes

Lagane e ceci is a common dish in the Italian South, especially in the regions of Basilicata, Campania, and Calabria. This comforting fresh pasta and chickpea soup has marked ancient Greek and Latin influences. It is as basic in its preparation and ingredients list as it is rich and complex in its taste. It begins with a very simple battuto of minced celery and onion, then chickpeas, fresh herbs, and fresh pasta are added. Lagane are large, short tagliatelle, made with durum wheat semolina flour and water. They simmer in the creamy chickpea soup, absorbing all the flavors: rosemary, bay leaves, and red pepper flakes. If you don't feel like making fresh pasta, use store-bought fresh pasta sheets (see the Note on page 189) or substitute about 1½ cups/12 ounces/340 g of your favorite short dried pasta.

————

Make the fresh pasta: Pour the flour onto a work surface and shape it into a mound with a large well in the center. Add the water and salt and, using a fork, stir slowly to incorporate the liquid, starting from the center and gradually picking up more flour from the edges. When the dough turns crumbly, switch to kneading with your hands. You want to knead the dough until it forms a ball and the gluten starts to develop, as this will render the sheets of pasta more elastic. The dough is ready when you have clean hands and a clean board and the dough is smooth, silky, and no longer sticky. If it is too stiff, add water a few drops at a time and continue kneading.

Alternatively, you can make the dough in a stand mixer fitted with the dough hook. Knead for about 5 minutes on low speed, then turn it out and finish kneading by hand for about 5 minutes. Shape the dough into a ball.

Cover the dough with an upturned bowl and let rest for 30 minutes.

Make the pasta sheets: Lightly flour a work surface with semolina flour. Cut the dough into 4 equal pieces.

To roll out the pasta by hand, work with one piece of dough at a time, keeping the rest covered with a clean towel. On the lightly floured surface, using a rolling pin, roll each piece of dough into a paper-thin sheet.

To roll out the dough using a pasta machine, on the lightly floured work surface, with a rolling pin, roll out one piece of dough into a ½-inch-thick/1.5 cm rectangle. (Keep the remaining pieces covered with a clean kitchen towel.)

(CONTINUED)

Turn the dial on your pasta machine to the widest setting. Feed the dough through the rollers once, then fold the sheet of pasta in three, as if you were folding a letter. Starting with one of the open sides, feed the pasta dough through the machine again. Repeat 3 times, lightly dusting the sheet of dough with semolina flour each time to prevent it from sticking and tearing.

Turn the dial to the next narrower setting. Roll the pasta through the machine, gently pulling it toward you as it comes out of the machine; hold the pasta sheet with the palm of one hand while you crank the machine with the other hand. Continue to reduce the settings and roll the dough through the machine again, lightly dusting the pasta sheet with semolina flour each time, until the dough is as thin as you'd like; I usually stop at the next to last setting.

Transfer the pasta sheet to a rimmed baking sheet dusted with semolina flour and repeat with the remaining dough; if you need to stack the sheets, dust each one with more semolina flour so they don't stick together.

Cut the lagane: Arrange the pasta sheets on a floured surface and cut them into strips approximately 8 inches by 1 inch/20 by 3 cm.

Make the chickpea soup: In a food processor or a blender (or in a large pot, with an immersion blender), process 2 cups/350 g of the chickpeas with 2 cups/480 ml of the reserved chickpea cooking water until pureed. Set aside.

Pour the olive oil into a large pot set over low heat and add the onion, celery, and a pinch of salt. Remove the needles from the rosemary sprigs (reserve the needles for another use, if desired) and tie the stems and bay leaves together with kitchen twine. Drop the bundle into the pot and cook, stirring, for about 5 minutes, until the onion and celery are soft and translucent.

Add the chickpea puree and the remaining 4 cups/650 g whole chickpeas to the pot, along with the remaining 4 cups/1 L chickpea cooking water, increase the heat to medium-high, and bring to a boil. Reduce the heat to medium and cook, stirring occasionally, for about 10 minutes. Taste and season with additional salt and red pepper flakes.

Add the lagane, stir, and cook for 2 to 3 minutes. Turn off the heat and let sit for 5 minutes, or until the pasta is tender. Remove and discard the herb bundle.

Ladle the soup into warmed bowls, drizzle with olive oil, and serve right away.

NOTE: *Instead of making the pasta, you can use 1 pound/455 g store-bought fresh pasta sheets and cut them into 8-by-1-inch/20 by 3 cm strips.*

VARIATION

Ciceri e tria comes from the fascinating gastronomy of Salento, my mother-in-law's birthplace. Very similar to lagane e ceci, it is traditionally prepared to celebrate Saint Joseph's Day on the nineteenth of March. Make thin tagliatelle, called *tria* in Salento. Cook most of the pasta in the chickpea soup and deep-fry the rest for garnish. Top each serving of soup with some fried tagliatelle for an unexpected crunchy note.

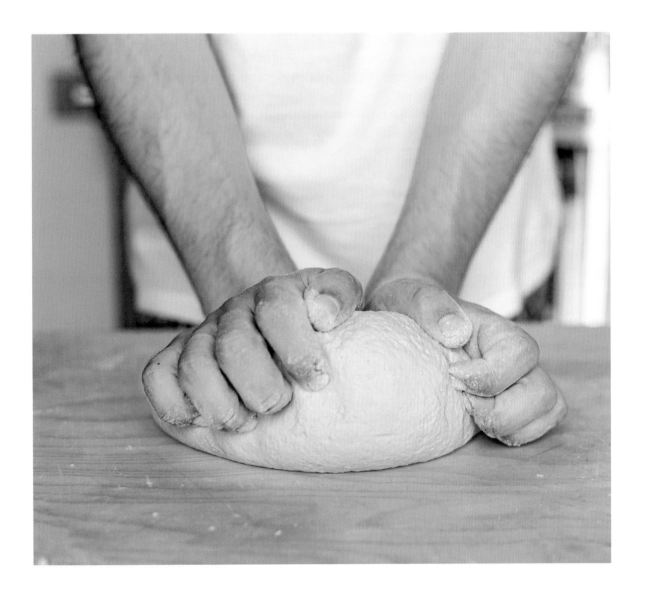

Zuppa di lenticchie umbra

UMBRIAN LENTIL STEW

SERVES 4 TO 6
AS A FIRST COURSE

1½ cups/300 g dried green lentils
1 fresh thyme sprig
1 fresh rosemary sprig
1 fresh mint sprig
2 bay leaves
¼ cup/60 ml extra-virgin olive oil, plus more for drizzling
1 small yellow onion, finely chopped
1 carrot, peeled and finely chopped
1 celery stalk, finely chopped
1 clove garlic, minced
2 ounces/60 g pancetta, cubed
Fine sea salt
3 medium tomatoes, peeled (see Note) and crushed
1 tablespoon tomato paste
4 cups/1 L hot water (see Note)
2 medium potatoes, peeled and cubed
Freshly ground black pepper
8 slices country bread, toasted, for serving

Lentils are the legume to choose when you don't have time for the long soaking and cooking that beans and chickpeas require. Most lentils can be cooked without soaking, and they often cook in less than an hour. Add them to soups or stews, serve as a side dish, or use them to make pasta e lenticchie, a popular dish in Neapolitan trattorias that follows in the footsteps of pasta e fagioli (page 185).

The most famous lentils in Italy come from Castelluccio di Norcia, the Umbrian village that was destroyed in the 2016 earthquake. The flowering plants attracted thousands of tourists and photographers every year. At the beginning of summer, the plateau where the lentils are still cultivated, in Monti Sibillini National Park, takes on a breathtaking rainbow of colors. In Castelluccio and the surrounding area, lentils are often stewed with the local red potatoes, tomatoes, and fresh herbs for a hearty, filling dish. Serve this as a main course with toasted country bread, or as a side dish to braised meats, such as sausages and guanciale (pork cheeks).

———

Rinse the lentils in a colander under cold running water, then drain and set aside.

With kitchen twine, tie together the thyme, rosemary, mint, and bay leaves into a bundle.

Pour the olive oil into a large pot set over low heat. Add the onion, carrot, celery, garlic, pancetta, and a pinch of salt and cook, stirring, for 5 minutes, or until the onion is soft. Add the lentils along with the tomatoes, tomato paste, and the herb bundle and stir thoroughly to combine. Pour in 3 cups/720 ml of the hot water, increase the heat, and heat until the mixture is simmering vigorously, then reduce the heat slightly and simmer for about 20 minutes, stirring occasionally.

Add the potatoes and the remaining 1 cup/240 ml water, season with 1 teaspoon salt and ½ teaspoon pepper, and cook for 20 more minutes, stirring often to prevent the soup from sticking to the bottom of the pot. Taste and season with additional salt and pepper if necessary.

Ladle into warmed bowls, add 2 slices of the toasted bread to each serving, and drizzle with olive oil.

The stew is even better the next day. Let cool completely, then cover and refrigerate. Reheat gently over low heat, adding a bit of water as necessary.

NOTES: *Peeling the tomatoes is easy and guarantees a smooth stew and no skins stuck between your teeth. Rinse the tomatoes and, with the tip of a knife, cut an X in the base of each one. Bring a medium saucepan of water to a boil and plunge the tomatoes into the water. Blanch them just until the skin begins to peel away at the X, about 30 seconds. Drain, immediately plunge them into a bowl of ice water to cool, and then drain and peel*

This stew has a thick, dense texture. If you'd like it a little soupier, add 1 to 2 cups/240 to 480 ml more water.

Ceci in zimino

CHICKPEA AND CHARD STEW

**SERVES 4
AS A MAIN COURSE**

1 ounce/30 g dried
  porcini
1 cup/240 ml hot water
¼ cup/60 ml extra-
  virgin olive oil, plus
  more for drizzling
1 small onion, finely
  chopped
1 carrot, peeled and
  finely chopped
1 celery stalk, finely
  chopped
1 clove garlic, minced
1 fresh parsley sprig,
  finely chopped
Fine sea salt
3 canned whole
  peeled tomatoes,
  crushed by hand,
  with their juices
1 tablespoon tomato
  paste
1 pound/455 g Swiss
  chard (1 large
  bunch), stems
  removed, leaves
  rinsed and cut into
  strips
6 cups/1 kg cooked
  chickpeas (see
  page 174)
6 cups/1.4 L reserved
  chickpea cooking
  water
Freshly ground black
  pepper
8 slices country bread,
  toasted, for serving

This is one of those soups that ticks all the boxes of flavor and umami, thanks to dried porcini mushrooms and tomato paste. It's also a balanced and nutritious dish that just happens to be vegan. Make it for a family meal and serve with slices of toasted country bread.

This stew was created in Genova, the busiest seaport in Italy, as a nutritious and digestible dish for Fridays and other lean days, when meat was forbidden. It was especially suited for workers at the local docks because it was cheap and hearty. The stew was served for lunch, then leftovers would be diluted in the evening with water and turned into a filling soup, with a handful of rice or pasta cooked in the broth. Now in Liguria, the stew is mainly prepared as a dish for Christmas Eve or for All Souls' Day, on the second of November. Make it with cooked dried chickpeas, soaked overnight and gently simmered on the stove until soft; then you can use the cooking water to stew the chard, adding flavor and creaminess to the stew.

———

Put the mushrooms in a small bowl and add the water. Let stand for 30 minutes.

Remove the mushrooms from the water and squeeze them over the bowl to remove the excess water. Strain the water and reserve. Finely chop the porcini and set aside.

Pour the olive oil into a large pot set over low heat, add the onion, carrot, celery, garlic, parsley, and a pinch of salt, and cook, stirring, for 5 minutes, or until the onion is soft. Add the crushed tomatoes, with their juices, the tomato paste, and chopped porcini. Stir thoroughly to combine, and cook over medium-low heat for 5 minutes.

Add the chard and reserved porcini soaking water, stir, bring to a simmer, and simmer for 10 minutes, or until the chard wilts and softens. Add half of the chickpeas and about 4 cups/920 ml of the chickpea cooking water, 1 teaspoon salt, and ½ teaspoon pepper, increase the heat, and cook until the mixture is simmering vigorously, then reduce the heat and simmer for about 15 minutes, stirring from time to time.

With a potato masher or the back of a fork, in a medium bowl, mash the remaining chickpeas with the remaining 2 cups/480 ml cooking water, then stir into the pot and cook for about 30 minutes, stirring often to prevent the soup from sticking to the bottom of the pot, until thickened to the consistency of a stew. Season with additional salt and pepper to taste.

Ladle into warmed bowls, add 2 slices of the toasted bread to each serving, and drizzle with olive oil.

The soup is even better the next day. Let cool completely, then cover and refrigerate. Reheat gently over low heat, adding a bit of water as necessary to thin it.

ZIMINO

The word *zimino* has an uncertain Arab origin and meaning, but today it refers to brothy stews and soups that usually have chard or, less often, spinach, among the ingredients. In Liguria, where zimino originated, it is often made with fish, such as cuttlefish or salt cod, snails, and legumes or chestnuts. Tuscany later adopted zimino, especially for cuttlefish, seppie in zimino, which can often be found on the menus of Florentine trattorias, along with lampredotto in zimino. It is not surprising, because lampredotto, the fourth stomach of the cow (see page 85), has an enjoyable chewy texture that is very similar to that of cuttlefish when cooked. If you are in Genova, you will most likely find zimino di ceci.

Ribollita

BEAN AND LACINATO KALE SOUP

**SERVES 6
AS A MAIN COURSE**

4½ cups/800 g
cooked cannellini
beans (see
page 174) or one
29-ounce/822 g can
cannellini beans,
rinsed and drained

7 cups/1.7 L reserved
bean cooking water
or warm water

¼ cup/60 ml extra-
virgin olive oil, plus
more for drizzling

1 small onion, finely
chopped

1 clove garlic, minced

Fine sea salt

2 carrots, peeled and
diced

1 celery stalk, diced

1 medium potato,
diced

1 small bunch/150 g
lacinato kale, tough
stalks removed and
discarded, leaves
sliced into ribbons

4 cups/250 g
shredded Savoy
cabbage

1 tablespoon tomato
paste

½ teaspoon freshly
ground black
pepper, or more
to taste

7 ounces/200 g stale
Tuscan Bread
(page 302) or crusty
country bread, cut
into thin slices

A flagship recipe of the Tuscan culinary tradition, ribollita truly embodies the spirit of cucina povera. It is always made with seasonal local ingredients—essentially whatever is growing in the garden or can be foraged in the wild. It's a hearty soup that is more filling than a simple minestrone (page 24), thanks to the addition of stale bread and beans.

Ribollita means reboiled: traditionally the thick bean, vegetable, and bread soup would be reheated the day after it is made, and it becomes so dense you can almost cut it with a knife. In Florentine trattorias, rather than reheating the soup on the stove, they sometimes spread it in a baking pan, top it with thinly sliced onions, and bake it until thickened. Another way to reheat ribollita is to pour it into a cast-iron skillet with some olive oil and cook it until a crisp crust forms on the bottom.

———

In a food processor or a blender (or in a pot using an immersion blender), process half of the beans with 1 cup/240 ml of the bean cooking water (or warm water) until pureed. Set aside.

Pour the olive oil into a large pot set over low heat, add the onion, garlic, and a pinch of salt, and cook, stirring, for 5 minutes, or until the onion is soft and translucent.

Add the carrots, celery, and potato to the pot, then add the kale and cabbage and stir thoroughly to combine. Cover the vegetables with the remaining 6 cups/1.4 L bean cooking water, then stir in the tomato paste, 1 teaspoon salt, and the pepper. Increase the heat and cook until the mixture is simmering vigorously, then reduce the heat and simmer for about 40 minutes, stirring from time to time.

Pour in the reserved bean puree and cook for 20 more minutes, stirring often to prevent the soup from sticking to the bottom of the pot.

Stir in the remaining whole beans. Taste, season with additional salt and pepper if necessary, and cook for 10 more minutes.

Add the bread, stir, and cook for 10 minutes. The soup will now be almost thick enough to cut with a knife. Ladle into warmed bowls and drizzle with olive oil.

(CONTINUED)

The soup is even better the next day. Let cool completely, then cover and refrigerate. Reheat gently over low heat, adding a bit of water as necessary to thin, or reheat in a baking pan with some sliced onions as described in the headnote.

THE INGREDIENTS THAT MAKE A TRADITIONAL RIBOLLITA

There are as many recipes for a traditional ribollita as there are home cooks in Tuscany, but there are three ingredients found in every version. The first is stale or day-old Tuscan bread, which gives ribollita its texture. Like panzanella (page 250) and pappa al pomodoro (page 239), ribollita is a way to upcycle stale bread. Once the bean and vegetable soup is ready, it is layered with the bread in a soup tureen. The bread absorbs the broth and its flavors and softens, thickening the soup. Because of the filling properties of the bread, historically, ribollita was a lean-day dish par excellence; it would be prepared on Fridays and then reheated and served as many times as possible until used up.

The second important element is cavolo nero, lacinato or Tuscan kale, a winter staple of the region. Cavolo nero has a starring role in ribollita, where it is immediately recognizable by its dark green color.

White beans, preferably cannellini or Toscanelli, are the third distinctive element of ribollita. Their cooking liquid is used for cooking the vegetables, and the beans are added partly whole and partly blended. They make the ribollita rich, creamy, and nutritious.

Along with these ingredients, other seasonal vegetables, foraged herbs, potatoes, and/or tomato paste are added for color and depth of flavor.

Farinata con le leghe

KALE AND BORLOTTI POLENTA

**SERVES 8
AS A MAIN COURSE,
12 AS A STARTER**

¼ cup/60 ml extra-virgin olive oil, plus more for drizzling

1 leek, trimmed and thinly sliced

1 clove garlic, minced

Fine sea salt

2¼ cups/400 g cooked cannellini beans (see page 174) or one 14-ounce/397 g can cannellini beans, rinsed and drained

9 cups/2.1 L reserved bean cooking water or warm water

1 large bunch/500 g lacinato kale, tough stalks removed and discarded, leaves sliced into ribbons

2½ cups/400 g polenta

¼ teaspoon freshly ground black pepper, plus more to taste

2½ ounces/75 g Pecorino Romano, grated (if baking the farinata)

When polenta is paired with a flavorful stock, beans, and kale, you get a nutritious, filling dish that is also gluten-free and vegan. Visit the Tuscan mountains, from Lunigiana to Garfagnana, Appennino Pistoiese, and Mugello, and you will find similar dishes in every area. It is the kale that gives the dish its name. *Leghe* means bonds or ties, and here it is ribbons of kale that twirl around the wooden spoon as you stir the polenta and that hold the farinata together.

Make farinata in winter, after kale has gone through the first frost: that is when its leaves are most tender and sweet. You can eat farinata as soon as it is made, when the polenta is still soft and creamy, or wait until the next day. With time, it thickens into a solid loaf that you can easily cut into neat slices. Grill the slices on a cast-iron griddle pan until nicely charred or bake them with a drizzle of extra-virgin olive oil and a sprinkle of grated pecorino. I always make a big batch of farinata because the crisp crust of a reheated leftover slice is simply addictive.

Pour the olive oil into a large pot set over low heat, add the leek, garlic, and a pinch of salt, and cook, stirring, for 5 minutes, or until the leek is soft and translucent.

Add the beans, reserved cooking water, and kale, increase the heat to medium-high, and bring to a boil, then reduce the heat to medium and cook for 10 minutes.

Gradually whisk in the polenta, stirring constantly to prevent lumps. Season with 2 teaspoons salt and the pepper and cook the polenta for 40 to 45 minutes, stirring vigorously and frequently with a wooden spoon to prevent it from sticking to the bottom of the pot, until it is thick, dense, and smooth. Taste, adjust the seasoning with salt and pepper as necessary, and remove from the heat.

You can serve the farinata immediately, scooping it into warm serving bowls and drizzling each serving with olive oil, or you can leave it for the next day.

In that case, lightly grease a 15-by-11-inch/38 by 28 cm baking dish with olive oil and pour in the farinata, spreading it into an even layer. Let cool to room temperature, then cover and refrigerate overnight.

The next day, preheat the oven to 425°F/220°C. The farinata will be very firm; turn it out onto a large cutting board and cut it into 1-inch-thick/3 cm slices. Arrange the farinata slices on an oiled baking sheet. Sprinkle with the grated pecorino, drizzle with 2 tablespoons olive oil, and bake until golden and crisp. Serve hot.

VARIATION

In the past, cooks would add a prosciutto bone to vegetable or legume-based soups to give them more flavor. To re-create that taste in the farinata, add 2 ounces/60 g cubed pancetta to the leek and garlic and cook for a few minutes, until the fat starts to render, then proceed as directed.

POTATOES, CORN, AND CHESTNUTS

STAPLES FROM THE MOUNTAIN REGIONS

Pasta, patate, e provola
Pasta with Potatoes and Cheese   204

Zuppa d'orzo trentina
Savoy Cabbage and Barley Soup   207

Zuppa di patate, castagne, e porcini
Potato, Chestnut, and Porcini Soup   208

Culurgiones
Sardinian Potato and Cheese Tortelli   211

Casunziei all'ampezzana
Beet Tortelli with Poppy Seed Sauce   214

Lasagne bastarde con sugo di porcini
Chestnut Flour Maltagliati with
Porcini Sauce   219

Polenta concia
Polenta with Butter and Cheese   223

Gnocchi alla sorrentina
Gnocchi Baked with Tomato Sauce and
Mozzarella   225

*Gnocchi di patate e castagne con sugo di
Gorgonzola e noci*
Chestnut and Potato Gnocchi with
Gorgonzola and Walnut Sauce   229

UNTIL A FEW DECADES AGO, LIVING IN THE ITALIAN MOUNTAINS
meant relying on a subsistence diet: chestnuts, potatoes, and polenta, along
with grains such as rye, buckwheat, and barley. These ingredients had to
feed and support people who mostly had draining jobs. Today, those same
ingredients are considered a source of identity in traditional recipes, smart
options when following a gluten-free diet, and the starting point for some of
the most comforting dishes in Italian culinary history.

Potatoes came to the Italian kitchen later than to other European
countries and were not common until the nineteenth century. In a relatively
short time, though, the potato became an essential ingredient of Italian
cucina povera. They are traditionally paired with other starches, as in
pasta, patate, e provola (page 204), zuppa d'orzo (page 207), and buckwheat
pizzoccheri (page 157), or used as a filling for fresh pasta parcels, as in
culurgiones (page 211) and casunziei (page 214). They assume a starring role
when turned into light, pillowy gnocchi (pages 225 and 229).

In Italy, potatoes are usually classified by the color of their skin or their
flesh. Those with yellow flesh are excellent fried, roasted, or boiled. Floury
potatoes with white flesh are suitable for gnocchi, purees, and soups, and
red-skinned potatoes are good for all uses but are best boiled, chopped, and
dressed in a drizzle of extra-virgin olive oil.

Corn cultivated in Northern Italy was once a staple food of the poor. It
is now the ultimate comfort food, especially in the form of polenta, paired
with butter and cheese (page 223). Any leftover polenta is given the cucina
povera no-waste approach: grilled, baked, or fried, it is a treat on its own, a
popular street food, or a delicious starter meant to be shared. Polenta flour
is also sometimes used to fortify hearty vegetable soups, such as farinata
con le leghe (page 198), a bean and kale soup that thickens enough when
chilled that it can be sliced and then baked until crisp.

Chestnuts are a staple ingredient in the cucina povera of the mountain
regions. In years of famine and poverty, chestnuts, high in calories and very
versatile, were an essential resource for the local populations. When fresh,
chestnuts can be boiled or roasted, and Italians love a paper cone of roasted
chestnuts bought street side: they warm you from the inside out.

Dried and then steamed, chestnuts give substance to soups, such as
the potato, chestnut, and porcini soup (page 208), and to seasonal stuffings
for fresh pasta and roast meat. Chestnut flour can be used for polenta,
porridges, breads, an autumnal cake (page 273), biscuits, fresh pasta
(page 219), and thin crepes. The flour is gluten-free, very nutritious, and
rich in fiber, minerals, and vitamins.

Pasta, patate, e provola

PASTA WITH POTATOES AND CHEESE

SERVES 4 TO 6
AS A FIRST COURSE

¼ cup/60 ml extra-
 virgin olive oil, plus
 more for drizzling
1 white onion, minced
1 celery stalk, minced
1 clove garlic, minced
Fine sea salt
1¼ pounds/565 g
 white potatoes,
 peeled and cut
 into ½-inch/1.5 cm
 cubes
2 ounces/60 g
 pancetta, diced
4 cups/1 L hot water,
 lightly salted
4 Roma (plum)
 tomatoes, diced
A Parmigiano-
 Reggiano rind,
 about 2 inches by
 ¾ inch/5 by 2 cm
2 cups/16 dry ounces/
 225 g pasta mista
 (see page 184) or
 ditali or other short
 dried pasta
1½ ounces/45 g
 aged provolone
 or Parmigiano-
 Reggiano, grated
5 ounces/140 g young
 provolone, cubed
Freshly ground black
 pepper

This pantry dish of pasta and potatoes, a winter staple, is sure to become a weeknight favorite in your family. The recipe is traditional in Neapolitan cuisine, but it is now popular all over Italy in different versions, from the brothier Roman dish to the Sicilian one spiced with saffron to the rich Calabrian pasta and potato casserole: baked layers of dried pasta, thinly sliced potatoes, and grated caciocavallo or provolone cheese with tomato puree. The Neapolitan version, neither a soup nor a simple plate of pasta, is usually described as *azzeccata*, dense, creamy, and well mixed, thanks to the stringy melted provolone cheese that binds it all together. A key ingredient is a Parmigiano-Reggiano rind that cooks with the pasta and potatoes, adding depth of flavor to the dish.

——

Pour the olive oil into a large pot set over low heat, add the onion, celery, garlic, and a generous pinch of salt, and cook, stirring occasionally, until the vegetables are soft, about 10 minutes.

Add the potatoes and pancetta, stir, and cook for about 5 minutes, taking care not to brown the potatoes. Pour in 2 cups/500 ml of the hot water (it should be enough to cover the potatoes), add the tomatoes and Parmigiano-Reggiano rind, and cook over medium heat for about 25 minutes, stirring occasionally, until you can easily mash the potatoes against the sides of the pot with a wooden spoon.

Pour in the remaining 2 cups/480 ml of hot water, add the pasta, and stir thoroughly. Bring to a simmer and cook until the soup has thickened and the pasta is al dente, about 10 minutes.

Remove the pot from the heat, add both cheeses, and stir energetically to melt them. Taste and adjust the seasoning with additional salt and with pepper.

Ladle the soup into warmed bowls, drizzle with olive oil, sprinkle with pepper, and serve. The Parmigiano-Reggiano rind can be cut into small pieces and added to the bowls.

Any leftover soup can be refrigerated for up to 2 days. Reheat gently over low heat, adding a bit of water as necessary to thin.

NOTE: *The Neapolitan pasta e patate usually calls for pasta mista (see page 184), but you can use ditali, another combination of short pasta shapes, or even broken spaghetti.*

Zuppa d'orzo trentina

SAVOY CABBAGE AND BARLEY SOUP

SERVES 4
AS A FIRST COURSE

1¼ cups/200 g pearled
   barley
⅓ cup/80 ml extra-
   virgin olive oil
1 medium onion, thinly
   sliced
1 leek, thinly sliced
3½ ounces/100 g
   speck or smoked
   pancetta or bacon,
   cut into strips
Fine sea salt
2 large carrots, peeled
   and diced
1 large potato, peeled
   and diced
½ Savoy cabbage
   (about 10½ ounces/
   300 g), thinly sliced
   (about 4 cups)
4 cups/1 L Vegetable
   Stock (page 307)
Freshly ground black
   pepper

Barley and cabbage are the stars of one of the favorite soups served in the Alpine lodges of Trentino–Alto Adige, the mountainous region in northeastern Italy. A steaming bowl of zuppa d'orzo usually welcomes you after hours spent hiking or skiing. Set on a wooden table next to a plate of dark bread, Alpine butter, and speck, it's a meal that warms you from the inside out and provides plenty of energy for outdoor activities.

I often make zuppa d'orzo in wintertime as a weeknight meal. I can put the soup on the stove and let it simmer away while I work or play with my daughter, and I know that in the evening, we will have a nutritious meal.

———

Bring a large pot of salted water to a boil, add the barley, and cook for about 40 minutes, or until tender. Drain in a colander set over a large bowl and reserve the cooking water.

Pour the olive oil into a large pot set over low heat, add the onion, leek, speck, and a pinch of salt, and cook, stirring, for 10 minutes, or until the onions and leeks are soft.

Add the carrots and potato, then add the cabbage and barley and stir thoroughly to combine. Add 4 cups/1 L of the reserved barley cooking water and the vegetable stock, increase the heat, and cook until the mixture is simmering vigorously, then reduce the heat slightly and simmer for about 1 hour, stirring from time to time. The soup is ready when the barley, potatoes, and carrots are soft and the cabbage is in silky ribbons.

Ladle the soup into warmed bowls, sprinkle with pepper, and drizzle with olive oil.

The soup is even better the next day. Let cool completely, then cover and refrigerate. Reheat gently over low heat, adding a bit of water as necessary to thin.

Zuppa di patate, castagne, e porcini

POTATO, CHESTNUT, AND PORCINI SOUP

**SERVES 4 TO 6
AS A FIRST COURSE**

¼ cup/60 ml extra-virgin olive oil, plus more for drizzling
1 white onion, minced
Fine sea salt
2 pounds/1 kg white potatoes, peeled and cubed
2 bay leaves
4 cups/1 L lightly salted warm water
10 ounces/285 g fresh porcini, brushed clean and chopped (see Note)
3½ ounces/100 g packaged cooked chestnuts
Freshly ground black pepper

This soup is the specialty of Ristorante Anna, a very traditional trattoria in Piancastagnaio, a Tuscan town famous for its tile-roofed houses and ancient chestnut trees. Warming, hearty, and nutritious, it is effortless enough to make on a weeknight. And once the winter holidays have passed, you might find yourself with all the ingredients you need to make the dish already on hand: dried chestnuts left over from making stuffing, cold roasted potatoes, and odd bits of dried porcini. Instead of serving it as a chunky soup, you can blend it with an immersion blender until creamy. If you want to go the extra mile, add a pour of cream, and serve it with homemade croutons.

———

In a large saucepan, heat the oil over low heat. When the oil is hot, add the onion with a generous pinch of salt and cook, stirring occasionally, until soft, about 8 minutes.

Add the potatoes and bay leaves, stir, and cook for about 5 minutes. Pour in the water, increase the heat to medium, and cook for about 25 minutes, stirring occasionally, until the potatoes start to soften.

Add the porcini and cook for about 5 minutes. When the porcini are soft, crumble the chestnuts into the pan and cook for about 5 minutes longer, stirring occasionally, until the potatoes are soft and the soup is thick and creamy. You should be able to easily mash the potatoes against the sides of the pan with a wooden spoon. Adjust the seasoning with more salt and with pepper to taste.

Ladle the soup into warmed bowls, drizzle with olive oil, sprinkle with more pepper, and serve.

Leftovers can be refrigerated for up to 2 days. Reheat gently over low heat, adding a little water as necessary to thin.

NOTE: *I've also made this soup with frozen or dried porcini. If using frozen mushrooms, don't thaw them first; just simmer the soup a bit longer, until they're completely cooked. If using dried porcini, 1 ounce/30 g will be enough: soak them in warm water for 30 minutes before cooking, then lift them out of the water and chop. If you can't find porcini, use other varieties, such as cremini or portobellos.*

Culurgiones

SARDINIAN POTATO AND CHEESE TORTELLI

**SERVES 6 TO 8
AS A FIRST COURSE**

FOR THE FILLING

2 pounds/1 kg Yukon
   Gold potatoes
⅓ cup/80 ml extra-
   virgin olive oil
4 cloves garlic,
   crushed and peeled
7 ounces/200 g aged
   pecorino sardo or
   Pecorino Romano,
   grated
3½ ounces/100 g
   Parmigiano-
   Reggiano, grated
About 30 fresh mint
   leaves, minced
Fine sea salt
½ teaspoon freshly
   ground black
   pepper

FOR THE FRESH PASTA

2¾ cups/500 g
   semolina flour, plus
   more for rolling
1 cup/240 ml water

2 cups/520 g
   Garlicky Tomato
   Sauce (page 308),
   reheated
A handful of fresh
   basil leaves for
   garnish
Grated Pecorino
   Romano for serving

Watching a Sardinian woman masterfully encasing a filling of boiled potatoes, garlic, cheese, and mint in an elegant, artful pasta pocket shaped like an ear of wheat makes you appreciate the enormous respect paid to even the poorest ingredients by cucina povera.

The traditional cheese used in culurgiones is a mixture of good-quality sheep, goat, and cow's-milk cheese and casu axedu, a fresh Sardinian cheese with a dense, pudding-like texture and a slightly acidic taste, similar to yogurt. For this recipe, I use pecorino sardo, for its sharpness and pungency, and Parmigiano-Reggiano, for its mildly acidic notes. A version of culurgiones from the Ogliastra region includes ricotta, saffron, onion, and chard.

———

The day before you plan to serve the culurgiones, start the filling: Rinse the potatoes and place them in a large pot. Add cold water to cover them by a few inches and bring to a boil over high heat. Reduce to a simmer and cook the potatoes until you can easily pierce them with a knife. Drain in a colander and cool under running water.

Peel the potatoes and pass them through the fine plate of a ricer into a bowl. Set aside.

In a large frying pan, heat the olive oil over medium-low heat. Add the garlic and cook, stirring, until golden and fragrant, about 2 minutes. Remove and discard the garlic.

Add the riced potatoes to the pan and mix well to incorporate the olive oil. Transfer to a bowl, cover with plastic wrap, and refrigerate overnight.

The next day, make the pasta dough: Pour the flour onto a work surface and shape it into a mound with a large well in the center. Add the water and, using a fork, stir slowly to incorporate it, starting from the center and gradually picking up more flour from the edges. When the dough turns crumbly, switch to kneading with your hands. You want to knead the dough until it forms a ball and the gluten starts to develop, as this will render the sheets of pasta more elastic. The dough is ready when you have clean hands and a clean board and the dough is smooth, silky, and no longer sticky.

(CONTINUED)

Alternatively, you can make the dough in a stand mixer fitted with the dough hook. Knead for about 5 minutes on low speed, then turn it out and finish kneading by hand for about 5 minutes. Shape the dough into a ball.

Cover the dough with an upturned bowl and let rest for 30 minutes.

While the dough rests, finish the filling: Remove the potatoes from the fridge, add the pecorino, Parmigiano-Reggiano, and mint, and mix to incorporate. Season with salt to taste and the pepper.

Make the culurgiones: Lightly flour a work surface with semolina flour.

To roll out the dough by hand, divide it into 2 pieces. On the floured surface, with a rolling pin, roll out one portion of dough into a paper-thin sheet of pasta. Keep the other piece of dough covered so it doesn't dry out.

To roll out the dough using a pasta machine, divide the dough into 6 equal portions. On the floured work surface, with a rolling pin, roll out one piece of dough into a ½-inch-thick/1.5 cm rectangle. (Keep the remaining pieces covered with a clean kitchen towel.)

Turn the dial on your pasta machine to the widest setting. Feed the dough through the rollers once, then fold the sheet of pasta in three, as if you were folding a letter. Starting with one of the open sides, feed the pasta dough through the machine again. Repeat 3 times, lightly dusting the sheet of dough with semolina flour each time to prevent it from sticking and tearing.

Turn the dial to the next narrower setting. Roll the pasta through the machine, gently pulling it toward you as it comes out of the machine; hold the pasta sheet with the palm of one hand while you crank the machine with the other hand. Continue to reduce the settings and roll the dough through the machine again, lightly dusting the sheet of dough with semolina flour each time, until the dough is as thin as you'd like; I usually stop at the next to last setting.

Once you've rolled out one sheet of dough (by hand or with the pasta machine), start to shape the culurgiones: With a round cutter, cut the sheet of pasta into 3-inch/ 8 cm circles. Collect any scraps of pasta dough and add to the covered dough.

Place 1 tablespoon of filling in the center of each circle. Holding one round in your hand, pinch the lower edges of the dough together with your other hand, fold them inward, and then continue pinching the dough first on one side and then on the other, folding it inward each time, until you have reached the other side, creating an ear of wheat (see the photos opposite). Transfer to a rimmed baking sheet dusted with semolina flour and repeat with the remaining circles. Cover with a clean, dry kitchen towel.

NOTE: *The shape of culurgiones may seem quite daunting even for those who can boast advanced pasta-making skills. Don't get discouraged, though. If you are fascinated by the idea of this Sardinian potato filling but don't feel like attempting the traditional shape, follow the instructions for making casunziei (page 214), tortelli folded into regular half-moon shapes.*

Repeat with the remaining dough, kneading the scraps together and rolling the remaining portion(s) out by hand or by machine, cutting out circles, and filling them.

Cook the culurgiones: Bring a large pot of salted water to a boil. Cook the culurgiones, in batches to avoid crowding the pot, for 3 to 5 minutes, until they float to the top. Remove from the water with a spider or slotted spoon and transfer to a warmed serving dish.

When all of the culurgiones are cooked, toss them with the tomato sauce, add fresh basil leaves, and sprinkle with pecorino. Serve immediately.

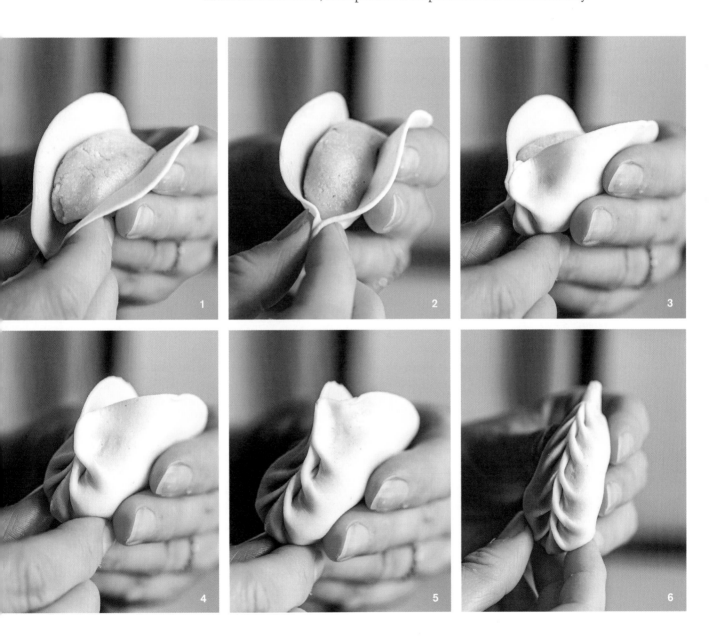

Casunziei all'ampezzana

BEET TORTELLI WITH POPPY SEED SAUCE

**SERVES 4 TO 6
AS A FIRST COURSE**

FOR THE FILLING

1 pound/455 g beets
2 tablespoons extra-
    virgin olive oil
2 medium potatoes
    (about 8 ounces/
    225 g)
2 tablespoons/30 g
    unsalted butter
½ white onion, finely
    minced
½ teaspoon grated
    nutmeg
1 teaspoon fine sea
    salt, or more to
    taste
¼ teaspoon freshly
    ground black
    pepper, or more
    to taste

FOR THE FRESH PASTA

2¼ cups plus
    2 tablespoons/
    300 g all-purpose
    flour
3 large/150 g eggs,
    lightly beaten
Semolina flour for
    rolling

FOR THE SAUCE

8 tablespoons/1 stick/
    115 g unsalted
    butter
3 tablespoons poppy
    seeds

Grated Parmigiano-
    Reggiano for
    serving

Wrapped in paper-thin sheets of fresh pasta that hint at their filling, casunziei change color from season to season. In winter, they are mostly ruby red, with a filling of beets, potatoes, and poppy seeds. In summer, they are green, the shade of wild spinach. In autumn, pumpkin gives a yellow hue to casunziei, and in spring, they are closer to purple, the color of wild radicchio.

The most famous version is the winter beet-based recipe of Cortina d'Ampezzo, where the filling is made with baked beets, boiled potatoes, and stewed onions. Once it has been pureed to a ruby-red thick paste, the filling is spiced with pepper and nutmeg.

The sauce is as simple as it is unique: about 3 tablespoons of poppy seeds drenched in melted butter are drizzled over the casunziei, along with a sprinkling of smoked salted ricotta, for a colorful, elegant dish.

——

The day before you plan to serve the casunziei, start making the filling: Preheat the oven to 400°F/200°C.

Scrub the beets. Place on a large piece of aluminum foil and drizzle with the olive oil. Fold the aluminum foil over to make a parcel and seal the seams, then put the parcel on a baking sheet. Transfer the beets to the oven and bake for about 1 hour, until you can easily pierce them with a knife. Carefully unwrap the beets, transfer to a colander, and let cool completely.

Peel the beets, grate them on the large holes of a box grater, and return to the colander, set over a bowl. Set a small plate on top of the grated beets to weight them down and let drain, refrigerated, overnight.

The next day, make the pasta: Pour the flour onto a work surface and shape it into a mound with a large well in the center. Add the beaten eggs to the well and, using a fork, stir slowly to incorporate them, starting from the center and gradually picking up more flour from the edges. When the dough turns crumbly, switch to kneading with your hands. You want to continue kneading the dough until it forms a ball and the gluten starts to develop, as this will render the sheets of pasta more elastic. The dough is ready when you have clean hands and a clean board and the dough is smooth, silky, and no longer sticky.

(CONTINUED)

Alternatively, you can make the dough in a stand mixer fitted with the dough hook. Knead for about 5 minutes on low speed, then turn it out and finish kneading by hand for about 5 minutes.

Cover the dough with an upturned bowl and let rest for 30 minutes.

While the dough rests, finish the filling: Peel the potatoes, transfer them to a medium pot, and add water to cover. Bring to a boil over high heat and salt the water, then reduce the heat to a simmer and cook the potatoes until you can easily pierce them with a knife, 20 to 25 minutes.

Drain the potatoes, pass them through a ricer, and transfer to a bowl.

In a large saucepan, melt the butter over low heat. Add the onion and cook, stirring, until translucent and soft but not browned, about 5 minutes. Add the drained grated beets and the riced potatoes and stir well, increase the heat to medium, and cook, stirring occasionally, to dry out the mixture, 5 to 8 minutes.

Transfer the mixture to a food processor, add the nutmeg, salt, and pepper, and process until smooth and thick. Transfer to a medium bowl, taste, and adjust the seasoning if necessary.

Make the casunziei: Lightly flour a work surface with semolina flour.

To roll out the dough by hand, divide the dough into 2 pieces. On the floured surface, with a rolling pin, roll out one portion of the dough into a paper-thin sheet. Keep the other covered so it won't dry out.

To roll out the dough using a pasta machine, divide the dough into 6 equal portions. On the lightly floured work surface, with a rolling pin, roll out one piece of dough into a ½-inch-thick/1.5 cm rectangle. (Keep the remaining pieces covered with a clean kitchen towel.)

Turn the dial on your pasta machine to the widest setting. Feed the dough through the rollers once, then fold the sheet of pasta in three, as if you were folding a letter. Starting with one of the open sides, feed the pasta dough through the machine again. Repeat 3 times, lightly dusting the sheet of dough with semolina flour each time to prevent it from sticking and tearing.

Turn the dial to the next narrower setting. Roll the pasta through the machine, gently pulling it toward you as it comes out of the machine; hold the pasta sheet with the palm of one hand while you crank the machine with the other hand. Continue to reduce the settings and roll the dough through the machine again, lightly dusting the sheet of dough with semolina flour each time, until the dough is as thin as you'd like; I usually stop at the next to last setting.

Once you've rolled out one sheet of dough (by hand or with the pasta machine), start to shape the casunziei: With a round cutter, cut the sheet of pasta into 2½-inch/6 cm circles. Collect any scraps of pasta dough and add to the covered dough.

Spoon 1½ teaspoons of filling into the center of one round, then fold it over to form a half-moon. Press the edges to seal the filling inside, trying to remove as much air as possible. Using the back of a fork, press the edges of the casunziei to seal. Transfer the casunziei to a rimmed baking sheet dusted with semolina flour as you shape them and cover with a clean, dry kitchen towel. Repeat the process with the remaining dough and filling.

Cook the casunziei and make the sauce: Bring a large pot of water to a rolling boil and salt it generously. While the water heats, in a medium frying pan, melt the butter over medium-low heat. When the butter stops foaming, add the poppy seeds and fry, stirring, for a couple of minutes. Set aside.

When the water is boiling, add the casunziei, in batches to avoid crowding the pot, and cook for 3 to 5 minutes, until they float to the surface. Remove from the water with a spider or slotted spoon and transfer to a warmed serving dish.

When all of the casunziei are cooked, drizzle them with the poppy seed sauce, sprinkle with Parmigiano-Reggiano, and serve immediately.

Lasagne bastarde con sugo di porcini

CHESTNUT FLOUR MALTAGLIATI WITH PORCINI SAUCE

SERVES 4 TO 6
AS A FIRST COURSE

FOR THE LASAGNE BASTARDE

2¼ cups plus
2 tablespoons/
300 g all-purpose
flour

¾ cup plus
2 tablespoons/100 g
chestnut flour

¾ cup plus
2 tablespoons/
200 ml water

1 teaspoon extra-virgin
olive oil

¼ teaspoon fine sea salt

Semolina flour for
rolling

FOR THE SAUCE

8 ounces/225 g fresh
Italian sausages,
casings removed

¼ cup/60 ml extra-
virgin olive oil

1 small white onion,
thinly sliced

1 clove garlic, crushed
and peeled

Fine sea salt

1¼ pounds/565 g porcini
or other mushrooms
(see Note), brushed
to remove any dirt
and sliced

½ cup/120 ml dry
white wine

⅓ cup/80 ml heavy
cream

Freshly ground black
pepper

Making fresh pasta doesn't have to be complicated. With their deceptive and irreverent name, the easy-to-make pasta shapes known as *lasagne bastarde* (*bastarde* means illegitimate) don't require a lot of precision. Unlike fresh lasagne sheets, in Lunigiana, the northern part of Tuscany where this recipe originated, lasagne noodles are irregularly shaped pieces of eggless pasta, made with just flour and water. All-purpose flour cut with a portion of chestnut flour results in pasta with a brownish hue and a subtly smoky taste.

Lasagne bastarde noodles are traditionally tossed with a simple walnut and cream sauce, or served with extra-virgin olive oil and grated pecorino cheese. But because of their rustic taste and appearance, I find a creamy porcini and sausage sauce the perfect complement.

——

Make the lasagne bastarde dough: Pour the two flours onto a work surface and shape into a mound with a large well in the center. Add the water, olive oil, and salt and, using a fork, stir slowly to incorporate the liquids, starting from the center and gradually picking up more flour from the edges. When the dough turns crumbly, switch to kneading with your hands. You want to continue kneading the dough until it forms a ball and the gluten starts to develop, as this will render the sheets of pasta more elastic. The dough is ready when you have clean hands and a clean board and the dough is smooth, silky, and no longer sticky.

Alternatively, you can make the dough in a stand mixer fitted with the dough hook. Knead for about 5 minutes on low speed, then turn out and finish kneading by hand for about 5 minutes. Shape the dough into a ball.

Cover the dough with an upturned bowl and let rest for 30 minutes.

Form the lasagne bastarde: Lightly flour a work surface with semolina flour.

To roll the dough out by hand, divide it into 2 pieces. On the lightly floured work surface, with a rolling pin, roll out one portion of the dough into a paper-thin sheet. Keep the other piece of dough covered while you work on the first piece so it won't dry out.

To roll out the dough using a pasta machine, divide the dough into 6 equal portions. On the lightly floured work surface, with a rolling pin, roll out one piece of dough into a ½-inch-thick/1.5 cm rectangle. (Keep the remaining pieces covered with a clean kitchen towel.)

Turn the dial on your pasta machine to the widest setting. Feed the dough through the rollers, then fold the sheet of pasta in three, as if you were folding a letter. Starting with one of the open sides, feed the pasta dough through the machine again. Repeat 3 times, lightly dusting the sheet of dough with semolina flour each time to prevent it from sticking and tearing.

Turn the dial to the next narrower setting. Roll the pasta through the machine, gently pulling it toward you as it comes out of the machine; hold the pasta sheet with the palm of one hand while you crank the machine with the other hand. Continue to reduce the settings and roll the dough through the machine again, lightly dusting the sheet of dough with semolina flour each time, until the dough is as thin as you'd like; I usually stop at the next to last setting.

Once you've rolled out one sheet of dough (by hand or with the pasta machine), cut the lasagne bastarde: Cut the pasta into maltagliati, irregular lozenges: First cut the sheet lengthwise into 2-inch-wide/5 cm strips, then cut these on the diagonal into 2-inch-long/5 cm parallelograms. Transfer the maltagliati to a rimmed baking sheet dusted with semolina flour.

Repeat the rolling and cutting process with the remaining piece(s) of dough.

Prepare the porcini mushroom sauce: Crumble the sausage into a large frying pan set over medium heat and cook, stirring often, until golden brown, about 10 minutes. Transfer the sausage to a plate and set aside.

Add the olive oil, onion, and garlic to the pan, season with a pinch of salt, and cook, stirring occasionally, until the onions are softened, about 5 minutes.

Add the porcini and cook for 5 minutes, stirring often. Pour in the wine, increase the heat to medium-high, and cook until the wine has almost completely evaporated. Add the reserved sausages and the cream, stir, and turn off the heat. Taste and adjust the seasoning with more salt and with pepper. Set aside.

Cook the lasagne bastarde: Bring a large pot of water to a rolling boil and salt it generously. Cook the lasagne bastarde, in batches to avoid crowding the pot, until they float to the surface. Remove from the water with a spider or slotted spoon as they are done and transfer to the pan with the porcini.

When all of the lasagne bastarde have been cooked, toss them to coat with the porcini sauce and serve immediately.

NOTES: *This fresh chestnut flour pasta can be cooked as soon as it's rolled out and cut or left to dry near the stove or another heat source. When it is completely dried, transfer the pasta to a paper bag. It can be stored in a cool, dry place for months.*

If fresh porcini are difficult to come by, substitute frozen porcini, or try a combination of cremini and portobellos. If the mushrooms are frozen, don't thaw them first: add them directly to the pan and cook them a bit longer.

VARIATION

Serve the lasagne bastarde with the Gorgonzola and walnut sauce on page 229.

Polenta concia

POLENTA WITH BUTTER AND CHEESE

**SERVES 4 TO 6
AS A MAIN COURSE**

5 cups/1.2 L water
2 teaspoons fine
    sea salt
1¾ cups/225 g polenta
8 tablespoons/1 stick/
    115 g unsalted
    butter
A handful of fresh
    sage leaves
8 ounces/225 g
    Fontina, diced
4 ounces/115 g
    Parmigiano-
    Reggiano, grated

Polenta concia is quintessential Alpine food, the dish you want to have for dinner after a cold day spent skiing. Every Italian Alpine region has its cheese of choice for making this dish: Fontina in Valle d'Aosta and Piedmont; latteria, Emmentaler, bitto, and Taleggio in Lombardia; and Asiago and puzzone, a local raw cow's-milk cheese with a strong smell (*puzzone* means stinky) in Trentino. It is traditionally served with local salumi such as speck and lucanica, a fresh sausage.

You can make polenta concia with any leftover cheese bits and rinds you have on hand: optimally a full-fat cheese that melts beautifully and a sharp grating cheese.

——

Pour the water into a large pot and bring to a boil. Add the salt, then slowly pour in the polenta, stirring constantly with a whisk to prevent lumps. Reduce the heat to the lowest setting and cook for about 45 minutes, stirring often. If the polenta becomes too thick, add more hot water a little at a time.

In the meantime, in a medium frying pan, melt half of the butter over medium-low heat. When the butter stops foaming, add the sage leaves and fry until they are crisp and the butter is lightly browned and smells nutty. With a slotted spoon, transfer the fried sage to a paper towel–lined plate; set the pan of butter aside.

When the polenta is almost ready, add the Fontina, the remaining butter, and the grated Parmigiano-Reggiano. Stir vigorously until the cheese is completely melted and the polenta starts to pull away from the sides of the pot.

Pour the brown butter over the polenta, add the fried sage leaves, and serve immediately, directly from the pot.

Any leftovers can be kept in the fridge for up to 2 days. Reheat gently in a heavy-bottomed saucepan with a bit of water or whole milk, stirring frequently until smooth, creamy, and hot.

(CONTINUED)

Polenta taragna: Typical of Valtellina, polenta taragna is made with a blend of cornmeal and buckwheat flour; substitute buckwheat flour for two-thirds of the polenta. Although it makes a main course on its own, it is often served with mushrooms, rich meat sauces, sausages, or cold cuts.

LEFTOVER POLENTA? HERE'S WHAT YOU CAN DO

Pour any leftover polenta into an oiled baking pan so that it is about 1½ inches/4 cm thick. Smooth it well, compacting it in the pan, cover with plastic wrap, and refrigerate overnight. The next day, you'll have a brick of polenta that you'll be able to easily turn out onto a cutting board and cut into slices.

You can grill polenta slices on a very hot cast-iron griddle pan, until you spot the charred marks of the pan, or you can even grill them outdoors on a hot grill. Or fry the polenta slices in a pan of hot oil until crisp and golden brown. In Naples, they cut the chilled polenta into thin wedges and fry them to make what are called *scagliozzi*, served in a brown paper cone, along with fried dough and fried zucchini flowers, breaded mozzarella, rice balls, and potato croquettes.

Or, if you don't want to fry the polenta, lay the slices on a baking sheet lined with parchment paper, drizzle with olive oil, and bake in a very hot oven until golden brown.

Serve the polenta with brandacujun, the Ligurian potato and cod puree (page 122) or with sarde in saor, Venetian sweet-and-sour sardines (page 119), or as a starter along with your favorite salumi and spreads like a spicy tomato sauce, mushroom sauce, or cheese sauce.

POLENTA, A SIDE OR A DISH ON ITS OWN?

To make enough plain polenta for 4 to 6 people, fill a large pot with 5 cups/1.2 L water and bring to a boil. Add 2 teaspoons fine sea salt, then slowly pour in 1¾ cups/8 ounces/225 g polenta, stirring constantly with a whisk. Reduce the heat to the lowest possible setting and cook for about 45 minutes, stirring often. If the polenta becomes too thick, add more water a little at a time.

The polenta can be served simply with a drizzle of olive oil and a dusting of grated Parmigiano-Reggiano, or with brown butter and crisp sage leaves.

If you want to serve polenta as a side dish, opt for hearty stews, like goulash and spezzatino; rustic meat sauces; grilled sausages; or fegato alla veneziana, the liver stew with onions (page 73).

If you want to grill or fry polenta slices, see Leftover Polenta? above.

Gnocchi alla sorrentina

GNOCCHI BAKED WITH TOMATO SAUCE AND MOZZARELLA

SERVES 6
AS A FIRST COURSE

FOR THE GNOCCHI

2 pounds/1 kg russet
   potatoes, peeled
   and cut into big
   chunks
2 teaspoons fine
   sea salt
Grated nutmeg
1 large/50 g egg,
   lightly beaten
1½ cups plus
   1 tablespoon/195 g
   all-purpose flour,
   plus more for rolling

TO FINISH

2½ cups/650 g
   Garlicky Tomato
   Sauce (page 308)
1 pound/455 g
   mozzarella, torn into
   bite-size pieces
6 tablespoons/30 g
   grated Parmigiano-
   Reggiano
A dozen fresh basil
   leaves
2 tablespoons extra-
   virgin olive oil

"Giovedì gnocchi, venerdì pesce, e sabato trippa." ("Gnocchi on Thursday, fish on Friday, tripe on Saturday.") This Roman saying dates back to the time after World War II, when families had to be very ingenious to make ends meet and cook nurturing meals on a budget. If Thursday was the time for an economical yet filling plate of potato gnocchi, often served with a simple tomato sauce, Friday was a day to abstain from meat, and fish, usually cod with chickpeas, was on the menu. Saturday was butchering day, as calves and beef were slaughtered for the Sunday meals of wealthy people. This tradition is still reflected on the menus of Roman trattorias, where you often find gnocchi served only on Thursdays and a special fish option on Fridays.

When making gnocchi, be sure to choose mature starchy potatoes, which have a low moisture content and high starch content, guaranteeing a soft, pillowy dough. Even more important, though, is how you cook the potatoes, as you want to prevent them from absorbing too much water, or you would have to add too much flour, resulting in heavy, gummy gnocchi. To avoid the problem, you can boil unpeeled whole potatoes just until you can easily pierce them with a knife, steam them (my favorite method, described in the recipe), or bake them on a bed of coarse sea salt (see page 229).

————

Make the gnocchi: Put the potatoes in a steamer basket set over simmering water or in a pressure cooker and steam them until you can easily pierce them with a knife, 10 to 15 minutes.

While they are still hot, pass the potatoes through the fine plate of a potato ricer onto a wooden cutting board or work surface.

Sprinkle the salt and nutmeg to taste over the potatoes and mix in with a fork. Gradually add the beaten egg and the flour, then combine gently but thoroughly. Knead the mixture briefly, stopping as soon as it comes together into a soft dough that doesn't stick to your hands; don't overwork the dough, or the gnocchi will be heavy. Roll the dough into a ball and set aside on the work surface, then clean the work surface with a spatula or dough scraper.

(CONTINUED)

Lightly dust a rimmed baking sheet with flour. With clean hands lightly dusted with flour, form the dough into long ropes about ½ inch/1.5 cm thick. Cut each rope into pieces slightly bigger than a hazelnut.

You can leave the gnocchi as they are, small chubby pillows, or round each one into a ball. If you want to go the extra mile, make ridged gnocchi by pressing them against a gnocchi board, or use a fork, tines facing downward: first press the gnocchi down quite hard against the fork, then drag it and pull it up the tines, forming a ridged gnocco with an indentation underneath. The ridges and the indentation are perfect vessels for catching the sauce.

Transfer the gnocchi to the prepared baking sheet as you shape them. (*The gnocchi can be made ahead and stored in the fridge for a few hours or frozen; see Note.*)

(CONTINUED)

Preheat the oven to 400°F/200°C.

Pour 1 cup/260 g of the tomato sauce into a large shallow bowl.

Cook the gnocchi: Bring a large pot of salted water to a boil. Add half of the gnocchi and cook for 3 to 5 minutes, until they float to the surface. Remove from the water with a spider or slotted spoon and transfer to the bowl with the tomato sauce. Add half of the mozzarella, 2 tablespoons of the grated Parmigiano-Reggiano, and a few basil leaves and gently fold into the gnocchi.

Let the water return to a boil and cook the remaining gnocchi, scooping them out when they float and adding them to the bowl, along with the remaining mozzarella, 1 cup/260 g of the tomato sauce, 2 tablespoons of the Parmigiano-Reggiano, and a few basil leaves. Stir gently to combine.

Transfer the gnocchi to a 10-inch/25 cm round casserole. Pour the remaining ½ cup/130 g tomato sauce on top, scatter over the remaining basil leaves, dust with the remaining 2 tablespoons Parmigiano-Reggiano, and drizzle with olive oil.

Transfer to the oven and bake for 8 to 10 minutes, until the mozzarella is melted. If you want a brown, crispy top, broil for 5 minutes or so. Serve immediately.

Any leftovers can be stored in the fridge for up to 2 days; reheat gently before serving.

NOTES: *Uncooked gnocchi can be frozen on a rimmed baking sheet dusted with semolina flour until firm and then transferred to a zip-top freezer bag and frozen for up to 2 months. Pop them into boiling water while still frozen and allow a couple of minutes more to cook them.*

You can use store-bought marinara sauce instead of the homemade tomato sauce, if you like.

VARIATIONS

You can also serve the gnocchi with a creamy cheese sauce with walnuts, such as the one used for the chestnut gnocchi (page 229), or with a porcini mushroom sauce (see page 219). But good gnocchi is delicious even just with some butter and grated Parmigiano-Reggiano. For an extra kick of flavor, try the cacio e pepe sauce on page 153.

Gnocchi di patate e castagne con sugo di Gorgonzola e noci

CHESTNUT AND POTATO GNOCCHI WITH GORGONZOLA AND WALNUT SAUCE

**SERVES 4 TO 6
AS A FIRST COURSE**

FOR THE GNOCCHI

2 pounds/1 kg russet
    potatoes
½ cup/140 g coarse
    sea salt
Grated nutmeg
1 large/50 g egg,
    lightly beaten
1 cup plus
    3 tablespoons/120 g
    chestnut flour
¾ cup plus
    1 tablespoon/100 g
    all-purpose flour
    or ½ cup plus
    2 tablespoons/100 g
    potato starch (see
    Notes) for dusting

**FOR THE GORGONZOLA
AND WALNUT SAUCE**

10½ ounces/300 g
    Gorgonzola or other
    creamy blue cheese
¼ cup/60 ml whole
    milk
4 tablespoons/60 g
    unsalted butter
A handful of fresh
    sage leaves
⅓ cup/40 g walnuts,
    lightly toasted and
    coarsely chopped
1 ounce/30 g
    Parmigiano-
    Reggiano, grated
Freshly ground black
    pepper

When making gnocchi, if you opt for baking the potatoes instead of steaming them (see page 225), expect a more pronounced potato flavor and very little moisture. For this recipe, you can swap in regular all-purpose flour for the chestnut flour, creating gnocchi with a rustic, slightly smoky flavor. They pair well with hearty, creamy sauces, like the Gorgonzola and walnut sauce in this recipe.

———

Make the gnocchi: Preheat the oven to 400°F/200°C.

Rinse the potatoes to remove any traces of dirt, drain, and pierce them all over with a knife.

Sprinkle half of the coarse salt on a rimmed baking sheet. Place the potatoes, still slightly damp, on the salt and sprinkle them with the remaining salt. Transfer to the oven and bake the potatoes until you can easily pierce them with a knife, about 50 minutes for medium potatoes. (The cooking time may vary, depending on the size of the potatoes.)

Remove the potatoes from the oven and let them cool briefly, just until you can handle them. While the potatoes are still hot, peel them, then cut them into chunks and pass them through a ricer onto a wooden cutting board or work surface.

Sprinkle grated nutmeg to taste over the potatoes and mix in with a fork. Drizzle the beaten egg over, then gradually add the chestnut flour and combine gently but thoroughly. Knead the mixture briefly, stopping as soon as it comes together into a soft dough that doesn't stick to your hands; do not overwork the dough, or the gnocchi will be heavy. Form the dough into a ball and set aside on the work surface, then clean the work surface with a spatula or dough scraper.

Lightly dust a rimmed baking sheet with all-purpose flour (or potato starch). With clean hands lightly dusted with flour, form the dough into long ropes about ½ inch/1.5 cm thick. Cut the ropes into pieces slightly bigger than a hazelnut. Because chestnut flour contains no gluten, you'll need to take extra care to make round gnocchi, as they are more delicate than those made with all-purpose flour. Roll the gnocchi into balls in the palms of your hands:

first press down hard when you start rolling, then finish rolling with a lighter touch.

Transfer the gnocchi to the prepared baking sheet as you shape them. (*The gnocchi can be prepared ahead and kept in the fridge for a few hours.*)

Prepare the sauce: Combine the Gorgonzola and milk in a medium saucepan set over low heat and cook, whisking constantly, until the cheese has completely melted. Set the pan aside.

In a medium frying pan, melt the butter over medium-low heat. When the butter stops foaming, add the sage leaves and fry until crisp. With a slotted spoon, transfer the fried sage to a paper towel–lined plate; set the pan of butter aside.

Cook the gnocchi: Bring a large pot of water to a rolling boil and salt it generously. Meanwhile, reheat the Gorgonzola sauce if it has cooled.

Add half of the gnocchi to the boiling water and cook for 3 to 5 minutes, until they float to the surface. Remove from the water with a spider or slotted spoon and transfer to a serving plate. Add half of the sauce, a drizzle of the butter, and half of the sage leaves and walnuts and toss to coat. Sprinkle with half of the grated Parmigiano-Reggiano and stir gently to combine.

Let the water return to a boil, then cook the remaining gnocchi, scoop them out, and add them to the serving plate, along with the remaining sauce, butter, sage leaves, walnuts, and grated Parmigiano-Reggiano and a few grinds of pepper. Fold gently to distribute the sauce, then serve immediately.

Any leftovers can be stored in the fridge for up to 1 day; reheat gently before serving.

NOTES: *If you are cooking for gluten-sensitive people, use potato starch or rice flour to shape the gnocchi rather than all-purpose flour.*

Chestnut gnocchi do not freeze as well as regular potato gnocchi, as they tend to fall apart in the water when you cook them.

LEFTOVERS

MAKING THE MOST OF WHAT YOU'VE GOT

Supplì al telefono
Roman Fried Rice Balls   236

Pappa al pomodoro
Tomato and Bread Soup   239

Arancine
Sicilian Fried Rice Balls   242

Smacafam
Sausage and Cheese Bake   246

Pancotto pugliese
Bitter Greens and Semolina Bread Soup   249

Panzanella
Tomato and Bread Salad   250

Canederli in brodo
Bread Dumplings   252

Strangolapreti
Spinach Bread Dumplings with
Butter and Sage Sauce   255

Mondeghili
Fried Beef and Mortadella Meatballs   257

Francesina
Beef Stew with Onions and Tomatoes   261

Frittata di spaghetti
Spaghetti Frittata   262

"To feed the planet,
first you have
to fight the waste."

—MASSIMO BOTTURA

THE WASTE-NOT APPROACH OF CUCINA POVERA IS CENTRAL TO MOST
Italian households; it's a way of thinking and acting that comes from
long-held customs. Upcycling leftovers has been a common practice for
all social classes throughout Italian history. It was a well-rooted habit
among the middle classes and even in the upper-level courts, where the
ostentatiousness of the food served never translated into waste. For the
lower classes, though, leftovers were never accidental. Peasant households
were usually composed of large patriarchal families, and the women would
cook large amounts of food to feed the many people living under the same
roof. The leftover food would be reheated, repurposed, and/or transformed
into something completely new.

That parsimonious approach applies to bread, of course, but also to fruit
and vegetable scraps: pea pods, boiled and pureed, are what make risi e bisi
(page 28) creamy; potato peelings are fried to become chips; carrot fronds or
radish leaves enrich soups and stews. In a society strongly dominated by the
Catholic culture, waste was intolerable from an ethical, social, and religious
perspective.

The same practice continues today. For example, I have a cotton bag
hanging behind my kitchen door, where I collect each and every scrap of
stale bread. It is an instinctive reflex, something I learned by watching my
grandmother and my mom do the same. Stale bread is as precious as gold: it
becomes breadcrumbs, gnocchi, breakfast cakes, or a stuffing for vegetables,
and it thickens soups, turning them into filling, satisfying meals. Eventually
that same stale bread can even feed your chickens and rabbits.

In Northern Italy, polenta is even more of a staple food than bread. Any
scraps are reused for meals from breakfast to dinner. In Friuli–Venezia
Giulia, for example, the polenta crusts left in the large cauldrons where
polenta has been patiently stirred are eaten with milk, just like modern-day
cornflakes. Leftover polenta can be fried or grilled; see Leftover Polenta? on
page 224.

Meat is expensive and so is typically stretched to cover more than one
meal, reheated, ground to make meatballs, or repurposed into salads,
soups, and stews. The remains of a roast can be turned into a stuffing for
fresh pasta. Leftover risotto made with meat can be baked or fried into
croquettes. Chicken and rabbit bones can be simmered with onion, celery,
carrots, and, sometimes, cheese rinds to make flavorful broths.

This old-school approach has been adopted even by today's haute
cuisine. In 2015, Milan hosted the World Expo. The Michelin-starred chef
Massimo Bottura took the challenge: he would collect all the leftovers from

the Expo and turn them into fine-dining dishes at Refettorio Ambrosiano, the soup kitchen managed by Caritas and the Diocese of Milan. Other chefs, from Alain Ducasse to René Redzepi, rotated into that kitchen, giving new life to ingredients that would have been otherwise wasted, in a true cucina povera approach. That is what a revolution looks like, according to Bottura: going back to the origins, to the traditions.

The same approach can simplify your own way of cooking. Prepare a large batch of risotto and make arancine (page 242) out of the leftovers. Make more bollito than you need for one meal, enjoy the fortifying homemade stock, and use the remaining meat for mondeghili (page 257). Follow the cucina povera way, and your cooking will become more resourceful and sustainable, you'll save time and money, and you'll discover how fun it can be to waste not in the kitchen.

Supplì al telefono
ROMAN FRIED RICE BALLS

**MAKES 16 SUPPLÌ;
SERVES 8 TO 16
AS A STARTER**

FOR THE RISOTTO
1 ounce/30 g dried
    porcini
2 tablespoons extra-
    virgin olive oil
1 medium yellow
    onion, minced
Fine sea salt
5 ounces/140 g
    ground beef
½ cup/120 ml dry
    white wine
2 cups/480 ml tomato
    puree (passata)
3⅓ cups/800 ml Beef
    Stock (page 305)
5 tablespoons/70 g
    unsalted butter
5 ounces/140 g
    chicken livers
2 cups plus
    2 tablespoons/225 g
    Arborio rice
3½ ounces/100 g
    Parmigiano-
    Reggiano, grated
7 ounces/200 g fresh
    mozzarella, cut into
    16 cubes

1 cup/125 g all-
    purpose flour
2 large/100 g eggs
1¾ cups/190 g dry
    breadcrumbs
6 cups/1.4 L vegetable
    or other neutral oil
    for deep-frying
Flaky sea salt
    (optional)

Supplì are a street food par excellence in Rome. They are a pizzeria's staple starter, along with fried zucchini blossoms and fried salt cod fillets: a heavenly triad of filling, greasy, salty, addictive food. These crisp hot fried rice balls were initially brought to Rome at the beginning of the nineteenth century by Napoleonic troops coming from Naples, where they had probably encountered pall 'e ris, the descendant of the Sicilian arancine (page 242). Their French origin is also evident in the name, as the word *supplì* comes from the French term for surprise, referring to the melted cheese filling hidden inside. Supplì are also known as *supplì al telefono*, because when you pull them open, that melted mozzarella creates strings of cheese, like telephone wires. The rice for this version is a risotto made with tomato sauce, dried porcini, ground beef, and chicken livers.

Channeling Roman cooks, you can make supplì with your leftover risotto, just as for arancine. A cube of mozzarella stuffed inside each rice ball ensures a delicious cheese-filled center.

———

Make the risotto: Put the dried porcini in a bowl and add boiling water to cover. Let stand for 20 minutes.

Meanwhile, in a medium frying pan, heat the olive oil over low heat. Add the onion with a pinch of salt and cook, stirring, until soft and translucent, about 8 minutes. Add the ground beef, increase the heat to medium, and cook, breaking up the chunks of meat with a wooden spoon, until the meat is nicely browned, about 10 minutes.

Pour in the wine and cook until evaporated, 5 to 10 minutes. Add the tomato puree, reduce the heat so the liquid is simmering, cover, and cook for 15 to 20 minutes, until the sauce is glossy and thick.

While the meat mixture cooks, pour the stock into a medium saucepan and bring to a simmer over medium-high heat.

In a medium frying pan, melt 1½ tablespoons/20 g of the butter over medium heat. Add the chicken livers and cook, stirring frequently, until browned but still pink inside, 5 to 8 minutes. Remove from the heat, and when the livers are cool enough to handle, roughly chop.

(CONTINUED)

Drain the porcini, discarding the soaking liquid, and finely chop. Add the livers and mushrooms to the meat mixture and stir to combine.

Stir in the rice and add a ladleful of the stock. Cook, stirring frequently, until most of the stock has been absorbed. Continue cooking and stirring, adding more stock by the ladleful as it is absorbed, until the rice is al dente, the risotto is very creamy, and you have used all of the stock, about 18 minutes in all.

Remove the risotto from the heat, add the remaining 3½ tablespoons/ 50 g butter and the grated Parmigiano-Reggiano, and stir vigorously. Taste and season with additional salt as necessary. Spread the risotto in an even layer on a rimmed baking sheet and let cool completely. You can make the risotto in advance and store it in the fridge, covered, for up to 1 day.

Form the supplì: Divide the cold risotto into 16 equal amounts. Lightly wet your hands and roll each portion into a ball.

Holding one ball in your hand, make a hole in the center and stuff it with a cube of mozzarella. Using your hands to enclose the filling in the rice, then roll into a smooth sausage shape and set on a rimmed baking sheet. Repeat with the remaining risotto and cheese.

Fry the supplì: Spread the flour in a cake pan or rimmed plate. Beat the eggs in a shallow bowl and put the breadcrumbs in another shallow bowl.

Preheat the oven to 200°F/95°C. Pour the oil into a large deep pot set over medium-high heat. Set a wire rack on a rimmed baking sheet and place nearby.

While the oil heats, bread the supplì: Roll one supplì in the flour to coat, then roll in the beaten eggs, turning to coat; lift it from the eggs, letting the excess drip off, add to the dish with the breadcrumbs, and roll to coat. Return to the baking sheet and repeat with the remaining supplì.

When the oil registers 350°F/175°C on a deep-frying thermometer, add some of the supplì to the pot, cooking them in batches; if you crowd the oil, the temperature will drop and the supplì will absorb too much oil. Fry, turning the supplì with two forks, until deep golden brown, about 6 minutes. Transfer to the wire rack set on the baking sheet, then transfer the whole setup to the oven to keep warm. Cook the remaining supplì in batches, allowing the oil to return to temperature between batches and transferring each batch of fried supplì to the wire rack in the oven to keep warm.

When all of the supplì have been fried, transfer to a platter, sprinkle with flaky sea salt, if desired, and serve immediately.

Pappa al pomodoro

TOMATO AND BREAD SOUP

SERVES 4 TO 6
AS A FIRST COURSE

One 28-ounce/794 g can whole peeled tomatoes or 8 ripe Roma (plum) tomatoes, peeled if desired (see headnote)

½ cup/120 ml extra-virgin olive oil

2 cloves garlic, finely chopped

¼ teaspoon red pepper flakes, plus more to taste

4 thick slices (about 12½ ounces/355 g) stale Tuscan Bread (page 302)

1 tablespoon tomato paste

2 cups/480 ml warm water

2 teaspoons fine sea salt, plus more to taste

A handful of fresh basil leaves, torn

Pappa al pomodoro is one of the most representative recipes of Tuscan cucina povera. The main ingredients are stale Tuscan bread—a bread that, according to the rest of Italy, is bland, because it is made without salt—and fresh tomatoes (but a can of good peeled tomatoes works just as well).

Pappa al pomodoro recipes differ from region to region: In Florence, the soup is bright red, as the bread is cooked in tomato puree with a battuto of minced onion, carrot, and celery as the flavor backbone. In Siena and the Chianti area, it is paler, made with just a few chunks of fresh tomatoes, along with the stale bread, and garlic instead of the onion. As for the aromatics, fresh basil is the most common herb, but near Pisa, they tend to use wild mint.

In summer, when ripe tomatoes cram the stalls of farmers' markets, make this soup with ripe Roma tomatoes. If you like, you can quickly peel them so that your pappa al pomodoro will be much more velvety. To do so, cut an X in the bottom of each tomato, plunge them into a pot of boiling water for 30 seconds, and then use a slotted spoon to transfer them to a bowl of cold water to cool; this will help the skins release from the tomatoes. This version of pappa al pomodoro is a thick, dense, porridge-like soup, glistening with extra-virgin olive oil and perfumed with the heady smell of basil. It is comfort food for many people in Tuscany, one of those dishes that wakes up childhood memories and soothes like a warm embrace.

———

Pour the tomatoes into a large bowl and crush them with your hands.

In a large pot, warm ¼ cup/60 ml of the olive oil over low heat. Add the garlic and red pepper flakes and cook, stirring, until the garlic is fragrant and golden, about 2 minutes. Pour in the tomatoes (set the bowl aside), increase the heat to medium-low, and cook, stirring occasionally, until the tomatoes start to break down into a sauce, about 15 minutes.

While the tomatoes cook, break the stale bread slices into big chunks and place in the tomato bowl. Add cold water to cover and let stand until the bread has soaked up enough water to become soft again, about 10 minutes.

(CONTINUED)

Remove the bread from the water, squeeze it between your hands to remove the excess water, and crumble into the tomato sauce. In a large measuring cup, stir together the tomato paste and warm water until well combined, then add to the pot. Season with the salt, reduce the heat to low, and cook for about 10 minutes, stirring vigorously from time to time with a whisk to give the pappa al pomodoro its typical creamy texture.

Remove from the heat, add the torn basil leaves and the remaining ¼ cup/ 60 ml olive oil, and stir to combine. Season to taste with additional salt as necessary.

Let the soup stand at room temperature for at least an hour to allow the flavors to mingle, then serve at room temperature or reheat gently over low heat to serve warm.

Arancine

SICILIAN FRIED RICE BALLS

MAKES 8 ARANCINE

FOR THE RISOTTO

4 cups/1 L boiling water

1 teaspoon fine sea salt, plus more to taste

Pinch of saffron threads

4 tablespoons/60 g unsalted butter

1 small onion, finely minced

2 cups/400 g Arborio rice (see Note)

3½ ounces/100 g Parmigiano-Reggiano cheese, grated

FOR THE FILLING

2 tablespoons/30 g unsalted butter

1 tablespoon extra-virgin olive oil

½ small onion, finely chopped

4 ounces/115 g lean ground beef

½ cup/35 g peas

2 tablespoons tomato paste

⅔ cup/160 ml hot water

1 hard-boiled egg, peeled and crumbled

Fine sea salt

2 ounces/60 g provolone, cut into 8 cubes

Strictly speaking, arancine were not born as a way to recycle leftover rice. Some think they date back to the period of Arab domination in Sicily, from the ninth to the eleventh centuries, when it was common practice to shape saffron rice into a ball in your hands and dress it with lamb meat before eating it. Yet there are no mentions of arancine, or arancini, in Italian literature, diaries, or cookbooks until the second half of the eighteenth century. The first mention of arancini is in Giuseppe Biundi's *Dizionario siciliano-italiano* (1857), which defines them as a sweet rice treat in the shape of a small orange—hence the name *arancino*. From there, they quickly evolved into the well-known savory fried rice balls.

Nowadays arancine are one of the favorite Sicilian street foods. You can buy them at the market stalls, where they are often fried on request, or in local shops. They crowd the counter next to other delicacies such as fried and stuffed pizza dough, rustici, focaccia, and sfoglie. At home, arancine are a practical way to use up risotto. You can cook the rice for the arancine as described below, or use leftover risotto (page 64; you would need about 8 cups/1.4 kg).

———

Make the risotto: In a medium saucepan, bring the water to a boil. Add the salt and saffron and stir to dissolve the salt, then turn off the heat.

In a medium saucepan, melt the butter over medium-low heat. Add the onion and cook, stirring occasionally, for about 8 minutes, until softened and golden. Add the rice and toast it, stirring often, until it is translucent, 2 to 3 minutes.

Add a ladleful of the saffron water to the rice and cook, stirring frequently with a wooden spoon, until it has evaporated. Continue cooking and stirring, adding saffron water to the rice by the ladleful as it is absorbed, until you have added all of the water, the rice is al dente, and the risotto is creamy, about 20 minutes.

Remove the pan from the heat and stir in the grated Parmigiano-Reggiano. Season to taste with additional salt as needed. Spread the risotto on a rimmed baking sheet and let it cool completely.

1 cup/125 g all-
   purpose flour
2 large/100 g eggs
1¼ cups/100 g dry
   breadcrumbs
6 cups/1.4 L vegetable
   or other neutral oil
   for deep-frying
Flaky sea salt

Meanwhile, prepare the filling: In a medium frying pan, melt the butter with the olive oil over medium heat. Add the onion and cook, stirring occasionally, until softened, about 8 minutes.

Add the ground beef and peas, stir well, reduce the heat to medium-low, and cook until the meat is nicely browned, about 6 minutes.

In a measuring cup, stir together the tomato paste and hot water, then add to the beef mixture and cook, stirring occasionally, for 10 to 15 minutes, until all the liquid has been absorbed. Stir in the hard-boiled egg and season to taste with salt. Set aside.

Form the arancine: Divide the cooled risotto into 8 equal portions. Lightly wet your hands and roll each portion of risotto into a ball (about the size of a small orange). Holding a ball in one hand, make a hole in the center and stuff it with a tablespoon of the meat filling and a cube of provolone. Using your hands, enclose the filling in the rice, roll again into a smooth ball, and set on a rimmed baking sheet. Repeat with the remaining risotto and filling.

Fry the arancine: Spread the flour in a cake pan or rimmed plate. Beat the eggs in a shallow dish and put the breadcrumbs in another shallow dish.

Preheat the oven to 200°F/95°C. Pour the oil into a large deep pot set over medium-high heat. Set a wire rack on a rimmed baking sheet and place nearby.

While the oil heats, bread the arancine: Roll one arancina in the flour to coat, then roll in the beaten egg to coat; lift it from the egg, letting the excess drip off, add to the breadcrumbs, and roll to coat. Return to the baking sheet and repeat with the remaining arancine.

When the oil registers 350°F/175°C on a deep-frying thermometer, add some of the arancine to the pot, cooking them in batches; if you crowd the oil, the temperature will drop and the arancine will absorb too much oil. Fry, turning the arancine with two forks, until deep golden brown, about 8 minutes. Transfer to the wire rack set on the baking sheet, then transfer the whole setup to the oven to keep warm. Continue to cook the remaining arancine in batches, allowing the oil to return to temperature between batches and transferring each batch of fried arancine to the wire rack in the oven.

When all of the arancine have been fried, transfer to a platter, sprinkle with flaky sea salt, and serve.

(CONTINUED)

NOTE: *This recipe calls for Arborio rice, but Carnaroli or Vialone Nano work as well. If you substitute another type of rice, keep in mind that different rices can absorb liquid differently, so you may need to add more water and cook your risotto for a few more minutes.*

VARIATIONS

The possibilities are endless when it comes to stuffing your arancine. The classic options are arancine al burro, with a filling of thick béchamel, mozzarella, and prosciutto cotto, and arancine agli spinaci, with spinach and mozzarella. Other variations evoke local specialties, such as arancine alla Norma, with fried eggplant, tomato, basil, and ricotta salata, or arancine con sarde e finocchietto, with sardines and wild fennel.

ARANCINE OR ARANCINI?

Is the name feminine, *arancine*, or masculine, *arancini*? It all depends on where you are in Sicily. On the western coast, especially in Palermo, they are arancine and have a round shape. On the eastern coast, they are arancini, and they often have a conical shape, probably recalling the Mt. Etna volcano. The Accademia della Crusca, the Italian literary academy founded in Florence in 1582, has stated that both names are correct. Even if the names apparently divide the island, Sicilians are united in their shared love for these golden fried rice treats.

ARANCINE AND SUPPLÌ

Arancine and supplì do look similar, delicious fried rice balls that are a quintessential street food or deli treat: cheap, filling, steaming hot, bursting with flavor. The main difference is their geographical origin: supplì are typically served as a starter in almost every Roman trattoria, and arancine have a strong Sicilian soul. But the rice used to make supplì is usually cooked in a tomato puree enriched with ground meat, chicken giblets, and dried porcini, while that used for arancine is simply spiced with saffron. Both supplì and arancine, though, now nod to local tradition with a modern gourmet approach that influences not only the flavor combination but also their choice of filling.

Smacafam

SAUSAGE AND CHEESE BAKE

**SERVES 8 TO 12
AS A STARTER**

Unsalted butter for
greasing the pan
2 cups/250 g all-
purpose flour
½ cup/50 g
buckwheat flour
2 cups/480 ml whole
milk
1 large/50 g egg,
lightly beaten
1 teaspoon fine
sea salt
½ teaspoon freshly
ground black
pepper
8 ounces/225 g sweet
Italian sausages,
casings removed
1½ ounces/40 g thinly
sliced pancetta
4 ounces/115 g
Fontina or Asiago,
cut into ½-inch/
1.5 cm cubes

A cross between an omelet and focaccia, smacafam is hearty Alpine comfort food hailing from the Trentino region. The recipe changes from valley to valley and from family to family, and it illustrates a basic rule of cucina povera: use whatever you have on hand. Originally made with stale bread, smacafam is now based on a thick batter of eggs, milk, flour, and buckwheat flour, enveloping cubes of cheese, sliced pancetta, and sausage. It follows the principle of collecting anything left in the pantry and turning it into a new dish. Consider smacafam a blank canvas for your own salumi leftovers.

The dish can be served hot or cold, along with salumi and cheese, or with a side of cooked vegetables. The name *smacafam* is dialect for "hunger crusher," which perfectly describes the satisfying quality of this rich, savory dish. There's also a sweet version of smacafam, known as *pinza de pomi*, where, instead of sausage and cheese, slices of apples and a few tablespoons of sugar are added to the batter.

⎯⎯

Preheat the oven to 450°F/230°C. Grease a 6-cup/1.4 L gratin or ceramic baking dish or 9-inch/23 cm pie plate.

In a large bowl, whisk together the all-purpose and buckwheat flours. In a small bowl, gently whisk the milk, egg, salt, and pepper until combined. Gradually add the wet ingredients to the flour, whisking until smooth. Set aside.

Place two-thirds of the sausage and the pancetta in a medium frying pan set over medium heat and cook, stirring and breaking up the sausage with a wooden spoon, until the pancetta is translucent and the sausage is golden brown, about 10 minutes.

Add the cooked sausage and pancetta, along with the accumulated fat, to the batter. Stir in the cubed cheese. Pour the batter into the prepared dish and crumble the remaining (raw) sausage on top.

Bake the smacafam for 35 to 40 minutes, until it is puffed and golden brown and a toothpick inserted in the center comes out clean. Serve hot or at room temperature.

Any leftovers can be stored, well wrapped, in the fridge for up to 3 days. Reheat in a hot oven before serving.

Pancotto pugliese

BITTER GREENS AND SEMOLINA BREAD SOUP

**SERVES 6
AS A FIRST COURSE**

2 large bunches/1 kg
  broccoli rabe or
  chicory
2 medium waxy
  potatoes, peeled
  and cut into 1-inch/
  3 cm cubes
8 cups/2 L water
6 cherry tomatoes,
  halved
2 cloves garlic
2 tablespoons extra-
  virgin olive oil, plus
  more for serving
3 bay leaves
1 tablespoon coarse
  sea salt, or more
  to taste
Red pepper flakes
7 ounces/200 g stale
  semolina bread
  (see Notes), cut into
  1-inch/3 cm cubes
  (4 cups cubed)

Pancotto is comfort food all over Italy, and there are many versions of it. In the North of Italy, the soup is made with stale bread, meat stock, grated cheese, and butter. It's considered a restorative food for women about to give birth, for the elderly, and for the sick, and it's also fed to young children as they are weaned from their mothers' milk.

In the South, the recipe omits the meat stock, swaps extra-virgin olive oil for the butter, and adds vegetables. In Tuscany, pancotto is like pappa al pomodoro stripped of tomatoes, while in Lazio, the bread is simmered with tomatoes and dusted with Pecorino Romano. In Apulia, the recipe changes from town to town, with one common denominator: slices of stale semolina bread, with a deep brown crust and a dense yellowish crumb.

This soup is a winter dish, yet you often find tomatoes in the ingredients list as pomodorini appesi, hung tomatoes. During summer, cooks hang small thick-skinned tomatoes in bunches from the ceiling in a dark room. The tomatoes keep through winter, a precious ingredient to use in salads and soups.

———

To clean the broccoli rabe (or chicory), remove the most rigid stalks, then rinse under cold running water and rip into large pieces.

Put the potatoes in a large pot and cover them with the water. Add the tomatoes, garlic, olive oil, bay leaves, salt, and red pepper flakes to taste. Bring to a boil, then reduce the heat to medium-low and simmer for 8 to 10 minutes, until the potatoes are almost done—you should be able to pierce them with the tip of a knife.

Add the broccoli rabe, submerge it with a wooden spoon, and simmer for 10 minutes, or until tender. Turn off the heat, taste, and add more salt, if desired.

Add the bread to the pot, stirring to moisten it, then let it soak for 2 minutes. With a slotted spoon, transfer the soup to a large shallow bowl. Drizzle generously with olive oil and serve immediately.

NOTES: *Buy a good crusty semolina loaf or bake your own (page 303).*

Make sure to use stale bread; fresh bread gives the soup a mushy texture. If your bread is still soft, toast it in a hot oven for about 10 minutes before using it in the recipe.

Panzanella

TOMATO AND BREAD SALAD

**SERVES 4 TO 6
AS A FIRST COURSE**

4 thick slices (about
   12½ ounces/355 g)
   stale Tuscan Bread
   (page 302)
1 small red onion,
   thinly sliced
2 large ripe tomatoes,
   chopped
1 cucumber, thinly
   sliced
Fine sea salt and
   freshly ground
   black pepper
⅓ cup/80 ml extra-
   virgin olive oil
¼ cup/60 ml red wine
   vinegar
A handful of fresh
   basil leaves

Panzanella is a Tuscan bread salad, an ancient yet still enormously popular recipe. It dates back to Renaissance times but is a staple on summer menus in trattorias and on family tables. Like pappa al pomodoro (page 239), it puts day-old bread and seasonal vegetables to good use. The bread is soaked in water until soft and spongy, then squeezed and crumbled into light breadcrumbs. The feathery crumbs are the starting point of a layered salad, soaking up the juices of ripe tomatoes, cucumbers, and onions. Dress the salad with your best extra-virgin olive oil, red wine vinegar, and plenty of fresh basil, then toss it with your hands. You can add or omit ingredients, depending on what's in your pantry and your own preferences. Possible add-ins are canned tuna, capers, anchovies, hard-boiled eggs, and olives.

Make the panzanella in advance and let it rest in the refrigerator so that the flavors can mix and mingle.

———

Break the stale bread into big chunks, transfer to a bowl, and add cold water to cover; set aside to soak. Put the red onion in a small bowl and add cold water to cover; let stand for 10 minutes, then drain.

After the bread has soaked for 5 minutes, check it; it should have soaked up enough water to become soft again. If it's still a bit hard, let it soak a few minutes longer. When the bread is soft, remove it from the bowl and squeeze it to remove the excess water. When you think you have squeezed it well, squeeze it again: there is nothing worse than a watery panzanella.

Crumble the bread into a large bowl. Add the onion, tomatoes, and cucumber and season generously with salt and pepper, then drizzle in the olive oil and vinegar and toss to combine. Add the basil and toss to mix, then taste again and season with additional salt and pepper as necessary.

Transfer the salad to the refrigerator and refrigerate for 30 minutes before serving.

Leftovers can be stored in the fridge for up to 1 day.

Canederli in brodo

BREAD DUMPLINGS

MAKES 16 CANEDERLI;
SERVES 4 TO 8 AS
A FIRST COURSE

13 ounces/370 g
    day-old bread (eight
    to ten 1-inch-thick/
    3 cm slices), crusts
    removed
2 cups/480 ml whole
    milk, warmed
8 ounces/225 g speck
    or pancetta
1 large/50 g egg
1 large/20 g egg yolk
2 tablespoons
    chopped fresh
    chives, plus more
    for serving
¾ teaspoon fine
    sea salt
¼ teaspoon freshly
    ground black
    pepper
1 to 2 tablespoons
    dry breadcrumbs
    (optional)
2 ounces/60 g Fontina,
    cut into 16 cubes
8 cups/2 L Beef Stock
    (page 305)
Grated Parmigiano-
    Reggiano for
    serving

Canederli, bread dumplings, are one of the best and oldest examples of the cucina povera of the Italian Dolomites, dating back at least to the twelfth century.

Canederli are made with stale bread along with eggs, milk, vegetables, fresh herbs, and any odd pieces of cheese and salumi, depending on what is on hand. In the past, canederli were most commonly made with rye bread, but now you find them made with spaccata, a local bread with a thin, crisp crust and a soft crumb. To substitute, you can use a few slices of day-old Tuscan Bread (page 302) or any stale wheat-based country bread.

———

Tear the bread into small pieces, transfer to the bowl of a food processor, and pulse to coarse crumbs. Transfer to a bowl and pour in 1¾ cups/420 ml of the warm milk. Set aside for about 30 minutes to soften.

Once the bread has softened, add the speck (or pancetta) to the bowl of the food processor and process to a paste. Add to the bowl of bread, then add the egg, egg yolk, chives, salt, and pepper. Mix everything together with your hands, squeezing the ingredients so they are well combined. If the mixture looks dry, add some or all of the remaining ¼ cup/60 ml milk. Or if it is very sticky, gradually add the breadcrumbs as needed, mixing until you have a soft, slightly sticky, moist dough. Let rest for about 15 minutes.

With wet hands, divide the mixture into 16 equal portions and roll each into a ball. Holding one of the canederli in your hand, make a hole in the center and place a cube of Fontina inside. Seal the bread mixture around the filling and roll it back into a ball. Set on a rimmed baking sheet and repeat with the remaining bread mixture and cheese.

In a large pot, bring the stock to a simmer over high heat. Add the canederli and simmer for 5 minutes, then turn off the heat and let them sit in the stock for 2 more minutes.

With a slotted spoon, transfer the canederli to bowls and ladle over some of the stock. Sprinkle with grated Parmigiano-Reggiano and chives and serve.

VARIATIONS

You can also cook the canederli in boiling salted water and serve them with brown butter and sage (see page 254), a rich cheese sauce, or even a mushroom sauce (see page 219).

Strangolapreti

SPINACH BREAD DUMPLINGS WITH BUTTER AND SAGE SAUCE

SERVES 4 TO 6
AS A FIRST COURSE

FOR THE
STRANGOLAPRETI

9 ounces/255 g
   crustless day-old
   bread (four to six
   1-inch-thick/3 cm
   slices), cut into
   1-inch/3 cm cubes
   (5 cups cubed)
1 cup/240 ml whole
   milk, warmed
One and a half
   10-ounce/283 g
   packages frozen
   chopped spinach,
   thawed, or 4 to
   5 bunches (650 g)
   fresh spinach, thick
   stems trimmed
2 tablespoons/30 g
   unsalted butter
¼ cup/25 g grated
   Parmigiano-
   Reggiano
1 large/50 g egg
Fine sea salt and
   freshly ground
   black pepper
Semolina flour for
   dusting

FOR THE SAUCE

8 tablespoons/1 stick/
   115 g unsalted
   butter
10 fresh sage leaves
5 tablespoons/30 g
   grated Parmigiano-
   Reggiano

Strangolapreti, dumplings made with stale bread, spinach, and cheese, are another example of Alto Adige cucina povera. They were once a favorite dish of bishops and other high-ranking clergy. The name translates as priest stranglers, and it probably refers to the gluttony of the priests who could never get enough of the dumplings. Do not mistake them for strozzapreti, a hand-rolled pasta made just with flour and water that is typical of Emilia-Romagna, Tuscany, Marche, and Umbria.

Today, strangolapreti are an easy recipe for the home cook, a simple but substantial dish. They're usually made with the regional bread known as *spaccata*, which becomes quite dry after a few days. You can use a few slices of stale Tuscan Bread (page 302) or any wheat-based country bread as a substitute.

———

Make the strangolapreti: Put the bread in a medium bowl, pour the warm milk over it, and set aside for about 30 minutes to soften.

Meanwhile, if using fresh spinach, rinse it thoroughly and transfer to a colander. Add 2 cups/480 ml water to a large pot and bring to a boil, then add the spinach, cover, and cook for 10 minutes, until very soft. Drain and, when it is cool enough to handle, squeeze handfuls of the spinach to remove the excess water. You should get about 1 cup/250 g of squeezed spinach. Or, if using frozen spinach, once it has thawed completely, squeeze to remove the excess water.

Finely chop the spinach, then transfer it to a frying pan, add the butter, and cook the spinach over medium heat for about 5 minutes to remove any remaining moisture. Remove from the heat.

Once the bread has softened, add the spinach to the bowl, add the Parmigiano-Reggiano and egg, and season with salt and pepper. Start mixing the ingredients together, squeezing them with your hands until a soft, moist dough forms, then continue to mix until the dough no longer sticks to your hands.

Lightly dust a rimmed baking sheet and your work surface with semolina flour. To form the strangolapreti, scoop up ½ tablespoon of the dough and, with slightly wet hands, roll into a ball. On the lightly floured work surface, gently roll the ball into an oval dumpling about 1 inch/3 cm long. Transfer to the prepared baking sheet and repeat with the remaining dough; you should end up with about 90 strangolapreti. Set aside.

Prepare the sauce: In a medium frying pan, melt the butter over medium-low heat. When the butter stops foaming, add the sage leaves and fry until crisp. With a slotted spoon, transfer the fried sage to a paper towel–lined plate; set the pan of butter aside.

Bring a large pot of water to a rolling boil and salt it generously. Cook the strangolapreti in batches for 3 to 5 minutes, until they float to the top. Remove from the water with a spider or slotted spoon and transfer to a warmed serving dish.

When all of the strangolapreti have been cooked, drizzle them with the reserved melted butter, sprinkle with the Parmigiano-Reggiano, and garnish with the fried sage leaves. Serve immediately.

NOTE: *Uncooked strangolapreti can be frozen on a rimmed baking sheet dusted with semolina flour until firm and then transferred to a zip-top freezer bag. Pop them into the pot of boiling water still frozen, and allow a couple of minutes more to cook them.*

Mondeghili

FRIED BEEF AND MORTADELLA MEATBALLS

**SERVES 4
AS A MAIN COURSE,
8 AS A STARTER**

2½ ounces/70 g
   day-old bread
   (about one and a
   half 1-inch/3 cm
   slices)
¾ cup/180 ml whole
   milk
1 pound/455 g leftover
   boiled beef (see
   page 305)
2 ounces/60 g
   mortadella or
   salami, in one
   thick slice
¾ cup/60 g grated
   Parmigiano-
   Reggiano
1 tablespoon finely
   chopped fresh
   flat-leaf parsley
Grated zest of
   ½ lemon
½ clove garlic, minced
1½ teaspoons fine
   sea salt
¼ teaspoon freshly
   ground black
   pepper
3 large/150 g eggs
1¼ cups/80 g
   breadcrumbs
7 tablespoons/100 g
   unsalted butter
½ cup/120 ml extra-
   virgin olive oil

In the middle-class households of Lombardy, bollito, a steaming-hot plate of boiled beef cuts, was quite commonly eaten on Sundays. The next day, the leftover meat would be repurposed in other hearty dishes, including a fresh salad made with diced bollito and lots of fresh herbs, boiled beef stewed with onions, or mondeghili, flattened meatballs with a crisp, golden-brown exterior and a soft, slightly lemony interior. Nowadays mondeghili are a fixture of Milan trattorias, where they are served as a main course or as a starter. The name comes from the Castilian word *albóndiga*, which means meatball, and probably dates back to the Spanish domination of Milan.

Mondeghili are made with boiled beef, day-old bread soaked in milk, eggs, grated Parmigiano-Reggiano, and fresh pork sausage or liver mortadella. You can substitute a few slices of pork mortadella or salami. Eat mondeghili steaming hot, as soon as they are fried, though leftovers are lovely cold too.

———

Crumble the bread into small pieces into a medium bowl. Add the milk and set aside to soak for about 10 minutes.

Grind the meat and mortadella (or salami) in a meat grinder fitted with the fine die, or cut into cubes and pulse in the food processor until finely minced but not a paste.

Transfer the meat to a medium bowl and add the Parmigiano-Reggiano, parsley, lemon zest, garlic, salt, and pepper. Squeeze the bread to release the excess milk and finely crumble it into the bowl; discard the milk.

Add one/50 g of the eggs to the mixture. Separate the remaining 2/100 g eggs and add the yolks to the meat mixture; transfer the whites to a small shallow bowl and set aside. Using your hands, mix all the ingredients together, squeezing and kneading until the mixture is homogeneous.

Pour the breadcrumbs onto a plate. Lightly beat the egg whites. Set a rimmed baking sheet or plate nearby for the finished meatballs.

(CONTINUED)

With wet hands, shape the meat mixture into 32 small meatballs, each slightly bigger than a walnut, then roll each one into an oval shape, and finally flatten them into fat ovals.

Dip one meatball in the beaten egg whites, letting the excess drip off, add to the breadcrumbs and turn to coat on all sides, and then transfer to the baking sheet. Repeat until all the meatballs have been breaded.

In a small frying pan, heat the butter and olive oil over medium heat. Line a plate with paper towels and set nearby. To check if the oil and butter are hot enough, insert a toothpick in the hot fat: when tiny bubbles surround it, you're ready to fry. Fry the meatballs, in batches, for 2 to 3 minutes per side, until crisp and golden brown, then use a slotted spoon to transfer them to the paper towel–lined plate to drain.

Transfer the meatballs to a serving platter and serve immediately.

Francesina

BEEF STEW WITH ONIONS AND TOMATOES

**SERVES 4
AS A MAIN COURSE**

¼ cup/60 ml extra-
virgin olive oil

4 red onions, thinly
sliced

1 teaspoon fine sea
salt, plus more to
taste

One 14.5-ounce/411 g
can whole peeled
tomatoes

1¼ pounds/565 g
leftover boiled flank
steak (from Beef
Stock, page 305),
thinly sliced against
the grain

½ cup/120 ml dry red
wine

2 cups/480 ml Beef
Stock (page 305),
heated

Freshly ground black
pepper

Crusty bread for
serving

When you make your own beef stock following the recipe on page 305, you are left with a piece of meat that is tough and stringy. That's when, once again, the ingenuity of cucina povera can really shine. The leftover boiled meat becomes the key ingredient for francesina, a rich and filling Tuscan meat stew that is anything but "poor." You use twice the amount of onions as beef and cook them together over low heat for at least an hour, until creamy. The meat, once tough and stringy, gains the texture of soft pulled pork thanks to the slow, gentle cooking.

You can find a similar dish in Roman cuisine, known as *lesso alla picchiapò*. Leftover boiled beef and onions are the main ingredients, but it includes chili pepper as well. Historically, Roman innkeepers would be heavy-handed with the chili pepper when making the dish, so they could sell more wine to their customers.

———

In a 12-inch/30 cm frying pan, warm the olive oil over low heat. Add the onions and salt and cook, stirring often, until the onions are soft and translucent but not browned, about 20 minutes.

Pour the tomatoes and their juices into a bowl and use your fingers or a fork to crush the tomatoes. Add the tomatoes to the onions, then rinse out the can with a little water and pour the liquid into the pan. Increase the heat to medium and cook, stirring occasionally, for 10 minutes.

Add the meat and wine, increase the heat to medium, and cook, stirring occasionally, until the wine has evaporated, about 15 minutes. Pour in the beef stock, adjust the heat so the liquid is simmering gently, and simmer for 30 minutes, or until the sauce is thick and the beef is falling apart. Taste and season with additional salt and with pepper.

Transfer the stew to a serving bowl and serve with plenty of crusty bread to mop up the sauce.

Frittata di spaghetti

SPAGHETTI FRITTATA

SERVES 4
AS A MAIN COURSE,
8 AS A STARTER

8 ounces/225 g
 spaghetti
1 cup/260 g Garlicky
 Tomato Sauce
 (page 308),
 reheated (see
 headnote)
4 large/200 g eggs
Fine sea salt
10½ ounces/300 g
 whole-milk
 mozzarella, torn into
 bite-size pieces
¾ cup/75 g grated
 Parmigiano-
 Reggiano, grated on
 the small holes of a
 box grater
Extra-virgin olive oil
1 clove garlic

NOTE: *If you want to add salami or another meat or cheese, dice it or cut into thin strips and add to the dressed spaghetti along with the beaten eggs, then proceed as instructed in the recipe.*

Born to make wise use of leftover pasta, frittata di spaghetti is an underrated, versatile, and fun recipe to add to your repertoire. You can serve it as part of a buffet; cut into generous slices, or cube it for an unusual starter. It makes a great packed lunch for day trips, picnics, and beach outings too.

The frittata is usually made with spaghetti, vermicelli, or bucatini, but short pasta such as penne or rigatoni will also work. Eggs are the ingredient that binds everything together: as a general rule, allow one egg per person, and maybe one more for the pan. As the recipe was created to use leftovers, consider it a blank canvas and use it to upcycle any leftover cheese that has been sitting at the back of your fridge for too long: grated Parmigiano-Reggiano or pecorino or cubed or sliced mozzarella, scamorza, or provola. You can also add salami, pancetta, or mortadella; see the Note.

If you don't have homemade sauce on hand, use 1 cup/260 g store-bought marinara sauce.

——

Bring a large pot of water to a rolling boil and salt it generously. Add the spaghetti and cook according to the package instructions until al dente. Drain and transfer to a large bowl. Add the tomato sauce and toss to coat. Let cool completely.

In a small bowl, beat the eggs with a pinch of salt.

When the spaghetti has cooled, add the beaten eggs, mozzarella, and Parmigiano-Reggiano and stir until thoroughly combined.

Heat an 8-inch/20 cm nonstick frying pan over medium heat until hot, then add a drizzle of olive oil and the garlic. Cook, stirring, until the garlic is golden; remove and discard the garlic.

Add the spaghetti to the pan, pressing it into an even layer with a spatula. Cook for 10 to 12 minutes, until a golden crust has developed on the bottom. Invert a large plate over the pan and, in one quick motion, flip the frittata onto the plate. Return the pan to the stove and add a drizzle of olive oil, then slide the frittata back into the pan and cook on the second side until golden brown, about 8 minutes. Serve hot.

DESSERTS

MAKING DO FOR CAKES, TARTS, PUDDINGS, AND COOKIES TOO

Torta di mele all'olio
Apple Olive Oil Cake   268

Torta di pane
Bread Pudding Cake   270

Castagnaccio
Chestnut Flour Cake   273

Schiacciata con l'uva
Grape Focaccia   274

Crostata alla marmellata
Short-Crust Pastry Tart with Jam   277

Torta di zucca gialla
Pumpkin Tart   281

Bonet bianco alla monferrina
Amaretti Pudding   283

Zuppa inglese
Pastry Cream and Chocolate Trifle   287

Biscotti con la frutta secca
Nut Biscotti   289

Biancomangiare di latte di mandorla
Sicilian Almond-Milk Pudding   292

Gelo di mellone
Sicilian Watermelon Pudding   295

Frittelle di fiori di sambuco
Elderflower Fritters   296

ITALY'S CUCINA POVERA IS FULL OF CAKES MADE WITH SEASONAL produce that perfectly embody the cuisine's spirit. A cake batter can incorporate what is abundant and in season in an inventive way, transforming poor ingredients into rich treats. Fruit is made into preserves, of course, but it also appears in simple puddings, like the Sicilian gelo di mellone (page 295).

The same principle applies to vegetables. Carrots, for example, a natural sweetener that can stand in for more expensive sugar or honey, are often paired with almonds or hazelnuts in desserts. But radicchio, eggplant, zucchini, and even Swiss chard are all part of the dessert scene, with pumpkin and butternut squash, for example, staple ingredients in fall, as in Pellegrino Artusi's torta di zucca gialla (page 281).

Day-old bread is turned into bread pudding cake (page 270), and dried-out sponge cake into a layered trifle (page 287). Most of the traditional cookies that appear at informal Italian dinners have a sturdy, durable character inherited from medieval biscuits, and so they should be accompanied by a glass of dessert wine.

As spices were once reserved for the wealthy classes, peasant cuisine learned to use whatever was available as flavorings for baking. Lemon and orange zest are used fresh when citrus is in season and are also dried for the following months. Elderflowers are dried to use in cakes, meringues, and cookies, along with lavender and rose petals. And be sure to use pure extracts rather than artificial ones; your baked goods will benefit from it.

Many sweet breads of peasant origins that celebrate festivities and seasonality are enriched by adding a handful of nuts, spices, and dried fruit to a simple dough, turning it into something out of the ordinary. And although these baked goods are steeped in tradition and reassuringly turn up year after year when the right time comes, their short seasonality makes their appearance much anticipated. Now you too can wait for September and the first bite of grape focaccia, schiacciata con l'uva (page 274), with a thrill.

Torta di mele all'olio

APPLE OLIVE OIL CAKE

SERVES 8

FOR THE CAKE

Butter for greasing
    the pan
1¾ cups plus
    3 tablespoons/
    240 g all-purpose
    flour, plus more for
    dusting the pan
4 firm tart apples
Juice of 1 lemon
1 cup /200 g
    granulated sugar,
    plus 4 tablespoons
    for sprinkling
1½ teaspoons/7 g
    baking powder
½ teaspoon ground
    cinnamon
¼ teaspoon fine
    sea salt
4 large/200 g eggs
½ cup/120 ml extra-
    virgin olive oil

FOR THE APPLE SYRUP

¾ cup/180 ml water
½ cup/100 g
    granulated sugar
Zest of ½ lemon,
    removed in strips
    with a vegetable
    peeler
Reserved apple peel
    (from above)

If there's a recipe that best represents the idea of Italian family and home, it is apple cake. It is one of the most popular desserts on the entire peninsula. Every family has its own favorite recipe for torta di mele, and they believe it's the perfect one. I am no exception. I worked on this recipe for years until I arrived at what I think is the ideal version. Not overly sweet, it is bursting with melting apples, with a hint of cinnamon and fresh lemon juice, and it has a soft, moist crumb thanks to extra-virgin olive oil.

During apple season, you can make this cake with any apples that need to be eaten or used immediately—even ones that are wrinkled or battered. Keep torta di mele out on the kitchen counter, ready to be sliced for breakfast along with an espresso, or for an afternoon snack with a cup of tea. For dessert, serve it warm with a scoop of vanilla gelato.

———

Make the cake: Preheat the oven to 350°F/175°C. Grease a 9-inch/23 cm or 10-inch/25 cm springform pan or round cake pan with butter and dust with flour, shaking out the excess.

Peel, core, halve, and thinly slice 3 of the apples. Put the slices in a bowl, add the lemon juice, and sprinkle with 2 tablespoons of the sugar. Give them a quick stir and set aside.

Sift together the flour, baking powder, cinnamon, and salt.

In a large bowl, whisk the eggs with the 1 cup/200 g sugar until light and foamy, then stir in the olive oil. With a rubber spatula, fold in the flour mixture until there are no dry patches, then add the apples and any accumulated juice and fold gently to combine.

Scrape the batter into the cake pan and smooth the surface with a spatula.

Peel, core, halve, and thinly slice the remaining apple, reserving the peel. Arrange the apple slices on top of the cake in concentric circles, slightly overlapping them, starting from the outer edge of the cake and working inward. Sprinkle the remaining 2 tablespoons sugar over the apples.

Transfer the cake to the oven and bake until a toothpick inserted in the center comes out clean and the cake is browned at the edges and beginning to pull away from the sides of the pan, 50 minutes to 1 hour (or slightly longer if using a 9-inch/23 cm pan). Remove from the oven and let cool on a wire rack for 10 minutes, then run a knife around the edges of the pan, release the springform ring, if using, invert the cake onto the rack, and invert again so it is apple side up.

NOTE: *If you don't want to make the apple syrup to brush the cake, just dilute 2 tablespoons of apricot jam with hot water to make a thick syrup, and brush the cake with that.*

While the cake is baking, prepare the apple syrup: In a small saucepan, combine the water, sugar, lemon zest, and reserved apple peel and bring to a boil, stirring to dissolve the sugar, then reduce the heat and simmer, covered, for about 20 minutes, until the syrup is thick and glistening. Remove from the heat.

While the cake is still hot, generously brush the surface with the apple syrup. Serve warm or at room temperature, cut into wedges.

The cake will keep for a couple of days at room temperature, covered with a kitchen towel or wrapped in aluminum foil.

VARIATIONS

Try this recipe with nectarines, apricots, or pears. Or make a chocolate olive oil pear cake by adding 2 tablespoons cocoa powder to the flour mixture and a handful of chocolate chips to the batter.

Torta di pane

BREAD PUDDING CAKE

SERVES 8

10½ ounces/300 g
    stale country bread
    (about 4 slices)
2 cups/480 ml whole
    milk, or as needed
½ tablespoon/10 g
    unsalted butter
    for the top of the
    cake, plus more for
    greasing the pan
¾ cup/150 g
    granulated sugar
2 large/100 g eggs,
    lightly beaten
3 tablespoons
    unsweetened cocoa
    powder, sifted
3½ tablespoons/50 g
    unsalted butter,
    melted
Grated zest of
    ½ orange
½ cup/85 g hazelnuts,
    lightly toasted and
    coarsely chopped
10 prunes, chopped
10 dried figs, chopped

Every region in Italy, or even every town, has its own bread, which can be turned into torta di pane, a cake made with stale bread, milk, and a handful of pantry ingredients.

The bread can be anything from dark rye, in Northern Italy, to durum wheat, in the South. Sometimes dry cookies, such as amaretti, or dry sponge cake are also used. The bread is soaked in milk until mushy; eggs ensure a dense pudding-like texture. The cake was traditionally sweetened with local honey, seasonal fruit, or dried figs, but sugar is now the most common sweetener.

———

Cut the bread into large cubes and put in a large bowl. Pour the milk into a medium saucepan and heat over medium heat until hot. Pour the milk over the bread and set aside for about 30 minutes to soften.

Preheat the oven to 350°F/175°C. Butter an 8-inch/20 cm round cake pan.

After the bread has soaked for 30 minutes, mash it with a fork into a soft, moist dough. If it still seems too dry, add a few more tablespoons of milk and blend with an immersion blender into a paste. Some pieces of crust may remain, but don't worry—they will give texture to the cake. Add the sugar, eggs, cocoa powder, melted butter, orange zest, hazelnuts, prunes, and figs and mix thoroughly.

Spoon the batter into the cake pan and smooth the surface with a spatula. Dot the top of the cake with the ½ tablespoon butter.

Bake the cake for about 40 minutes, until crisp on the surface but still moist inside; a toothpick inserted in the center of the cake should come out with a few crumbs clinging to it. Let cool completely on a wire rack.

Run a knife around the edges of the cake pan and invert the cake onto the rack, then invert again onto a serving plate.

This dense cake will keep well for days on the counter, covered with a kitchen towel or wrapped in aluminum foil.

Incorporate other roughly chopped nuts, such as almonds, pine nuts, or walnuts, and other dried fruits, like raisins and apricots: they all give flavor and texture to the cake. Cubed apples or pears (2 medium) can stand in for dried fruit when in season.

Castagnaccio

CHESTNUT FLOUR CAKE

SERVES 8

⅓ cup/50 g raisins
1 tablespoon vin santo, Marsala, passito, or port (optional; see Note)
2¼ cups/250 g chestnut flour
Pinch of fine sea salt
1½ cups/360 ml water
½ cup/50 g walnuts, roughly chopped
¼ cup/30 g pine nuts
¼ cup/60 ml extra-virgin olive oil
1 fresh rosemary sprig
Sweetened whipped ricotta for serving

NOTE: *If you do not have vin santo, the dessert wine from Tuscany, you can substitute any sweet wine, like Marsala, passito, or port, or simply omit it.*

This Tuscan cake marks the arrival of autumn. Barely sweet, with a dense pudding-like texture and a crisp exterior, castagnaccio has a subtle smoky flavor from the chestnut flour and a savory herbal note from the rosemary and olive oil. (Because the batter is made with just chestnut flour, water, and olive oil, castagnaccio is both vegan and gluten-free.) This version includes pine nuts and walnuts, but you can stud the batter with raisins, chopped candied citrus peel, and/or dried fruit, if you like. The rustic cake benefits from a dollop of sweetened whipped ricotta served on the side.

————

Put the raisins in a small bowl, add warm water to just cover, and stir in the vin santo, if using. Let stand for 10 minutes.

Preheat the oven to 350°F/175°C. Set out a 10-inch/25 cm round cake pan (you can use a springform pan if you have one).

Sift the chestnut flour into a large bowl and stir in the salt. Pour about two-thirds of the water into the chestnut flour and whisk until smooth. Add the remaining water and whisk to combine.

Drain the raisins, squeeze them dry, and add to the bowl, along with half of the walnuts and pine nuts. With a wooden spoon or spatula, stir to combine.

Pour 3 tablespoons of the olive oil into the cake pan and tilt the pan to distribute the oil evenly. Pour the batter into the pan and sprinkle the surface with the remaining walnuts and pine nuts. Scatter the rosemary needles on top and drizzle with the remaining 1 tablespoon olive oil. The batter will be almost floating on the olive oil: that's the point. This will prevent it from sticking to the pan and give the castagnaccio a crunchier bottom and sides.

Transfer to the oven and bake for 40 to 45 minutes, or until the cake is crisp at the edges and the top is covered with fine wrinkles.

Remove from the oven and let the cake cool for about 10 minutes on a wire rack, then remove from the pan and transfer to a serving plate. Serve warm or at room temperature with sweetened whipped ricotta.

Schiacciata con l'uva

GRAPE FOCACCIA

SERVES 6

FOR THE DOUGH

¼ cup/60 ml
    lukewarm water
1 teaspoon granulated
    sugar
¼ teaspoon active
    dry yeast
1 cup plus
    2 tablespoons/
    150 g bread flour
1¼ cups/150 g
    all-purpose flour
1 tablespoon
    granulated sugar
¾ cup/180 ml room-
    temperature water
1 teaspoon fine sea
    salt
1 tablespoon extra-
    virgin olive oil

TO FINISH

12 ounces/340 g
    Concord grapes or
    red wine grapes
2 tablespoons
    granulated sugar
Needles from 1 fresh
    rosemary sprig
2 tablespoons extra-
    virgin olive oil

Come September, everything in the Tuscan countryside revolves around the grape harvest: the vineyards are dotted with people picking grapes in the early morning, and big tractors brimming with grapes slow the traffic around the local wineries. Fat clusters of wine grapes appear in market stalls, and bakeries add a seasonal treat to their menus: sticky, sweet focaccia topped with jammy grapes and rosemary.

Schiacciata con l'uva (*schiacciata* is the Tuscan term for focaccia) belongs to that special category of enriched breads that celebrates various festivities by adding nuts, spices, and dried fruit to the dough. Among these are pan co' santi, the spiced bread studded with raisins and walnuts that Italians bake for All Saints' Day, and schiacciata di Pasqua, a speckled domed aniseed bread that announces the arrival of Easter. These baked goods, steeped in tradition, are made for only a short period of time, and their appearance is much anticipated. Every September, I can't wait to bake this schiacciata con l'uva to celebrate the beginning of the harvest season.

⸻

Make the dough: In a large bowl, stir together the ¼ cup/60 ml lukewarm water, sugar, and yeast. Let stand for about 10 minutes, until foamy.

Add the bread flour, all-purpose flour, sugar, and all but 1 tablespoon of the room-temperature water to the yeast mixture and mix with a wooden spoon, or knead by hand until you have incorporated all the flour. The dough will be very sticky and not homogeneous. Cover with a damp towel and let rest for 20 minutes.

Add the salt and the reserved tablespoon of room-temperature water to the dough and mix by squeezing the dough between your hands. The dough should become less sticky and more elastic.

Add the olive oil. With wet hands, pick up one edge of the dough, stretch it gently upward, and fold it over itself. Give the bowl a quarter turn and repeat. Continue until you have come full circle to complete four "folds" around the bowl. Let the dough rest for 20 minutes, then repeat the stretch-and-fold technique 3 more times, letting the dough rest for 20 minutes each time. The dough should be soft, elastic, and velvety.

(CONTINUED)

Cover with plastic wrap and refrigerate for 20 to 22 hours, until the dough has doubled in size.

Remove the dough from the fridge and bring to room temperature.

Oil a 9-by-13-inch/23 by 33 cm baking pan. Prepare the grapes by detaching them from the stems.

Oil your hands and gently deflate the dough, then turn it out into the baking pan and stretch it to fit. Press the grapes into the dough and sprinkle with the sugar and rosemary. Drizzle the olive oil over the dough and let rise again at room temperature for 1 hour.

Arrange one rack in the lower third of the oven and a second rack in the center and preheat the oven to 400°F/200°C.

Transfer the baking pan to the lower rack of the oven and bake for 15 minutes, then move it to the middle rack and bake for 15 to 20 more minutes, until the focaccia is golden brown and the grapes have collapsed into a bubbling, caramelized jam.

Remove the focaccia from the oven and transfer to a wire rack to cool. Serve warm or cold.

The focaccia can be stored at room temperature for a couple of days, wrapped in aluminum foil.

NOTE: *Grape seeds are essential to the grape focaccia, where they provide a natural crunch. But if you cannot find red wine or Concord grapes, you can make it with blackberries or blueberries instead. It works perfectly with ripe figs and rosemary too.*

Crostata alla marmellata

SHORT-CRUST PASTRY TART WITH JAM

SERVES 8

2¼ cups plus
2 tablespoons/
300 g all-purpose
flour, plus more for
dusting

½ cup plus
2 tablespoons/
125 g granulated
sugar

¼ teaspoon fine
sea salt

Grated zest of
½ lemon

11 tablespoons/
5½ ounces/155 g
unsalted butter or
lard, cubed, at room
temperature, plus
more for greasing
the pan

1 large/50 g egg,
beaten

1 cup/12 ounces/340 g
jam (see Note)

Pasta frolla, the rich, buttery Italian short-crust pastry, is a versatile dough and the starting point for many humble recipes, from shortbread cookies to rustic jam-filled crostatas. A crostata is the Italian version of a fruit pie, though instead of fresh fruit, it is filled with jam. Rustic, homey, and versatile, it is one of the most classic Italian desserts. Bake it for breakfast (yes, in Italy, cake for breakfast is not only allowed, it is recommended!) or as an afternoon snack, or serve thick slices after a family meal.

———

In a large bowl or on a wooden board, mix together the flour, sugar, salt, and lemon zest. Add the cubed butter (or lard) and use your fingertips to rub it into the flour mixture until fine crumbs form, similar to grated Parmigiano-Reggiano. (You can also use a stand mixer fitted with the paddle attachment to do this.) Add the beaten egg and use your hands (or the mixer) to quickly mix the ingredients, until the dough just comes together. It will still be slightly sticky and not completely homogeneous, but there shouldn't be any visible streaks of flour.

Shape the dough into a disk, wrap it in plastic wrap, and stash it in the fridge to rest for at least a few hours, or, ideally, overnight.

When ready to make the crostata, remove the pasta frolla from the fridge and leave it at room temperature for about 20 minutes. This will make it easier to roll it out.

Preheat the oven to 350°F/175°C. Butter a 12-inch/30 cm tart pan with a removable bottom.

Lightly flour a work surface. Separate the dough into large pieces and then quickly knead them back together. This will make rolling out the dough much easier.

Divide the dough into 2 pieces, one twice as big as the other (two-thirds and one-third of the dough). With a floured rolling pin, roll the larger piece into a 13-inch/33 cm round about ⅓ inch/8 mm thick.

Gently lift the dough, with the help of the rolling pin, and lay it in the tart pan. Use your fingers to press the dough over the bottom of the pan and up the sides. Roll the rolling pin over the edges of the pan to trim the dough; reserve the scraps.

Spoon the jam into the crust and, with an offset spatula or spoon, spread it evenly over the bottom of the crust.

Knead the dough scraps into the reserved piece of dough. Roll it out on a sheet of parchment paper to a round that is ¼ inch/6 mm thick. With a sharp knife, cut it into ¾-inch-wide/2 cm strips (alternatively, you can use your favorite cookie cutter to cut out shapes to decorate the crostata). If the dough is getting warm, transfer the dough strips (still on the parchment) to a baking sheet and freeze for 5 minutes.

Lay half of the strips vertically across the tart and the other half horizontally, to form a lattice top (there is no need to weave the lattice; the dough strips will melt together as they bake). Press the ends of each strip into the dough on the sides of the pan to seal.

Bake the crostata for 40 minutes, or until golden brown. Let cool completely on a wire rack, then cut into slices to serve.

The crostata can be kept on the counter for a few days, covered with a clean dish towel, ready for you to slice as needed.

NOTE: *Although the Italian name translates as crostata with marmalade, the filling is usually jam. Flavors can range from apricot or blackberry jam, the most common options, to more refined sour cherry, plum, or blueberry jam.*

VARIATIONS

Blind-bake the pasta frolla shell and let cool completely. (You can use the second portion of dough to make cookies; see the instructions below.) Fill the tart shell with pastry cream (see page 287) and top it with sliced seasonal fruit or berries to make crostata di frutta, a standard at Italian birthday celebrations and summer garden parties.

To make pasta frolla biscotti (cookies), roll out the dough about ⅓ inch/ 8 mm thick and cut out cookies with your favorite cutters. Bake them until pale golden. Dust with confectioners' sugar, or pair up the cookies and fill with jam for sandwich cookies.

Torta di zucca gialla

PUMPKIN TART

SERVES 8

FOR THE TART DOUGH

2 cups/250 g all-purpose flour

½ teaspoon fine sea salt

9 tablespoons/1 stick plus 1 tablespoon/ 125 g unsalted butter, cubed, at room temperature

¼ cup/60 ml cold water

FOR THE PUMPKIN FILLING

1 small sugar pumpkin (about 2 pounds/ 1 kg), peeled, halved, and seeded

2 cups/480 ml whole milk

1 cup/100 g almond flour

½ cup plus 2 tablespoons/125 g granulated sugar

¼ cup/30 g fine dry breadcrumbs

2 tablespoons/30 g unsalted butter, cut into pieces, at room temperature

3 large/150 g eggs, beaten

1 teaspoon ground cinnamon

¼ teaspoon fine sea salt

Unsalted butter for greasing the pan

Confectioners' sugar for dusting

Even Pellegrino Artusi, the father of Italian cuisine, had a recipe for torta di zucca gialla, Italy's version of pumpkin pie. The pumpkin is grated, drained, and cooked in milk, then mixed with sugar, finely minced almonds, butter, breadcrumbs, eggs, and cinnamon. The batter is poured into a pie shell and baked into a pudding-like filling encased in a buttery crust.

———

Prepare the tart dough: In a large bowl or on a wooden board, mix together the flour and salt. Add the cubed butter and use your fingertips to rub it into the flour until the mixture forms fine crumbs, similar to grated Parmigiano-Reggiano. (You can also use a stand mixer fitted with the paddle attachment to do this.) Slowly pour in the cold water, using your hands (or the mixer) to quickly mix the ingredients until the dough just comes together. It will still be slightly sticky and not completely homogeneous, but there shouldn't be any visible streaks of flour.

Shape the dough into a disk, wrap it in plastic wrap, and put it in the fridge to rest for at least a few hours, or, ideally overnight.

Prepare the filling: Grate the pumpkin flesh using the large holes on a box grater or a food processor fitted with the grating disk. Transfer it to a clean kitchen towel, wrap it up in the towel, and squeeze the water from the pumpkin pulp.

In a large saucepan, bring the milk to a boil over medium-high heat. Add the pumpkin pulp, stir, reduce the heat, and simmer, stirring often, for about 30 minutes, until the pumpkin is cooked through and soft.

Remove from the heat and transfer to a fine-mesh sieve set over a bowl to drain, pressing on the solids to release as much liquid as possible (set the pan aside). Return the pumpkin puree to the saucepan, add the almond flour, granulated sugar, breadcrumbs, and butter, and stir thoroughly, then set aside to cool completely. (*The filling can be prepared in advance to this point, covered, and refrigerated for up to 2 days.*)

Assemble and bake the pie: Remove the dough from the fridge. Preheat the oven to 350°F/175°C. Butter a 10-inch/25 cm round tart pan with a removable bottom.

(CONTINUED)

Stir the eggs, cinnamon, and salt into the pumpkin mixture until well combined. Set aside.

On a floured surface, with a floured rolling pin, roll out the dough into a 13-inch/33 cm round about ¼ inch/6 mm thick.

Gently lift up the dough, with the help of the rolling pin, and lay it in the tart pan. Use your fingers to press the dough over the bottom of the pan and up the sides. Roll the rolling pin over the edges of the pan to trim the dough.

Pour the pumpkin filling into the prepared shell. Transfer to the oven and bake for 55 minutes to 1 hour, until the filling is set, golden brown, puffed, and beginning to crack on top.

Let the pie cool completely on a wire rack, then dust with confectioners' sugar, cut into slices, and serve.

BUTTER OR LARD?

Most Italian cooks now use unsalted butter to make pasta frolla. In older recipes, though, as in two of the variations of pasta frolla listed by Pellegrino Artusi in his 1891 cookbook *Science in the Kitchen and the Art of Eating Well*, you find lard instead of butter. Even today, lard is still very common in Southern Italian versions of pasta frolla, including that for the shell of the Easter pastiera from Naples, a tart filled with ricotta, boiled wheat berries, and candied citrus peel, and pasticciotti, small pastries from Salento with a heart of thick pastry cream.

If you can find snowy-white artisanal lard, try it in pasta frolla in place of the butter. You'll get a rich, delicately crumbly pastry, which is especially good paired with creamy fillings, such as rich vanilla pastry cream, and a topping of sour cherries.

Bonet bianco alla monferrina

AMARETTI PUDDING

SERVES 8 TO 10

3½ ounces/100 g
 amaretti cookies
 (about 30 cookies)
4 cups/1 L whole milk
8 large/400 g eggs
1½ cups plus
 2 tablespoons/
 325 g granulated
 sugar
¼ cup/60 ml dark rum

A Sunday lunch in a Piedmontese household most likely includes a thick slice of bonet drizzled with caramel for dessert. Bonet, bunèt in the local dialect, is a chocolate pudding whose original recipe dates back to the thirteenth century. Dense and silky, it is made with crumbled amaretti, eggs, milk, sugar, cocoa powder, and rum.

This white bonet is based on an older recipe born in Monferrato, before cocoa was imported to Italy. Despite its short, basic ingredients list, bonet bianco has an elegant, rich taste, with intense notes of bitter almond from the amaretti, rounded out by the caramel.

The secret to a bonet is patience. Resist mixing the eggs and sugar with a whisk; opt for a wooden spoon or silicone spatula and a careful folding, to avoid incorporating too much air. Then a long, gentle cooking in a water bath in the oven does its magic and sets the pudding, giving it its characteristic silky consistency. Let the bonet rest overnight in the refrigerator before turning it out onto a serving plate. This will allow time for the caramel to melt into a thick sauce.

Put the amaretti in a zip-top plastic bag, press out the air, and seal the bag. With a rolling pin, gently pound the amaretti to reduce them to fine powder.

In a large saucepan, bring the milk to a simmer over medium heat. Turn off the heat, add the powdered amaretti, stir, and let stand at room temperature until cool.

Preheat the oven to 325°F/165°C.

In a large bowl, combine the eggs and 1 cup plus 2 tablespoons/225 g of the sugar. Mix with a silicone spatula, pressing the mixture against the sides of the bowl. Don't be tempted to use a whisk, as it would incorporate too much air into the mixture, resulting in a bubbly pudding. The aim is a very smooth texture.

Pour the cooled milk mixture into the eggs in a thin stream, stirring constantly with the spatula, then add the rum and gently stir until smooth.

Set out a 9-by-5-by-3-inch/23 by 13 by 8 cm loaf pan. Put the remaining ½ cup/100 g sugar in a nonstick frying pan set over medium-low heat and heat until it becomes an amber caramel. Don't stir, but swirl the pan for more even cooking and watch closely to prevent the caramel from burning.

Pour the caramel into the loaf pan, tilting the pan to cover the bottom and sides, then wait for a few seconds, until the caramel sets.

Pour the milk and egg mixture into the pan, gently set the loaf pan inside a larger baking dish, and add enough cold water to the baking dish to come halfway up the sides of the loaf pan. Transfer to the oven and bake for 1½ hours, or until the bonet is set; the surface should no longer look moist, and it will still be a bit jiggly in the center.

Remove the baking pan from the oven, carefully lift the loaf pan from the water bath, and let the custard cool completely. Transfer the bonet to the refrigerator, cover, and refrigerate overnight.

To serve the bonet, gently shake the pan so that the liquid caramel will help release the pudding. Should the bonet appear to be sticking to the pan, run a knife around the edges of the pan. Invert a serving plate over the top of the loaf pan and turn the bonet out onto the serving dish, letting any excess caramel from the pan drip over the top of the bonet. Cut into slices to serve.

Any leftover bonet can be stored in the refrigerator for a couple of days.

NOTE: *While the bonet is baking, the crumbled amaretti will rise to the top of the pudding, forming a sort of crust. Once the pudding is turned out, the amaretti crust becomes the bottom, a trademark of a perfectly executed bonet.*

Zuppa inglese

PASTRY CREAM AND CHOCOLATE TRIFLE

SERVES 8

FOR THE PASTRY CREAM
4 cups/1 L whole milk
1 lemon
6 large/120 g egg
  yolks
1¼ cups/250 g
  granulated sugar
½ cup plus
  2 tablespoons/
  80 g cornstarch
3½ ounces/100 g dark
  chocolate (60 to
  70 percent cacao),
  finely chopped

1 cup/240 ml alkermes
  (see the sidebar
  on the following
  page) or cherry
  brandy or 2 cups/
  480 ml cold strong
  coffee
1 cup/240 ml water if
  using alkermes or
  brandy
10½ ounces/about
  36/300 g savoiardi
  (Italian ladyfingers)
1 tablespoon
  unsweetened cocoa
  powder
1 tablespoon shaved
  chocolate

Zuppa inglese literally means English soup, but it is a very traditional cucina povera sweet, especially in Tuscany and Emilia-Romagna. It can be found on the menus of classic trattorias, or served at home to end Sunday lunch on a sweet note. In my family, trifle is a favorite afternoon snack.

Created in sixteenth-century Renaissance courts as an homage to England's trifle, zuppa inglese slowly evolved into a peasant concoction. You can make zuppa inglese with Italian ladyfingers (savoiardi), or use day-old slices of sponge cake or digestive biscuits that are turning on the dry side. If you can, make zuppa inglese in a clear glass bowl or, even better, a festive trifle bowl. That way, you can see the colorful layers: yellow pastry cream, darker chocolate pastry cream, and, in between, the pinkish savoiardi dunked in alkermes, a crimson liqueur. Serve zuppa inglese in small bowls.

———

Make the pastry cream: Pour the milk into a medium saucepan. With a vegetable peeler, remove the zest from half of the lemon in wide strips, then tie the strips of zest together with kitchen twine and add to the milk. Bring the milk just to a simmer over medium heat; remove from the heat.

In a large saucepan, whisk the egg yolks with the sugar and cornstarch until smooth. Slowly pour the hot milk into the egg mixture in a thin stream, whisking constantly; add the lemon zest too.

Put the saucepan over medium-low heat and cook, whisking constantly. As soon as you spot the first bubbles and the mixture starts to thicken, remove it from the heat and divide it evenly between two heatproof bowls. Remove and discard the lemon zest.

Add the chopped dark chocolate to one bowl and whisk until smooth.

Assemble the zuppa inglese: Pour the alkermes (or cherry brandy) into a medium bowl and add the water (if you are using coffee, there is no need to dilute it).

Working with one at a time, dip one-quarter of the ladyfingers into the alkermes for a few seconds, just to moisten, and arrange in a single layer in the bottom of a medium serving bowl or a trifle bowl. Top with half of the chocolate pastry cream, spreading it gently over the ladyfingers. Dip another one-quarter of the ladyfingers into the alkermes and lay in a single layer on top of the chocolate cream, then spoon on half of the vanilla pastry cream and spread it gently over the cookies. Repeat the process with the remaining ladyfingers and chocolate and vanilla pastry creams.

Put the cocoa powder in a fine-mesh strainer and dust generously over the top of the zuppa inglese, then sprinkle with the shaved chocolate. Transfer to the refrigerator and refrigerate for at least a few hours before serving. (*The zuppa inglese can be made ahead and refrigerated for up to 2 days.*)

To serve, use a large spoon to scoop out individual servings.

ALKERMES

The key ingredient of a traditional zuppa inglese is alkermes. This bright crimson liqueur was once considered an elixir for long life and a pick-me-up for fragile women. It is still made today by the Santa Maria Novella Pharmacy in Florence, with the original recipe created in 1743, along with many other artisanal and refined liqueurs.

Alkermes is infused with spices, time and tradition, and a handful of dried insects—cochineals—which give it its characteristic color and also its name (*alquermes* means cochineals in Spanish). Open a bottle of alkermes and inhale: you will recognize cardamom, coriander seeds, mace, orange peel, star anise, and vanilla, and then a subtle aroma of rose. If you cannot find alkermes, you can substitute cherry brandy, which will approximate the flavor but lack the crimson color, or opt for coffee, which will produce a different result, more similar to tiramisu, but still delicious.

Biscotti con la frutta secca

NUT BISCOTTI

**MAKES ABOUT
30 BISCOTTI**

2 large/100 g eggs
1 cup/200 g
    granulated sugar
1 tablespoon honey
2 tablespoons/30 g
    unsalted butter,
    melted
2¼ cups/280 g
    all-purpose flour
1 teaspoon/5 g baking
    powder
Grated zest of
    ½ lemon
Grated zest of
    ½ orange
¼ teaspoon fine
    sea salt
1½ cups/7 ounces/
    200 g mixed nuts,
    such as hazelnuts,
    almonds, pistachios,
    and/or walnuts
1 large/20 g egg yolk

When a Tuscan meal comes to an end, the table is swiftly cleared and the vin santo appears, with tiny glasses and a plate of almond biscotti alongside. At our house, it's a simple way to finish an improvised dinner, because we always have a bottle of aged vin santo, the local dessert wine, and a jar of home-baked biscotti in the pantry. For those who prefer coffee, biscotti are a great accompaniment to espresso too.

Biscotti are baked first as a loaf, then sliced and baked a second time cut side down; biscotti means twice-baked. This double baking extends the cookies' life. Biscotti is a most versatile recipe: with one basic dough, you can make endless variations, choosing your favorite combination of pantry ingredients such as nuts, dried fruit, and/or spices. Bake the biscotti as gifts for the holidays; they can be made well in advance and stored in a jar for a couple of weeks.

—————

Preheat the oven to 475°F/250°C. Line a baking sheet with parchment paper.

In the bowl of a stand mixer fitted with the paddle attachment, combine the eggs, sugar, and honey and beat on medium-high speed until light and fluffy, about 2 minutes. Reduce the speed to low, add the butter, flour, baking powder, lemon and orange zests, and salt, and mix until a dough forms. Add the nuts and mix until incorporated.

With the help of a spatula or with wet hands, form the dough into two loaves on the prepared baking sheet, each about 12 inches/30 cm long and no wider than 2 inches/5 cm, leaving space between them. Whisk the egg yolk with a teaspoon of water, then brush it onto each dough loaf.

Reduce the oven temperature to 350°F/175°C and transfer the baking sheet to the oven. (The very high temperature at the start of baking will prevent the dough from expanding too much as it bakes.) Bake the loaves for about 25 minutes, until they are golden but still slightly soft to the touch.

Remove from the oven and let the loaves cool for about 5 minutes, then carefully transfer to a cutting board. With a very sharp knife, slice the loaves into biscotti about ¾ inch/2 cm thick.

(CONTINUED)

Arrange the biscotti on the baking sheet, cut side down, and bake for 13 to 15 minutes, until golden. Remove the biscotti from the oven and let cool completely on a wire rack.

The biscotti will keep for weeks stored in a cookie jar or tin.

VARIATIONS

If you want to make the original Tuscan cantucci, use only almonds. Opt for unblanched nuts, which will give the biscotti their authentic look.

If you like the idea of chocolate biscotti, add a tablespoon of cocoa powder to the dough, then swap ¾ cup/100 g hazelnuts and ⅔ cup/100 g chocolate chips for the mixed nuts. Or use ¾ cup/100 g pistachios and ⅔ cup/100 g roughly chopped white chocolate for elegant biscotti.

If you'd like a sweet, fruity version, substitute ⅓ cup/100 g chopped candied orange peel, dried apricots, or dried figs for half of the nuts.

Biancomangiare di latte di mandorla

SICILIAN ALMOND-MILK PUDDING

SERVES 6

1 organic lemon
¾ cup minus
   1 tablespoon/
   140 g granulated
   sugar
½ cup/65 g cornstarch
3 cups/720 ml
   unsweetened
   almond milk (see
   Note)
2 tablespoons shelled
   raw pistachios,
   finely chopped, for
   garnish

Biancomangiare, literally translated as white food, is a recipe with a long history. In the past it could include chicken breast along with sugar, ground almonds, rice, breadcrumbs, and spices such as ginger and cinnamon. Nowadays in Sicily, biancomangiare is a delicate almond-milk pudding, as wobbly as a panna cotta, flavored with orange blossom water, lemon peel, or rose water and thickened with cornstarch. Biancomangiare is a quick, straightforward dessert, and it's naturally gluten-free and vegan.

––––

With a vegetable peeler, remove the zest from the lemon in wide strips. Stack the strips and tie together with a piece of kitchen string.

In a large saucepan, combine the sugar and cornstarch, then whisk in ½ cup/120 ml of the almond milk until smooth. Whisk in the remaining almond milk and drop in the bundle of lemon zest. Bring to a simmer over medium-low heat, stirring constantly, and cook, stirring, until the mixture begins to thicken. When you spot the first bubbles, cook for 1 more minute, then remove from the heat.

Fish out the lemon zest and discard, then pour the pudding into six ½-cup/120 ml ramekins or soufflé molds, cover, and refrigerate overnight (or for up to 2 days).

Just before serving, invert the biancomangiare onto small saucers or serving plates; should the biancomangiare stick to the ramekins, run a knife around the edges of the ramekins or dip them in hot water for a few seconds to release them. Decorate with the chopped pistachios and serve.

NOTE: _Use homemade almond milk (see sidebar) if possible, since it will consist of just two ingredients: water and almonds, without sugar and/or additives. But in a pinch, whole cow's milk will do, although the flavor will be slightly different._

VARIATIONS

Serve the biancomangiare topped with seasonal fruit, or use it as a filling for a crostata (page 277), blind-baking the crust first.

   To decorate, sprinkle the top with cinnamon, the chopped pistachios or other nuts, or sliced almonds, or spoon a lemon syrup or fruit compote on top.

HOW TO MAKE ALMOND MILK

**MAKES ABOUT
4 CUPS/1 L**

1 cup/5 ounces/140 g
   raw unblanched
   almonds
5 cups/1.2 L water
Pinch of fine sea salt

You can easily make almond milk at home. If you're making it for the biancomangiare (opposite), don't sweeten it, but if you want to drink it, you can add some sugar or a date along with the soaked almonds. Play with spices too: cinnamon and vanilla are nice add-ins.

——

Put the almonds in a small bowl, cover with water, and soak overnight.

The next day, drain the almonds and peel them by gently squeezing each one between your fingers to pop it out of the skin.

Put the almonds in the jar of a blender (preferably a high-speed blender) and add the water and salt. Blend until creamy and smooth, 3 to 4 minutes.

Strain the milk through a nut milk bag or cheesecloth into a bowl, squeezing the bag until all the liquid is released. Discard the almond pulp, or save it to add to cookies or spreads.

Pour the almond milk into a glass bottle or jar. It will keep in the refrigerator for 4 to 5 days.

Gelo di mellone

SICILIAN WATERMELON PUDDING

SERVES 6

1 cup/240 ml water
1 cinnamon stick
2 pounds/1 kg
   watermelon flesh
   (from a 3½-pound/
   1.6 kg watermelon,
   if starting with a
   whole melon)
5 tablespoons/65 g
   granulated sugar
7 tablespoons/55 g
   cornstarch
2 tablespoons shelled
   raw pistachios,
   finely chopped
1 ounce/30 g
   semisweet
   chocolate, roughly
   chopped

Gelo di mellone smells of the Sicilian summer. *Gelo*, which means bitter cold, holds promises of refreshment and respite from summer's heat. The texture sits somewhere between that of a pudding and that of a fruit gelatin. Light and bright, this gelo is made with just a handful of ingredients, including watermelon, sugar, and cornstarch. The gelo needs to chill overnight, then you can serve it as a dolce al cucchiaio, a pudding to be eaten with a spoon, topped with pistachios and chocolate, or use it as a filling for tarts or pastries.

––––

Pour the water into a small saucepan, add the cinnamon stick, and bring to a simmer. Simmer for about 15 minutes, until the water is reduced to ¼ cup/60 ml. Discard the cinnamon stick and set the water aside.

If using a blender, cut the watermelon into wedges; remove and discard the seeds. Puree the watermelon in the blender, strain the puree through a sieve placed over a bowl, and discard the pulp. Or, if you have a juicer, cut the watermelon into chunks and juice it. You need about 3 cups/720 ml watermelon juice for the gelo; save any extra for another use.

In a medium saucepan, combine the sugar and cornstarch, stirring well, then stir in ½ cup/120 ml of the watermelon juice. Add the rest of the watermelon juice and the cinnamon water and bring to a simmer over medium-low heat, stirring constantly. When you spot the first bubbles, cook for 1 more minute, then remove from the heat.

Pour the mixture into six ½-cup/120 ml ramekins or glasses and smooth the surface. Cover and refrigerate overnight (or for up to 2 days).

Just before serving, garnish the puddings with the chopped pistachios and chocolate.

VARIATION

If you find yourself with a basket of lemons, make gelo di limone. Squeeze the juice of 4 lemons into 4 cups/1 L of water. Increase the sugar to 1¼ cups/250 g and the cornstarch to ½ cup plus 2 tablespoons/80 g. Follow the same procedure for making gelo di mellone, and decorate the puddings with chopped pistachios, thin lemon slices, or fresh mint leaves.

Frittelle di fiori di sambuco

ELDERFLOWER FRITTERS

SERVES 4

FOR THE BATTER

¼ cup/30 g all-purpose flour

1 tablespoon granulated sugar, plus more for sprinkling

Pinch of fine sea salt

7 tablespoons/105 ml water

¼ cup/60 ml beer, cold

12 clusters elderflowers

2 cups/480 ml vegetable or other neutral oil for frying

As soon as April arrives, the first white elderflowers appear, announcing the blooming of spring, the best time for foraging. The creamy white parasol-shaped clusters of tiny flowers, with a heady aroma, punctuate the countryside, especially along little streams and at the edges of cultivated fields or woods.

One of the most common uses of elderflowers is to steep them in hot water and sugar with some lemons to make a syrup or cordial. The cordial can be diluted with still or sparkling water for a refreshing summer drink, or with Prosecco and tonic water to make a Hugo, a spritz-like aperitivo from Alto Adige, in the North of Italy.

Elderflowers can also be battered and fried to make fritters, either sweet, like these, or savory. Or they can also be infused overnight in cream or milk to make gelato or panna cotta, or simply to enjoy as a seasonal custard with a heady unmistakable smell. When they are in season, try substituting elderflowers for the lemon zest in the pastry cream for zuppa inglese (page 287).

Use elderflowers as quickly as possible after picking them, before they start smelling like cat pee!

——

Make the batter: In a medium bowl, whisk together the flour, sugar, and salt, then slowly add the water, whisking constantly to prevent lumps. Whisk in the beer little by little until incorporated. Refrigerate the batter for about 30 minutes.

Shake the elderflowers to remove dust and unwanted insects. Do not wash them, or they will get soggy and it will be difficult to fry them, as the hot oil will spit everywhere.

Pour the vegetable oil into a large high-sided pot and heat until it registers 350°F/175°C on a deep-frying thermometer. If you don't have a thermometer, dip the handle of a wooden spoon into the oil: if tiny bubbles immediately surround it, the oil is ready. Line a plate with paper towels and set nearby.

Working in batches, dip a few of the elderflowers at a time into the beer batter, shake them to remove the excess batter, add to the hot oil, and fry, turning once, for 2 minutes per side, or until crisp and golden. With a spider or slotted spoon, remove the flowers from the oil, transfer to the prepared plate, and sprinkle with sugar. Fry the remaining elderflowers, letting the oil return to temperature between batches.

Enjoy the fritters while they are hot.

VARIATIONS

The same beer batter can also be used to fry robinia flowers and wisteria flowers, if you can get them. If you prefer savory fritters, skip the sugar in the ingredients and finish your fritters with a sprinkling of flaky sea salt; in that case, batter and fry some sage leaves too. The savory fritters make for a quick and tasty starter.

COFFEE, BARLEY COFFEE, AND CHICORY COFFEE

In Italy, coffee is as much of an institution as pasta is. Nothing beats the experience of standing at the counter in a busy café in the morning while the barista masterfully juggles the shouted orders of espresso, macchiato, cappuccino, caffè ristretto, and caffè lungo. Even at home, there are sacred rituals related to brewing coffee: some swear by the old, reliable Moka pot; others prefer an espresso, made just like at the local café; and then there are those who insist on a more modern approach, with a filtered coffee. But coffee wasn't always ubiquitous.

Over the centuries, during times of scarcity, especially in the Italian countryside, coffee was substituted with beverages brewed from beans and chickpeas, chestnuts and acorns, rye, barley, chicory, malt, or dried figs—which were used mainly for their naturally sweet taste. Although most of these beverages disappeared as soon as difficult times were over, some of them are still appreciated today.

Barley coffee is still the most common coffee substitute in Italy, thanks partly to its low cost, but above all to its pleasing taste. At a café in the morning, it is common to hear someone asking for *orzo in tazza grande*, barley coffee served in a large cup, often with an orange peel. You can even order cappuccino d'orzo, where barley coffee replaces espresso in the quintessentially Italian morning drink made with coffee and foamy milk. In my family, caffè d'orzo is consumed every evening after dinner: my mom prefers instant barley coffee, quickly stirred into a cup of steaming-hot water, while I brew it in a Moka pot. It is often the first coffee-like beverage children experience too, with a little of it diluted in their mugs of milk in the morning.

Caffè di cicoria, chicory coffee, is made with toasted and ground dried chicory root. It has a long history, dating back to the nineteenth century. When coffee was not readily available, farmers would brew this hot, slightly bitter beverage to enjoy on their breaks. In Italy, caffè di cicoria became popular between the two World Wars, when resources were scarce.

Although it was born out of adversity, chicory coffee is now widely sold in organic and herbalist shops as a caffeine-free substitute for coffee, associated with several health benefits, such as improving digestive health, lowering blood sugar, and decreasing inflammation. During winter, it is comforting to brew a steaming cup of chicory coffee after dinner: it tastes similar to coffee, without the caffeine and with pleasant woody, nutty notes. A teaspoon of honey tames the bitter chicory taste, making it the perfect drink to enjoy before bed.

BASICS

BREADS, STOCKS, AND SAUCE

Pane sciocco toscano
Tuscan Bread   302

Pane di grano duro
Semolina Bread   303

Brodo di carne
Beef Stock   305

Brodo di pollo
Chicken Stock   306

Brodo vegetale
Vegetable Stock   307

Sugo di pomodoro all'aglio
Garlicky Tomato Sauce   308

Pane sciocco toscano

TUSCAN BREAD

Traditional Tuscan bread is famous for its lack of salt. Legend says that Florentine people started baking their bread without salt in order to avoid paying the high tax that the government in Pisa had placed on it. The real reason, though, probably lies in the intensely savory well-cured prosciutto and aged pecorino toscano that were often served as companions to the bread. The other striking characteristic of Tuscan bread is its longevity. Because it is made without salt, it doesn't get moldy when stale; it simply dries out. That's why Tuscan cuisine is teeming with recipes to upcycle stale bread, such as pappa al pomodoro (page 239) and panzanella (page 250).

Pane sciocco is made with a biga, a pre-fermented starter dough that includes just flour, water, yeast, plus a pinch of sugar to help activate the yeast. You make it the day before and then knead it into the bread dough the following day. It gives strength to weak flours and, thanks to the secondary fermentation, lends a fragrant aroma to the loaf and a unique porosity to the bread's crumb, which is honeycombed with irregular holes.

To enjoy pane sciocco like a Tuscan, eat it with sharp cheese and prosciutto, with a selection of sottoli, vegetables preserved in oil, like giardiniera; or toasted, rubbed with garlic, and finished with a drizzle of intense extra-virgin olive oil and a sprinkle of salt; or, for an afternoon snack, with jam.

MAKES 1 LOAF

FOR THE BIGA

⅛ teaspoon active
　dry yeast
⅓ cup/80 ml room-
　temperature water
1 teaspoon granulated
　sugar
1 cup plus
　2 tablespoons/
　150 g bread flour
Extra-virgin olive oil for
　greasing the bowls

FOR THE BREAD DOUGH

4 cups/500 g all-
　purpose flour
1¼ cups/300 ml
　lukewarm water

The night before you want to bake the bread, make the biga: In a medium bowl, stir together the yeast, 2 tablespoons of the water, and the sugar and let stand until creamy and frothy, about 10 minutes.

Add the bread flour and the remaining water to the yeast mixture and stir until roughly combined. Turn out onto a work surface and knead the dough into a ball; it will be sticky and rough.

Transfer the biga to a lightly oiled large bowl and cover with plastic wrap. Let rise at room temperature overnight (8 to 12 hours).

The next day, make the bread: The biga should be doubled in size and have numerous bubbles. Tear it into bite-size pieces, returning the pieces to the bowl. Add the all-purpose flour and water and knead, squeezing the dough between your fingers, until you have incorporated all the flour and a rough ball of dough has formed.

Alternatively, knead the dough in a stand mixer fitted with the dough hook for about 5 minutes on low speed, then turn out and finish kneading by hand for about 5 minutes. Shape the dough into a ball.

Transfer to a lightly greased bowl and cover with plastic wrap. Let rest for about 20 minutes at room temperature.

With wet hands, pick up one edge of the dough, stretch it gently upward, and fold it over itself. Give the bowl a quarter turn and repeat. Continue until you have come full circle to complete four "folds" around the bowl. Let rest for 20 minutes, then repeat the stretch-and-fold technique 3 more times, letting the dough rest for 20 minutes each time. The dough should be soft, elastic, and velvety.

Turn the dough out onto a lightly floured surface. Flatten it gently with your hands and shape it into a fat round disk. Fold the upper third of the disk over the middle third and press to seal the seam, then stretch the right and then the left sides of the disk over into the center. Roll the dough toward you over the bottom third of the disk so the edges meet and press to seal again.

Turn the loaf seam side up with a long side facing you. Fold the upper third of the dough over the middle third and press to seal the seam, fold over the left and right sides of the dough, and then pull the dough toward you over the bottom third of the loaf and press to seal again. Then pull the loaf toward you, allowing the surface tension between the work surface and the dough to tighten it into a firm, tight loaf.

Transfer the dough seam side down to a 5½-by-10-inch/ 14 by 25 cm oval bread basket lined with a well-floured tea towel. Wrap it loosely in the tea towel and let rest at room temperature, away from drafts, until doubled in size, about 2 hours.

While the dough rises, position a rack in the lower third of the oven and preheat the oven to 475°F/250°C. If you have a baking stone, place it in the oven while it preheats. If you don't have a stone, line a rimmed baking sheet with parchment paper.

Gently turn out the loaf onto the baking stone or prepared pan. Bake for 20 minutes, then lower the oven temperature to 400°F/200°C and bake for 30 to 40 more minutes, until the loaf is golden and sounds hollow when tapped on the bottom.

Turn off the oven and leave the bread in the oven for 10 minutes, then transfer to a wire rack and let cool completely before slicing.

Pane di grano duro

SEMOLINA BREAD

In the South of Italy, the most common bread has a thick, crunchy dark crust and a dense, aromatic yellow crumb. It is made with semolina flour and lievito madre, or sourdough starter, and baked in large loaves in enormous communal wood-burning ovens (for this simpler version, I use a biga rather than a sourdough starter). Semolina bread has always been a source of pride and identity in Southern Italy and, in times of famine, an invaluable resource.

Semolina bread is the perfect choice for mozzarella in carrozza (page 147), bread-and-cheese-stuffed eggplant (page 46), and pancotto (page 249). Or rub slices with halved ripe tomatoes for an afternoon snack, or use it to mop up the juices of a tomato and mozzarella caprese salad.

MAKES 1 LOAF

FOR THE BIGA	FOR THE BREAD DOUGH
⅛ teaspoon active dry yeast	1⅔ cups/300 g semolina flour (see Note)
⅓ cup/80 ml room-temperature water	1½ cups/360 ml lukewarm water
1 teaspoon granulated sugar	1½ cups/200 g bread flour
1 cup plus 2 tablespoons/ 150 g bread flour	1 tablespoon plus 1 teaspoon/20 g fine sea salt
Extra-virgin olive oil for greasing the bowls	

The night before you want to bake the bread, make the biga: In a medium bowl, stir together the yeast, 2 tablespoons of the water, and the sugar and let stand for about 10 minutes, until creamy and frothy.

Add the bread flour and the remaining water to the yeast mixture, stir well, and knead the dough into a ball; it will be sticky and rough.

Transfer the biga to a lightly oiled large bowl and cover with plastic wrap. Let rise at room temperature overnight (8 to 12 hours).

The next day, make the bread: Early in the day, put the semolina flour in a bowl, drizzle with 1 cup/240 ml of the water, and quickly mix to start hydrating the flour. Set aside to rest for 1 hour.

The biga should be doubled in size and have numerous bubbles. Tear it into bite-size pieces and add it into the bowl with the semolina flour. Add the bread flour and ⅓ cup/80 ml of the remaining water and knead, squeezing the dough between your fingers, until you have incorporated all the flour.

Add the salt and the remaining 3 tablespoons water and knead to incorporate, then transfer to a wooden board and keep kneading, pushing, and stretching the dough for at least 10 minutes, until it is elastic, slightly moist, and smooth.

Alternatively, make the dough in a stand mixer fitted with the dough hook: Knead it for about 5 minutes on low speed, then turn it out and finish kneading by hand for about 5 minutes.

Shape the dough into a ball, transfer to a lightly greased bowl, and cover with plastic wrap. Let rest at room temperature for 1 hour.

Stretching and folding the dough will improve the quality of the bread: With wet hands, pick up one edge of the dough, stretch it gently upward, and fold it over itself. Give the bowl a quarter turn and repeat. Continue until you have come full circle to complete

four "folds" around the bowl. Let the dough rest for another hour and repeat the stretch-and-fold technique, then let rest for another hour, or until doubled in size.

When the bread has doubled in size, turn it out onto a lightly floured surface. Flatten it gently with your hands and shape it into a fat round disk. Fold the upper third of the disk over the middle third and press to seal the seam, then stretch the right and then the left sides of the disk over into the center. Roll the dough toward you over the bottom third of the disk so the edges meet and press to seal again.

Turn the loaf seam side up with a long side facing you. Fold the upper third of the dough over the middle third and press to seal the seam, tuck in the left and right sides of the dough, and then pull the dough toward you over the bottom third of the loaf and press to seal again. Then pull the loaf toward you, allowing the surface tension between the work surface and the dough to tighten into a firm, tight loaf.

Transfer the loaf seam side up to a 5½-by-10-inch/14 by 25 cm oval bread basket lined with a well-floured tea towel. Wrap it loosely in the tea towel and let rest at room temperature, away from drafts, until doubled in size, about 2 hours.

Position a rack in the lower third of the oven and preheat the oven to 475°F/250°C. If you have a baking stone, place it in the oven as it preheats. If you don't have a stone, line a rimmed baking sheet with parchment paper.

Gently turn out the loaf onto the baking stone or prepared baking sheet. For an open and better-structured bread, using a lame or another very sharp blade, score the loaf with a single, smooth cut.

Bake the bread for 10 minutes, then lower the oven temperature to 450°F/230°C and bake for 10 more minutes. Lower the temperature to 400°F/200°C and bake for 30 more minutes, or until the loaf is golden brown and sounds hollow when tapped on the bottom.

Turn off the oven and leave the bread in the oven for 10 minutes. Then transfer to a wire rack to cool completely before slicing.

NOTE: *It is trickier to knead a dough made with semolina flour rather than regular wheat flour. So combine the flour and water for the dough an hour before adding the pre-fermented biga and kneading the bread. This helps fully hydrate the flour, making it more manageable and easier to knead and shape.*

Brodo di carne

BEEF STOCK

Brodo is homemade stock; lesso is the meat resulting from making the stock, which is usually quite stringy. The best beef cuts for making homemade stock and lesso are flank steak, chuck, and brisket. Another budget-friendly cut is beef cheek, which also requires a long cooking time. If you want to make bollito, a feast of juicy, tender mixed boiled meats, served with traditional sauces and vegetables, choose pricier lean cuts of beef; see the sidebar.

When boiling meat, you usually have a choice to make: either a flavorful stock or a tender piece of meat. To make a good-quality stock, start the meat in cold water, so that the beef will release all its flavor into the liquid, making it rich and sapid. If what you want is juicy, tasty boiled beef for bollito, plunge the meat into boiling water. The resulting stock will be quite bland and lacking flavor, but the beef will be tastier.

If you don't want to have to choose between flavorful meat and good stock, there's a trick: make the stock starting with a smaller piece of meat. It could even be a bone, like a beef knee. Add this, along with the carrot, celery, tomatoes, fresh herbs, and onion, to a pot of cold water. Turn on the heat and then, when the water is boiling, plunge in your chosen cut of beef, reduce the heat to a simmer, and gently cook the meat for at least 2 hours. Eat it on its own or use it to make francesina (page 261) or mondeghili (page 257).

**MAKES 2½ QUARTS/ 2.4 L STOCK,
WITH ENOUGH BOILED MEAT TO SERVE 4 TO 6**

- 4 quarts/4 L water
- 1 carrot, peeled and cut into thirds
- 1 celery stalk, halved crosswise
- 2 whole cloves
- 1 yellow onion, halved
- 2 cherry tomatoes
- 1 fresh parsley sprig
- 1 fresh basil leaf
- 1 beef knee bone or shank
- 2 pounds/1 kg boneless chuck steak, flank steak, or brisket
- 1 tablespoon coarse sea salt, or more to taste

Fill a large pot with the water. Add the carrot and celery, then stick the cloves into the onion and add that too, along with the cherry tomatoes, parsley, and basil. Add the knee bone and bring the water to a boil over medium-high heat.

Add the beef and salt, then reduce the heat so the liquid is simmering gently and simmer for 2 hours, or until the meat is fork-tender and the stock is flavorful.

With tongs, remove the knee bone and meat from the pot; transfer the meat to a platter and discard the bone. Strain the stock through a fine-mesh sieve into a large bowl and season to taste with additional salt if necessary. If using the stock immediately, let stand for 10 minutes, then skim off the fat that has risen to the surface and discard. If not, let the stock cool to room temperature, then refrigerate. Once cold, the fat will harden on the surface and be easy to skim off and discard.

Use the boiled meat immediately, or store in the refrigerator submerged in the stock to keep it moist.

If you want to freeze the stock, ladle it into zip-top freezer bags, press out the air from the bags, seal, and lay flat on a rimmed baking sheet. Transfer to the freezer and freeze until solid, then stack the bags in the freezer and store for up to 3 months.

BOLLITO MISTO

Bollito misto is a convivial meal, a feast of mixed boiled meats, something that you would make for a holiday or a big gathering. The selection of meats included in bollito misto varies from region to region, but the extravagant gran bollito from Piedmont deserves special mention. It is made with seven high-quality beef cuts, including flank steak, chuck steak, brisket, and round, and seven ammennicoli, meaning less noble cuts, such as veal tongue, oxtail, testina, calf's head, pig's trotter, cotechino, hen or capon, and pork loin, and it is served with seven sauces, including salsa verde (see page 60).

Brodo di pollo

CHICKEN STOCK

Good chicken stock is a kitchen staple, of course, but it's also a cure-all elixir. Make chicken stock to use in stracciatella in brodo (page 94), to gently simmer some passatelli (page 159) or tortellini, to give body to a risotto, or to make a Fontina and Savoy cabbage casserole (page 162). The cooked chicken left from the stock makes a tasty chicken salad (page 97).

In the past in the countryside, when meat consumption was minimal, a chicken would usually be slaughtered and boiled to make a stock for one of two reasons: there was a severely ill person in the house who needed the fortification or there was a chicken whose time had come. The arrival of a newborn in the family would be another excellent excuse to butcher a chicken, as a mug of chicken stock, or even squab stock, was considered the perfect nourishing food for a woman who had just given birth. When famine and poverty were not so relentless, homemade tagliolini in chicken broth was a typical Sunday lunch.

MAKES 2½ QUARTS/2.4 L

16 cups/4 L water
2 carrots, peeled and cut into thirds
1 celery stalk, cut in half
1 yellow onion, halved
1 fresh parsley sprig
1 fresh thyme sprig

1 chicken (2½ to 3 pounds/1.1 to 1.4 kg), split in half (you could ask the butcher to do this)
1 tablespoon coarse sea salt, or more to taste

Fill a large pot with the water. Add the carrots, celery, onion, parsley, and thyme and bring the water to a boil over medium-high heat. Add the chicken and salt, reduce the heat to low, and simmer for 2 hours. With tongs, transfer the chicken to a large plate or rimmed baking sheet to cool. Set the stock aside.

When the chicken is cool enough to handle, remove the meat from the bones and discard the skin and bones; you should have about 1 pound/455 g of meat.

Strain the stock through a fine-mesh sieve into a large bowl and season to taste with additional salt if necessary. If using the stock immediately, let stand for

10 minutes, then skim off the fat that has risen to the surface and discard. If you are not using the stock right away, let cool to room temperature, then refrigerate. Once cold, the fat will harden on the surface and be easy to remove and discard.

If you want to freeze the stock, ladle it into zip-top freezer bags, press out the air from the bags, seal, and lay flat on a rimmed baking sheet. Transfer to the freezer and freeze until solid, then stack the bags in the freezer and store for up to 3 months.

If you are not eating the chicken meat immediately, store it in the fridge in a small container with some of the stock to keep it tender and juicy.

Brodo vegetale

VEGETABLE STOCK

A good homemade stock is often the secret ingredient of a standout dish. And if it is true for beef stock (page 305) and chicken stock (opposite), it is the same for vegetable stock.

Make the stock from scratch using fresh vegetables—carrots, celery, onion, and the like—or channel cucina povera resourcefulness and make a zero-waste stock with vegetable scraps: collect spinach and chard stalks; the outer leaves of cabbage; the harder parts of broccoli stalks; trimmed ends from green beans and zucchini; carrot, tomato, potato, and onion peels; the green parts of leeks and spring onions; celery leaves; the outer layers of fennel; and any wilted herbs like parsley, basil, or thyme. Avoid asparagus and artichokes, as they will make a bitter stock. Make sure the vegetables are rinsed thoroughly and dried before you prepare them for another dish, then freeze all the scraps in a zip-top freezer storage bag. When you have about 2 pounds/1 kg scraps, turn them into this flavorful stock (the frozen scraps can be added right to the pot), perfect for a light meal on its own or used to make risotto or a soup.

The key here is to add a piece of Parmigiano-Reggiano rind: as it slowly simmers with the vegetable scraps, it releases its salty, umami flavor into the stock. When your stock is done, don't discard the rind: cube it and add it to a soup, or eat it as a snack.

MAKES 10½ CUPS/2.5 L

6 quarts/6 L water
About 2 pounds/1 kg
   mixed vegetable
   scraps (see headnote)

A 2-ounce/60 g
   Parmigiano-Reggiano
   rind
1 tablespoon coarse sea
   salt, or more to taste

Pour the water into a large pot. Add the vegetable scraps and Parmigiano-Reggiano rind, bring to a boil over medium-high heat, and add the salt. Reduce the heat to low and simmer for 3 hours, or until the stock has reduced by half.

Strain the stock through a fine-mesh sieve into a large bowl and season to taste with additional salt if necessary. If you don't plan to use the stock right away, let cool to room temperature, then refrigerate for up to 4 days.

If you want to freeze the stock, ladle it into zip-top freezer bags, press out the air from the bags, seal, and lay flat on a rimmed baking sheet. Place in the freezer and freeze until solid, then stack the bags in the freezer and store for up to 6 months.

NOTE: *If you want to make a vegan vegetable stock, skip the Parmigiano-Reggiano rind and add a handful of dried mushrooms—porcini or shiitake would do.*

Sugo di pomodoro all'aglio

GARLICKY TOMATO SAUCE

Discussing tomato sauce ingredients with any Italian will give you a good indication of where they are from. In Northern Italy, tomato sauce includes butter; from Tuscany down to Sicily, it's olive oil. Marcella Hazan's signature tomato sauce requires a good knob of butter and a white onion; the sauce of another Marcella, my grandmother, calls for extra-virgin olive oil and a crushed garlic clove. The two recipes share the same basic ingredients list—tomato, some kind of fat, and aromatics—and the same emphasis on quality, but with completely different results tastewise.

It's so simple to make tomato sauce from scratch. This garlicky, bright red sauce can be used immediately or preserved and stored in the pantry (or just frozen) to enjoy in the winter months with fresh orecchiette (page 35), gnocchi alla sorrentina (page 225), or ricotta gnudi (page 151). Feel free to scale down the recipe to make just a small batch, or to scale it up so you will have enough tomato sauce to sustain you until the next summer. There are certain shortcuts you can take too. Start with peeled fresh tomatoes, or with tomato puree, to make a quicker sauce on the spur of the moment (see the sidebar).

**MAKES 3 CUPS/720 ML,
ENOUGH FOR THREE ½-PINT/240 ML JARS**

5½ pounds/2.5 kg ripe
   tomatoes
1 teaspoon fine sea salt,
   plus more to taste
⅓ cup/80 ml extra-virgin
   olive oil

4 cloves garlic, crushed
   and peeled
A small handful of fresh
   basil leaves

Bring a large pot of water to a boil. Prepare a large bowl of ice water and set it in the sink.

Rinse the tomatoes and, with the tip of a knife, cut an X in the base of each tomato. Working in batches, plunge the tomatoes into the boiling water and blanch just until the skin begins to peel away at the cut, about 30 seconds. Remove them from the pot and immediately plunge them into the bowl of ice water to stop the cooking. Drain the tomatoes again and peel them, discarding the skins.

Gently squeeze each tomato to remove most of the juices and the seeds, then transfer them to a colander set over a bowl. Sprinkle the tomatoes with the salt and let them drain for about 1 hour to release excess liquid.

Squeeze the tomatoes one last time, then pass them through a food mill into a bowl. Alternatively, blend the tomatoes with an immersion blender until smooth.

In a large saucepan, heat the olive oil over medium-low heat, then add the garlic. Cook, stirring, until the garlic is golden and fragrant, about 2 minutes. Pour in the tomato puree and simmer for about 20 minutes, until the sauce is thick, bright red, and glossy. Add the basil, then taste and add salt as necessary. You can use the sauce immediately to dress a bowl of pasta, or preserve it for winter.

If you want to preserve the sauce, pour the hot tomato sauce into three sterilized ½-pint/240 ml jars and add a couple of basil leaves to each jar. Tightly seal each jar. Place the jars in a large pot and add water to cover the jars by a few inches. Bring the water to a boil; once the water is boiling, set a timer for 20 minutes.

After 20 minutes, turn off the heat and let the jars cool in the water before removing. The jarred sauce will keep in a cool, dark place for 1 year. Once you open a jar, use what you need and refrigerate any extra sauce for up to a week.

Alternatively, you can freeze the sauce: Let the sauce cool, then ladle it into zip-top freezer bags. Press out the air from each bag, seal, and lay on a rimmed baking sheet. Transfer to the freezer and freeze until solid, then stack in the freezer and store for up to 3 months.

NOTE: *The tomato sauce yield depends on the ripeness of the tomatoes and on the weather. Dry summers make for tomatoes that are less watery, with firmer pulp, while a rainy season would require a longer drain time to get rid of all the tomato juices.*

A QUICK TOMATO SAUCE MADE WITH PASSATA

If you are in a hurry, or fresh tomatoes are out of season, you can quickly put together this easy, aromatic tomato sauce using passata, tomato puree.

MAKES 4 CUPS/1 L

⅓ cup/80 ml extra-virgin olive oil
½ yellow onion, thinly sliced
1 clove garlic, finely chopped
Fine sea salt

4 cups/1 L tomato puree (passata)
A handful of fresh basil leaves, torn
Freshly ground black pepper

———

In a medium saucepan, heat the olive oil over medium heat. Add the onion, garlic, and a pinch of salt and cook, stirring, until the onion is soft and translucent, 5 minutes.

Pour in the tomato puree, reduce the heat to medium-low, and cook, stirring occasionally, for 25 to 30 minutes, until the sauce is thick and glossy. Add the basil and season to taste with additional salt and with pepper.

Use immediately to dress your favorite pasta, or let cool and store in the fridge, covered, for up to 3 days. This sauce can also be preserved or frozen for longer storage as in the recipe for Garlicky Tomato Sauce (opposite).

THE MANY WAYS TO PRESERVE TOMATOES

It is impossible to imagine a life without tomatoes, even though they only became part of Italian cuisine during the nineteenth century. There are different types of canned tomatoes found in any Italian pantry, occupying significant space on our shelves. Here is a guide to the preserved tomatoes that play a key role in everyday Italian cooking.

Pomodori pelati: This is probably the easiest way to preserve tomatoes. Blanch them for just a couple of minutes to make it easier to remove the skins, then peel them, halve them, and let drain before preserving them in sterilized jars with a couple of basil leaves. Crush them with your hands before using them to add body to a meat sauce, as in vincisgrassi (page 104); to make the Tuscan pappa al pomodoro; or to stew chicken, as in pollo alla cacciatora (page 98). Tomatoes preserved this way are the most versatile.

Passata: Once you have drained peeled tomatoes, you can puree them to make passata, a raw tomato puree that can be preserved in jars or bottles, a pantry shortcut to a hundred different recipes. Use passata to make a tomato sauce with your favorite herbs and aromatics (page 309); to cook a meat stew, as in frittata trippata (page 101); or to top homemade pizza.

Sugo di pomodoro: Keep a jar of tomato sauce, homemade or store-bought, in your pantry, and you'll know you can serve dinner in 15 minutes, the time it takes to boil a pot of spaghetti. It is also the starting point for more complex and deeply flavored sauces, such as sugo di vongole, with clams; sugo alla Norma, with fried eggplant and grated ricotta salata; sugo alla puttanesca, with anchovy fillets and olives; or sugo al tonno, with canned tuna.

Pomarola: For pomarola, raw tomatoes are cooked with the basic Italian aromatics: carrots, celery, and onion. Once all the vegetables are soft, they are passed through a food mill, resulting in a deep red sauce. This technique ensures a layering of flavors and a more complex sauce that should be paired only with pasta: don't use pomarola for stewing meat or, God forbid, on pizza. A jar of pomarola, a knob of butter to round out its taste, and a good amount of grated Parmigiano-Reggiano over pasta makes one of the best meals.

Concentrato di pomodoro: Tomato paste provides the umami kick in many traditional Italian dishes, from ribollita (page 195) to robust meat ragùs. It is also the trickiest preserve to make: a thick tomato sauce seasoned with a generous amount of salt is first reduced on the stove, and then, traditionally, spread onto large tables and left to dry under the scorching Mediterranean sun. Then the concentrato is scraped into jars to store for winter. In climates that are not as hot and dry as an Italian summer, you can dry the tomato paste in the oven at a low temperature.

Pomodori secchi: These sun-dried tomatoes have their taste concentrated by the hot Italian summer sun and a good sprinkle of salt. All of the moisture is leached from the tomatoes, leaving chewy, meaty tomato halves that can be stored in the pantry for months. A dehydrator or an oven set at a low temperature can work the same magic, albeit in a less poetic way. These dried tomatoes can be preserved in olive oil and served as a starter, chopped into a salad, or blended into a Sicilian pesto with almonds and basil.

Confettura: Made with either tart green tomatoes or ripe red ones, this tomato jam is a more modern, yet brilliant way to preserve tomatoes with the help of a good amount of sugar. I am partial to a spicy red tomato jam made with chili pepper and cumin.

ACKNOWLEDGMENTS

I love food for its force of attraction, and thanks to food, I have met some of the most significant people in my life. My husband, Tommaso, and I want to say *grazie*, a big heartfelt thank-you, to all our family and friends, and everyone who helped us bring this book to reality.

As the saying goes, it takes a village, and this is the village that actually helped us not only make a book but also raise a child. Our daughter, Livia, was born a couple of months after we started working on the book, right at the beginning of the recipe testing process, and we weaned her with fave e cicorie and gnocchi alla sorrentina.

To my friends Emanuela Regi, Gaia Innocenti, Simonetta Masangui, and Simona Quirini, who encouraged the making of this book in many precious ways, from brainstorming their favorite cucina povera recipes to shaping orecchiette on a hot August day, from scaling kilos of sardines to happily eating all the food with their families afterward.

To Luciano, Nieri, and Stefania Capocasa, my favorite butchers and friends, who unveiled all their secrets, from which is the best cut to make stracotto to how to roast tender, juicy pork liver skewers.

To Andrea Ghini and Jessica Inzirillo, our trustworthy fruit and vegetable vendors at the local market, who found the best, ripest produce, including a lush bunch of cime di rapa when the season was already over.

To Giulia Scappaticcio and Francesca Belfiglio, who helped me with the recipes from Abruzzo. Now my pallotte cacio e ova dance in hot oil, just like yours!

To Beppe Piovano, Franca Chiesa, and Francesca Miccoli from Azienda Agricola Agrimani—I've learned to make a mean bagna caoda following your advice.

To Giovanna and Giovanni Porcu from the dairy farm Podere Paugnano in Radicondoli, who taught me how to make culurgiones, and who make the best Tuscan pecorino in the world.

To Vea Carpi, a cook and a mountain farmer, for not only her knowledge about recipes from Trentino but also her support in the quest to make the best passatelli.

To Enrica Monzani, a friend, a brilliant cooking teacher in Genoa, and my go-to source for any Ligurian recipe, I owe you the crispest crust in my torta pasqualina.

To Manuela Conti, my bread guru and the reason why the cassoeula in this book might be one of the most comforting dishes you have ever eaten.

To Claudia Renzi, for your knowledge of foraging.

To Valeria and Arduina Grasselli; you first made us fall in love with erbazzone, then helped us perfect the recipe. Now I know that lardo is never enough.

To Lorenzo Colloreta, our Adobe Lightroom guru, and Andrea Palei, a brilliant photographer, who gave us advice, tips, and food for thought.

To Regula Ysewijn, who's been our greatest supporter since we first met through our blogs, thank you for your smart advice, and for being always right by our side.

To Šárka Babická, who flew twice across Europe to spend some time with us. Our days together are always brimming with food, photography, laughter, chats, and yet more food. Our friendship is precious.

To our editor, Judy Pray, who chose us for this project, turned the first draft of the manuscript into an organic collection of stories and recipes, and helped me find my voice, and to the Artisan Books team for believing in this project.

To Jessica Battilana, who tested all our Italian recipes in her American kitchen, making sure they would work with different ingredients, pans, and measurements—even without a scale!

To our families, both those who are here and those who are gone, who encouraged us throughout the making of this book with time, support, babysitting, dishwashing, and love, so much love.

INDEX

Note: Page numbers in *italics* refer to illustrations.

Agnello cacio e ova, 80, *81*
alkermes (note), 288
Almond Milk, 293
Amaretti Pudding, 283–84, *285*
anchovies:
    Anchovy and Garlic Dip, 116–18, *117*
    Bread-and-Anchovy–Stuffed Sweet Green Peppers, 48–49, *49*
    note, 118
    Pasta with Anchovy, Onion, and Black Pepper Sauce, 124, *125*
    Tuna and Bean Salad, 172–73, *173*
Apple Olive Oil Cake, 268–69, *269*
Apple Syrup, 268–69
Arancine, 242–45, *244*
aromatic bouquet (note), *93*
artichokes:
    Artichoke, Fava Bean, Pea, and Lettuce Stew, 50–53, *51*
    how to clean, *53*
    Jerusalem: Anchovy and Garlic Dip, 116–18, *117*

Baccalà al forno con le patate, *136*, 137
Bagna caoda, 116–18, *117*
barley: Savoy Cabbage and Barley Soup, 206, *207*
barley coffee, 298
basics, 300–312
    beef stock, 305
    chicken stock, 306
    Garlicky Tomato Sauce, 308
    Semolina Bread, 303–4, *304*
    Tuscan Bread, 302–3, *302*
    Vegetable Stock, 307
beans, 168–71
    Artichoke, Fava Bean, Pea, and Lettuce Stew, 50–53, *51*

Bean and Lacinato Kale Soup, 195–96, *197*
Fava Bean Puree with Chicory, 181–82, *183*
how to cook, 174–75
Kale and Borlotti Polenta, 198–99, *199*
Pasta and Bean Soup, *184*, 185
Pork Braised in White Wine, 76, *77*
Tuna and Bean Salad, 172–73, *173*
Vegetable Soup, 24–25
beef:
    Beef Stew with Onions and Tomatoes, *260*, 261
    Beef Stock, 305
    Florentine Beef Stew, 70, *71*
    Fried Beef and Mortadella Meatballs, 257–58, *259*
    Roman Fried Rice Balls, 236–38, *237*
    Sicilian Fried Rice Balls, 242–45, *244*
Beet Tortelli with Poppy Seed Sauce, 214–17, *215*
Besciamella, 105
Biancomangiare di latte di mandorla, 292–93, *293*
Bigoli in salsa, 124, *125*
Biscotti con la frutta secca, 289–90, *291*
bollito misto (note), 305
bone marrow (note), 63
Bonet bianco alla monferrina, 283–84, *285*
Brandacujun, 122–23, *123*
bread, 17
    Bitter Greens and Semolina Bread Soup, 248, *249*
    Bread-and-Anchovy-Stuffed Sweet Green Peppers, 48–49, *49*
    Bread-and-Cheese-Stuffed Eggplant, 46–47, *47*
    Bread Dumplings, 252, *253*
    Bread Pudding Cake, 270–71, *271*
    croutons, 24
    Flatbread with Tomato Sauce and Poached Eggs, 102, *103*

Fontina and Savoy Cabbage Bread Casserole, 162–63, *163*
Semolina Bread, 303–4, *304*
Spinach Bread Dumplings with Butter and Sage Sauce, *254*, 255–56
Tomato and Bread Salad, 250, *251*
Tomato and Bread Soup, 239–41, *240*
Tuscan Bread, 302–3, *302*
broccoli rabe:
    Bitter Greens and Semolina Bread Soup, 248, *249*
    Broccoli Rabe Dressing, 35–36
    Orecchiette with Broccoli Rabe, *34*, 35–36, *37*
Brodetto marchigiano, 131–33, *132*
Brodo di carne, 305
Brodo di pollo, 306
Brodo vegetale, 307
Buckwheat Pasta with Cabbage and Cheese, *156*, 157–58
Butter and Sage Sauce, *254*, 255–56
butter or lard? (note), 282

cabbage:
    Bean and Lacinato Kale Soup, 195–96, *197*
    Buckwheat Pasta with Cabbage and Cheese, *156*, 157–58
    Fontina and Savoy Cabbage Bread Casserole, 162–63, *163*
    Pork Stew with Savoy Cabbage, 74–75, *75*
    Savoy Cabbage and Barley Soup, 206, *207*
    Vegetable Soup, 24–25
cakes:
    Apple Olive Oil Cake, 268–69, *269*
    Bread Pudding Cake, 270–71, *271*
    Chestnut Flour Cake, 272, *273*
cakes, savory:
    Cheese and Potato Cake, 148, *149*
    Tuscan Chickpea Cake, *178*, 179–80

Canederli in brodo, 252, *253*

Cassoeula, 74–75, *75*

Castagnaccio, *272*, 273

Casunziei all'ampezzana, 214–17, *215*

cavolo nero (note), 196

Ceci in zimino, *192*, 193–94

cheese, 140–67

    Bread-and-Cheese-Stuffed Eggplant, 46–47, *47*

    Buckwheat Pasta with Cabbage and Cheese, *156*, 157–58

    Cheese-and-Egg Balls Stewed in Tomato Sauce, 144–45, *145*

    Cheese and Potato Cake, 148, *149*

    Fontina and Savoy Cabbage Bread Casserole, 162–63, *163*

    Foraged-Herb Tortelli with Walnut Pesto, 38–40, *41*

    Fried Mozzarella Sandwiches, *146*, 147

    Gnocchi Baked with Tomato Sauce and Mozzarella, 225–28, *227*

    Gorgonzola and Walnut Sauce, 229–31, *230*

    Hand-Pulled Pici Pasta with Cheese and Black Pepper, 153–54, *155*

    Ligurian Spinach and Ricotta Pie, *164*, 165–67

    Mussel, Potato, and Rice Gratin, 128–30, *129*

    Nettle and Ricotta Gnudi, *150*, 151–52

    Onion Soup from Calabria, 26, *27*

    Parmigiano-Reggiano Sauce, 159–60, *161*

    Pasta with Potatoes and Cheese, 204, *205*

    Polenta with Butter and Cheese, *222*, 223–24

    Sardinian Potato and Cheese Tortelli, *210*, 211–13, *213*

    Sausage and Cheese Bake, 246, *247*

    Savory Swiss Chard and Parmigiano-Reggiano Pie, 82, 83–84

    Spaghetti Frittata, 262, *263*

    Stewed Lamb with Eggs and Cheese, 80, *81*

Chestnut Flour Cake, *272*, 273

Chestnut Flour Maltagliati with Porcini Sauce, *218*, 219–21

chestnuts, 202

    Chestnut and Potato Gnocchi with Gorgonzola and Walnut Sauce, 229–31, *230*

Potato, Chestnut, and Porcini Soup, 208, *209*

chicken:

    Boiled Chicken Salad, *96*, 97

    Chicken and Pork Lasagne, 104–8, *106*, *108*

    Chicken Cacciatore, *98*, 99

    Chicken Stock, 306

Chicken Liver Spread, 90, *91*

chickpea flour, 180

chickpeas:

    Chickpea and Chard Stew, *192*, 193–94

    Chickpea Flour Fritters in Sesame Seed Buns, 176, *177*

    Fresh Pasta and Chickpea Soup, 186–89, *187*

    how to cook, 174–75

    Tuscan Chickpea Cake, *178*, 179–80

chicory: Fava Bean Puree with Chicory, 181–82, *183*

chicory coffee, 298

chocolate:

    Pastry Cream and Chocolate Trifle, *286*, 287–88

    Sicilian Watermelon Pudding, *294*, 295

Ciambotta, 54, *55*

cod:

    Baked Salt Cod with Potatoes, *136*, 137

    Potato and Dried Stockfish Puree, 122–23, *123*

    stoccafisso (note), 123

coffee, 298

corn, 202

Crostata alla marmellata, 277–78, *279*

croutons, 24

cucumber: Tomato and Bread Salad, *250*, 251

Culurgiones, *210*, 211–13, *213*

desserts, 264–97

dumplings:

    Bread Dumplings, 252, *253*

    Spinach Bread Dumplings with Butter and Sage Sauce, *254*, 255–56

eggplant:

    Bread-and-Cheese-Stuffed Eggplant, 46–47, *47*

    grilled, 179

    Summer Vegetable Stew, 54, *55*

eggs:

    Amaretti Pudding, 283–84, *285*

    Cheese-and-Egg Balls Stewed in Tomato Sauce, 144–45, *145*

    Flatbread with Tomato Sauce and Poached Eggs, 102, *103*

    Frittata Cooked in Tomato Sauce, *100*, 101

    Ligurian Spinach and Ricotta Pie, *164*, 165–67

    Roman Egg Drop Soup, 94, *95*

    Spaghetti Frittata, 262, *263*

    Stewed Lamb with Eggs and Cheese, 80, *81*

Elderflower Fritters, 296–97, *297*

Erbazzone reggiano, *82*, 83–84

Farinata con le leghe, 198–99, *199*

Fave e cicorie, 181–82, *183*

Fegato alla veneziana, *72*, 73

fennel: Anchovy and Garlic Dip, 116–18, *117*

figs: Bread Pudding Cake, 270–71, *271*

fish and seafood, 112–39

Fish Soup, 131–33, *132*

Flatbread with Tomato Sauce and Poached Eggs, 102, *103*

Florentine Beef Stew, 70, *71*

flour, 17

Focaccia, Grape, *264*, 274–76, *275*

Fontina and Savoy Cabbage Bread Casserole, 162–63, *163*

Francesina, *260*, 261

Frico friulano, 148, *149*

Frittata di spaghetti, 262, *263*

Frittata trippata, *100*, 101

Frittelle di fiori di sambuco, 296–97, *297*

fritters:

    Chickpea Flour Fritters in Sesame Seed Buns, 176, *177*

    Elderflower Fritters, 296–97, *297*

Garlicky Tomato Sauce, 308

Gelo di mellone, *294*, 295

giardiniera (note), 97

gnocchi:

    Chestnut and Potato Gnocchi with Gorgonzola and Walnut Sauce, 229–31, *230*

    Gnocchi Baked with Tomato Sauce and Mozzarella, 225–28, *227*

    Gnocchi alla sorrentina, 225–28, *227*

Gnocchi di patate e castagne con sugo di
Gorgonzola e noci, 229–31, *230*
Gnudi di ricotta e ortiche, *150*, 151–52
Gorgonzola and Walnut Sauce, 229–31,
230
Grape Focaccia, *264*, 274–76, *275*
greens, 40
Artichoke, Fava Bean, Pea, and
Lettuce Stew, 50–53, *51*
Bitter Greens and Semolina Bread
Soup, 248, 249
Fava Bean Puree with Chicory, 181–82,
183
Foraged-Herb Tortelli with Walnut
Pesto, 38–40, *41*
Gremolata, 63–64

herbs and spices, 16
aromatic bouquet (note), 93
Foraged-Herb Tortelli with Walnut
Pesto, 38–40, *41*

Insalata di pollo lesso, *96*, 97
Insalata di tonno e fagioli, 172–73, *173*
Involtini di peperoni alla piemontese,
22, *23*
Italian street food, 85, 180

jam: Short-Crust Pastry Tart with Jam,
277–78, *279*
Jerusalem artichoke: Anchovy and
Garlic Dip, 116–18, *117*

kale:
Bean and Lacinato Kale Soup, 195–96,
197
Kale and Borlotti Polenta, 198–99, *199*

Lagane e ceci, 186–89, *187*
lamb: Stewed Lamb with Eggs and
Cheese, 80, *81*
lard and lardo (notes), 83, 84, 282
lasagne: Chicken and Pork Lasagne,
104–8, *106, 108*
Lasagne bastarde con sugo di porcini, *218*,
219–21
leftovers, 232–63
Beef Stew with Onions and Tomatoes,
260, 261
Bitter Greens and Semolina Bread
Soup, 248, 249
Bread Dumplings, 252, *253*

Fried Beef and Mortadella Meatballs,
257–58, *259*
Roman Fried Rice Balls, 236–38, *237*
Sausage and Cheese Bake, 246, *247*
Sicilian Fried Rice Balls, 242–45, *244*
Spaghetti Frittata, 262, *263*
Spinach Bread Dumplings with Butter
and Sage Sauce, *254*, 255–56
Tomato and Bread Salad, 250, *251*
Tomato and Bread Soup, 239–41, *240*
legumes, 168–99
dried, 17
how to cook, 174–75
see also specific legumes
Lentil Stew, Umbrian, 190–91, *191*
Licurdia, *26*, 27
Ligurian Spinach and Ricotta Pie, *164*,
165–67
Lingua con salsa verde, 60, *61*
liver:
Chicken Liver Spread, 90, *91*
Onion-Stewed Calf's Liver, 72, *73*
Roasted Pork Liver Skewers, 78–79,
79

macco di fave, 182
mackerel: Baked Mackerel with
Salmoriglio Sauce, 138, *139*
Maiale ciffe e ciaffe, 76, *77*
meatballs: Fried Beef and Mortadella
Meatballs, 257–58, *259*
meats, 56–84
bollito misto (note), 305
Meat Sauce, 104–8, *106, 108*
see also specific meats
Melanzane ripiene alla calabrese, 46–47,
47
Milanese-Style Braised Veal Shank with
Saffron Risotto, *62*, 63–64
milk:
Almond Milk, 293
Amaretti Pudding, 283–84, *285*
Bread Dumplings, 252, *253*
Bread Pudding Cake, 270–71, *271*
Pumpkin Tart, 280, 281–82
Sicilian Almond-Milk Pudding, 292–93,
293
Minestrone di verdure, 24–25
Mondeghili, 257–58, *259*
mortadella: Fried Beef and Mortadella
Meatballs, 257–58, *259*
Mozzarella in carrozza, *146*, 147

mushrooms:
Chestnut Flour Maltagliati with Porcini
Sauce, *218*, 219–21
Potato, Chestnut, and Porcini Soup,
208, *209*
Potato-and-Mushroom-Stuffed
Zucchini, 44–45, *45*
mussels:
Fish Soup, 131–33, *132*
Mussel, Potato, and Rice Gratin,
128–30, *129*

Nettle and Ricotta Gnudi, *150*, 151–52
nuts:
Chestnut Flour Cake, *272*, 273
Gorgonzola and Walnut Sauce, 229–31,
230
Nut Biscotti, 289–90, *291*
Sicilian Watermelon Pudding, *294*, 295
Walnut Pesto, 38

olive oil, 15
onions:
Beef Stew with Onions and Tomatoes,
260, 261
Onion Soup from Calabria, *26*, 27
Onion-Stewed Calf's Liver, 72, *73*
Pasta with Anchovy, Onion, and Black
Pepper Sauce, 124, *125*
Savory Swiss Chard and Parmigiano-
Reggiano Pie, *82*, 83–84
Sweet-and-Sour Sardines with Onions,
119–21, *120*
Orata all'acqua pazza, 134–35, *135*
Orecchiette con le cime di rapa, 34,
35–36, *37*
Orecchiette with Broccoli Rabe, 34,
35–36, *37*
Ossobuco alla milanese con risotto allo
zafferano, *62*, 63–64
Oxtail Stew with Rigatoni, 65–67, *66*

Pallotte cacio e ova, 144–45, *145*
Pancotto pugliese, 248, 249
Pane di grano duro, 303–4, *304*
Pane e panelle, 176, *177*
Pane frattau, 102, *103*
Pane sciocco toscano, 302–3, *302*
Pansoti con salsa di noci, 38–40, *41*
Panzanella, 250, *251*
Pappa al pomodoro, 239–41, *240*
Parsley Sauce, 60, *61*

Passatelli asciutti con crema di
   Parmigiano-Reggiano, 159–60, *161*
pasta:
   Beet Tortelli with Poppy Seed Sauce,
      214–17, *215*
   Buckwheat Pasta with Cabbage and
      Cheese, *156*, 157–58
   Chestnut and Potato Gnocchi with
      Gorgonzola and Walnut Sauce,
      229–31, *230*
   Chestnut Flour Maltagliati with Porcini
      Sauce, *218*, 219–21
   dry, 17
   Fresh Pasta and Chickpea Soup,
      186–89, *187*
   Gnocchi Baked with Tomato Sauce
      and Mozzarella, 225–28, *227*
   Hand-Pulled Pici Pasta with Cheese
      and Black Pepper, 153–54, *155*
   Passatelli with Parmigiano-Reggiano
      Sauce, 159–60, *161*
   Pasta and Bean Soup, *184*, 185
   pasta mista, 184
   Pasta with Anchovy, Onion, and Black
      Pepper Sauce, 124, *125*
   Pasta with Potatoes and Cheese, 204,
      205
   Sardinian Potato and Cheese Tortelli,
      210, 211–13, *213*
Pasta, patate, e provola, 204, *205*
Pasta e fagioli, *184*, 185
Pasta matta, *164*, 165–67
Pastry Cream and Chocolate Trifle, *286*,
   287–88
Patè di fegatini, 90, *91*
peas:
   Artichoke, Fava Bean, Pea, and Lettuce
      Stew, 50–53, *51*
   Rice and Pea Soup, 28, *29*
Peperoni ripieni alla lucana, 48–49, *49*
peppers:
   Bread-and-Anchovy-Stuffed Sweet
      Green Peppers, 48–49, *49*
   Roasted Pepper Rolls Stuffed with
      Tuna and Capers, 22, *23*
   Summer Vegetable Stew, 54, *55*
pesto: Walnut Pesto, 38
Petto di tacchino ripieno, 109–11, *110*
Pici cacio e pepe, 153–54, *155*
pies, savory:
   Ligurian Spinach and Ricotta Pie, *164*,
      165–67

Savory Swiss Chard and Parmigiano-
      Reggiano Pie, 82, *83*–84
Pizzoccheri, *156*, 157–58
polenta:
   Kale and Borlotti Polenta, 198–99,
      199
   notes, 224
   Polenta with Butter and Cheese, *222*,
      223–24
Polenta concia, *222*, 223–24
Pollo alla cacciatora, 98, *99*
Pomodori ripieni di riso alla romana,
      42, 43
Poppy Seed Sauce, 214–17, *215*
pork:
   Chicken and Pork Lasagne, 104–8,
      106, *108*
   Pork Braised in White Wine, 76, *77*
   Pork Stew with Savoy Cabbage, 74–75,
      75
   Roasted Pork Liver Skewers, 78–79, *79*
potatoes, 200–202
   Anchovy and Garlic Dip, 116–18, *117*
   Baked Salt Cod with Potatoes, *136*, 137
   Beet Tortelli with Poppy Seed Sauce,
      214–17, *215*
   Bitter Greens and Semolina Bread
      Soup, *248*, 249
   Buckwheat Pasta with Cabbage and
      Cheese, *156*, 157–58
   Cheese and Potato Cake, 148, *149*
   Chestnut and Potato Gnocchi with
      Gorgonzola and Walnut Sauce,
      229–31, *230*
   Fava Bean Puree with Chicory, 181–82,
      183
   Gnocchi Baked with Tomato Sauce
      and Mozzarella, 225–28, *227*
   Mussel, Potato, and Rice Gratin,
      128–30, *129*
   Onion Soup from Calabria, *26*, 27
   Pasta with Potatoes and Cheese, 204,
      205
   Potato, Chestnut, and Porcini Soup,
      208, *209*
   Potato and Dried Stockfish Puree,
      122–23, *123*
   Potato-and-Mushroom-Stuffed
      Zucchini, 44–45, *45*
   Rice-Stuffed Tomatoes, *42*, 43
   Sardinian Potato and Cheese Tortelli,
      210, 211–13, *213*

Summer Vegetable Stew, 54, *55*
Umbrian Lentil Stew, 190–91, *191*
Vegetable Soup, 24–25
poultry, 86–111
prunes: Bread Pudding Cake, 270–71, *271*
puddings:
   Amaretti Pudding, 283–84, *285*
   Sicilian Almond-Milk Pudding, 292–93,
      293
   Sicilian Watermelon Pudding, 294, *295*
Pumpkin Tart, *280*, 281–82

rabbit, 88
   Rabbit Preserved in Olive Oil, 92, *93*
raisins:
   Boiled Chicken Salad, 96, *97*
   Sweet-and-Sour Sardines with Onions,
      119–21, *120*
Ribollita, 195–96, *197*
rice, 17
   culture of, 33
   Mussel, Potato, and Rice Gratin,
      128–30, *129*
   Rice and Pea Soup, 28, *29*
   Rice-Stuffed Tomatoes, *42*, 43
   Roasted Squash Risotto, 30, *31*–32
   Roman Fried Rice Balls, 236–38, *237*
   Saffron Risotto, 64
   Sicilian Fried Rice Balls, 242–45, *244*
   Squid Ink Risotto, *126*, 127
   varieties of, 33
ricotta:
   Ligurian Spinach and Ricotta Pie, *164*,
      165–67
   Nettle and Ricotta Gnudi, *150*, 151–52
Rigatoni alla vaccinara, 65–67, *66*
Risi e bisi, 28, *29*
Riso al nero, *126*, 127
Riso al salto, 32
Risotto alla zucca, 30, *31*–32
Risotto allo zafferano, 64
Roman Egg Drop Soup, 94, *95*
Roman Fried Rice Balls, 236–38, *237*

Saffron Risotto, 64
salads:
   Boiled Chicken Salad, 96, *97*
   Tomato and Bread Salad, 250, *251*
   Tuna and Bean Salad, 172–73, *173*
Salmoriglio Sauce, 138
Salsa verde, 60, *61*
salt, 15

sandwiches:
  Chickpea Flour Fritters in Sesame
    Seed Buns, 176, *177*
  Fried Mozzarella Sandwiches,
    146, 147
Sarde in saor, 119–21, *120*
sardines: Sweet-and-Sour Sardines with
    Onions, 119–21, *120*
Sardinian Potato and Cheese Tortelli,
    210, 211–13, *213*
sauces:
  Anchovy and Garlic Dip, 116–18, *117*
  Besciamella, 105
  Broccoli Rabe Dressing, 35–36
  Butter and Sage Sauce, *254*, 255–56
  Garlicky Tomato Sauce, 308
  Gorgonzola and Walnut Sauce, 229–31,
    230
  Meat Sauce, 104–8, *106*, *108*
  Parmigiano-Reggiano Sauce, 159–60,
    161
  Parsley Sauce, 60, *61*
  Pasta with Anchovy, Onion, and Black
    Pepper Sauce, 124, *125*
  Poppy Seed Sauce, 214–17, *215*
  Porcini Sauce, *218*, 219–21
  Salmoriglio Sauce, 138
  Tomato Sauce, 144–45, *145*
  Tomato Sauce with Passata, 309, *309*
sausages:
  Chestnut Flour Maltagliati with Porcini
    Sauce, *218*, 219–21
  Sausage and Cheese Bake, 246, *247*
Schiacciata con l'uva, *264*, 274–76, *275*
Sea Bream Stewed with Tomatoes,
    134–35, *135*
Semolina Bread, 303–4, *304*
Sgombro al salmoriglio, 138, *139*
Short-Crust Pastry Tart with Jam, 277–78,
    279
shrimp: Fish Soup, 131–33, *132*
Sicilian Almond-Milk Pudding, 292–93,
    293
Sicilian Fried Rice Balls, 242–45, *244*
Sicilian Watermelon Pudding, *294*, 295
Smacafam, 246, *247*
soups:
  Bean and Lacinato Kale Soup, 195–96,
    197
  Bitter Greens and Semolina Bread
    Soup, *248*, 249
  Fish Soup, 131–33, *132*

Fresh Pasta and Chickpea Soup,
    186–89, *187*
  Onion Soup from Calabria, 26, *27*
  Pasta and Bean Soup, *184*, 185
  Potato, Chestnut, and Porcini Soup,
    208, *209*
  Rice and Pea Soup, 28, *29*
  Roman Egg Drop Soup, 94, *95*
  Savoy Cabbage and Barley Soup, *206*,
    207
  Tomato and Bread Soup, 239–41, *240*
  Vegetable Soup, 24–25
Spaghetti Frittata, 262, *263*
Spiedini di fegatelli di maiale, 78–79, *79*
spinach:
  Ligurian Spinach and Ricotta Pie, *164*,
    165–67
  Spinach Bread Dumplings with Butter
    and Sage Sauce, *254*, 255–56
  Vegetable Soup, 24–25
squash: Roasted Squash Risotto, 30, 31–32
squid: Fish Soup, 131–33, *132*
squid ink, 126
Squid Ink Risotto, *126*, 127
stews:
  Artichoke, Fava Bean, Pea, and Lettuce
    Stew, 50–53, *51*
  Beef Stew with Onions and Tomatoes,
    260, 261
  Chickpea and Chard Stew, *192*, 193–94
  Florentine Beef Stew, 70, *71*
  Onion-Stewed Calf's Liver, *72*, 73
  Oxtail Stew with Rigatoni, 65–67, *66*
  Pork Stew with Savoy Cabbage, 74–75,
    75
  Sea Bream Stewed with Tomatoes,
    134–35, *135*
  Stewed Lamb with Eggs and Cheese,
    80, *81*
  Stewed Tripe, 68, *69*
  Summer Vegetable Stew, 54, *55*
  Umbrian Lentil Stew, 190–91, *191*
stoccafisso (note), 123
stocks:
  Beef Stock, 305
  Chicken Stock, 306
  Vegetable Stock, 307
stracciatella (cheese), 94
Stracciatella in brodo, 94, *95*
Stracotto di manzo alla fiorentina, 70, *71*
Strangolapreti, *254*, 255–56
Sugo di pomodoro all'aglio, 308

Summer Vegetable Stew, 54, *55*
supplì (note), 245
Supplì al telefono, 236–38, *237*
Swiss chard:
  Chickpea and Chard Stew, *192*, 193–94
  Savory Swiss Chard and Parmigiano-
    Reggiano Pie, *82*, 83–84
Syrup, Apple, 268–69

tarts:
  Pumpkin Tart, *280*, 281–82
  Short-Crust Pastry Tart with Jam,
    277–78, *279*
Testaccio Market, Rome, 67
Tiella di patate, riso, e cozze, 128–30, *129*
tomatoes:
  Baked Salt Cod with Potatoes, *136*, 137
  Beef Stew with Onions and Tomatoes,
    260, 261
  Bitter Greens and Semolina Bread
    Soup, *248*, 249
  canned or preserved, 17
  Cheese-and-Egg Balls Stewed in
    Tomato Sauce, 144–45, *145*
  Chicken and Pork Lasagne, 104–8,
    106, *108*
  Chicken Cacciatore, 98, *99*
  Chickpea and Chard Stew, *192*, 193–94
  Fish Soup, 131–33, *132*
  Flatbread with Tomato Sauce and
    Poached Eggs, 102, *103*
  Florentine Beef Stew, 70, *71*
  Frittata Cooked in Tomato Sauce, *100*,
    101
  Garlicky Tomato Sauce, 308
  Gnocchi Baked with Tomato Sauce
    and Mozzarella, 225–28, *227*
  Mussel, Potato, and Rice Gratin,
    128–30, *129*
  Pasta and Bean Soup, *184*, 185
  Pasta with Potatoes and Cheese, 204,
    205
  preserving, 311
  Rice-Stuffed Tomatoes, *42*, 43
  Roman Fried Rice Balls, 236–38, *237*
  Sea Bream Stewed with Tomatoes,
    134–35, *135*
  Spaghetti Frittata, 262, *263*
  Stewed Tripe, 68, 69
  Summer Vegetable Stew, 54, *55*
  Tomato and Bread Salad, 250, *251*
  Tomato and Bread Soup, 239–41, *240*

Tomato Sauce with Passata, 309, *309*
Tuna and Bean Salad, 172–73, *173*
Umbrian Lentil Stew, 190–91, *191*
tongue: Veal Tongue with Parsley Sauce, 60, *61*
Tonno di coniglio, *92, 93*
Torta di ceci, *178*, 179–80
Torta di mele all'olio, 268–69, *269*
Torta di pane, 270–71, *271*
Torta di zucca gialla, *280*, 281–82
Torta pasqualina, 165–67, *165*
tortelli:
    Beet Tortelli with Poppy Seed Sauce, 214–17, *215*
    Foraged-Herb Tortelli with Walnut Pesto, 38–40, *41*
    Sardinian Potato and Cheese Tortelli, *210*, 211–13, *213*
trifle: Pastry Cream and Chocolate Trifle, *286*, 287–88
tripe: Stewed Tripe, 68, *69*
Trippa al sugo, 68, *69*

tuna:
    Roasted Pepper Rolls Stuffed with Tuna and Capers, 22, *23*
    Tuna and Bean Salad, 172–73, *173*
turkey: Stuffed Turkey Breast Roulade, 109–11, *110*
Tuscan Bread, 302–3, *302*
Tuscan Chickpea Cake, *178*, 179–80

Umbrian Lentil Stew, 190–91, *191*

veal:
    Milanese-Style Braised Veal Shank with Saffron Risotto, *62*, 63–64
    Veal Tongue with Parsley Sauce, 60, *61*
vegetable oil, 15
vegetables, 18–55
    Summer Vegetable Stew, 54, *55*
    Vegetable Soup, 24–25
    Vegetable Stock, 307
    see also specific vegetables

Vignarola, 50–53, *51*
Vincisgrassi marchigiani, 104–8, *106, 108*
vin cotto (note), 108

Watermelon Pudding, Sicilian, *294, 295*

zimino (note), 194
zucchini:
    Potato-and-Mushroom-Stuffed Zucchini, 44–45, *45*
    Summer Vegetable Stew, 54, *55*
    Vegetable Soup, 24–25
Zucchini ripieni alla ligure, 44–45, *45*
Zuppa alla valpellinese, 162–63, *163*
Zuppa di lenticchie umbra, 190–91, *191*
Zuppa di patate, castagne, e porcini, 208, *209*
Zuppa d'orzo trentina, *206*, 207
Zuppa inglese, *286*, 287–88

GIULIA SCARPALEGGIA is a Tuscan-born and -bred home cook, food writer, podcaster, and cooking school instructor who has written five cookbooks in Italian. In 2009, she founded the blog *Juls' Kitchen* to collect family recipes and stories, and now she shares Tuscan and Italian regional recipes both in Italian and in English.

Since 2016, *Juls' Kitchen* has become a family project, with Giulia's husband, Tommaso Galli, lending his photography. In 2019, *Saveur* magazine named it the best food culture blog.

In 2019, Giulia launched a podcast, *Cooking with an Italian Accent*, and in 2021, a weekly newsletter, *Letters from Tuscany*. Her work has been featured in numerous news outlets in Italy and abroad, including Food52, *The Simple Things*, *What Women Cook*, BBC Good Food, *Corriere della Sera*, and *Bake from Scratch*.

Giulia and Tommaso live in Tuscany with their daughter, Livia, and two dogs. Find Giulia on Instagram at @julskitchen and on her blog, en.julskitchen.com.

TOMMASO GALLI is a Tuscan-based photographer. Born and raised in the mountain area of Mugello, he moved to Florence as a teenager and happily lived in the city until he met his wife, Giulia Scarpaleggia. Now he lives in the countryside of Colle Val d'Elsa, where he shares a family and business with her. Find him online at @tommyonweb.